P9-AOT-712

THE HISTORY OF THE NEW YORK CITY LEGISLATURE

NUMBER 581
COLUMBIA STUDIES
IN THE SOCIAL SCIENCES
EDITED BY
THE FACULTY OF
POLITICAL SCIENCE
OF COLUMBIA UNIVERSITY

THE HISTORY OF THE NEW YORK CITY LEGISLATURE

By FREDERICK SHAW

AMS PRESS
NEW YORK

COLUMBIA UNIVERSITY
STUDIES IN THE
SOCIAL SCIENCES

581

The Series was formerly known as
Studies in History, Economics and Public Law.

Reprinted with the permission of Columbia University Press
From the edition of 1954, New York
First AMS EDITION published 1968
Manufactured in the United States of America

Library of Congress Catalogue Card Number: 75-76659

AMS PRESS, INC.
NEW YORK, N. Y. 10003

PREFACE

No GOVERNMENT offers such abundant opportunities for direct participation and first-hand knowledge of the political process as municipal government. Conducted far from the typical citizen's personal observation, federal and state governments are likely to appear remote and obscure. Municipal government, however, is highly visible; it affects the citizen's life in a multitude of ways; it is on the job every minute of the time. That is why local government has been called a "school for self-government in larger affairs."

The general purpose of this book is to explore the history of a municipal institution—New York's legislature—since the consolidation of the city. Its specific aim is to compare the work of the City Council that began its deliberations in 1938 with that of the defunct Board of Aldermen. I did not propose, however, to confine the scope of this volume to the scrutiny of a single municipal body. For this reason I have not limited the narrative to events within the legislative chamber, but have endeavored to integrate it with the city's political history. Thus Chapter V, "The Alderman and His Bailiwick," is concerned not merely with relations between the typical alderman and his constituency, but also with his services to his political organization and the manner in which the daily performance of those services helped maintain the organization's power. So, too, the section on the collapse of Tammany Hall describes the events that made possible a thorough overhauling of the city charter in the 1930's; it may also be considered a segment of the city's political history.

In the past New York was often called the "Metropolis of America"; today it is known as the "World's Capital City." Is it not a singular fact that while this city outstrips most members of the United Nations in wealth and population, a definitive history of it, particularly in the twentieth century, has yet to be written? It is my hope that this work will contribute to such a history.

I am indebted to the late Professor Joseph P. Chamberlain, former counsel to two Charter Revision Commissions, and to Professor Allan Nevins, my constant advisors while the book was in preparation, for their invaluable advice and assistance. I am also grateful to Professors Harry J. Carman and Arthur W. MacMahon for their gracious encouragement. Miss Elsie S. Parker placed the files of the National Municipal League at my disposal and read the chapter on the origins of Proportional Representation. The staff of the Municipal Reference Library extended more than the usual courtesies.

This volume would not have been possible without the indulgence and active cooperation of my wife, Daisy K. Shaw. For the preparation of the index and other invaluable assistance in the manuscript itself I am deeply obliged to Miss Dorothy H. Schwartz. For all matters of fact and opinion in the pages which follow I am personally responsible.

FREDERICK SHAW

New York City

June 15, 1954

CONTENTS

TABLES

THE HISTORY OF THE NEW YORK CITY LEGISLATURE

1. A DISCREDITED LEGISLATURE, 1851–1901

The name "alderman" has become such a byword that it ought to be blotted from the municipal dictionary.[1]

OLD NEW YORK AND BROOKLYN

THE CLOSING DECADES of the nineteenth century witnessed a Dark Age in American municipal history. "With very few exceptions," wrote the first President of Cornell University in 1890, "the city governments of the United States are the worst in Christendom—the most expensive, the most inefficient, and the most corrupt." Rapid industrial expansion was accompanied by a mushroom growth of cities. Hitherto predominantly rural, American communities were unprepared for the complex problems of city life. An unprecedented need for new municipal services and public utilities placed many a city government under an unbearable strain.[2]

No branch of municipal government declined more dramatically than the city legislature. None offered more convincing proof of Lord Bryce's celebrated observation that city government was the "one conspicuous failure of the United States." Professor John R. Commons characterized the typical municipal law-making body of 1893 as a "sickening failure." "The name alderman is now a synonym for boodler and embezzler," he wrote. The New York Board of Aldermen achieved greater notoriety

[1] *New York Daily Tribune,* April 8, 1890.

[2] Andrew D. White, "The Government of American Cities," *Forum,* X (1890), 357: Quoted in Arthur M. Schlesinger, "The City in American History," *Mississippi Valley Historical Review,* XXVII (1940), 59; Clifford W. Patton, *The Battle for Municipal Reform* (Washington, 1940), p. 7.

than most only because the city's size made it more conspicuous.[3]

Rapid city growth had created an urgent need for new transportation facilities. Here lay lush opportunities for predatory politicians, on the one hand, and recipients of public grants on the other. With the bestowal of the first trolley franchise in 1851 the Board of Aldermen embarked on a career of spoliation. The body in which "Boss" Tweed served his apprenticeship the following year was known as the "Forty Thieves." It was said that an enterprising alderman could make his fortune in a single term; few were backward in the pursuit of pelf. "I seen my opportunities and I took 'em," was the famous boast of George Washington Plunkitt, alderman in the seventies. "Boss" Tweed spoke more plainly: "There never was a time when you couldn't buy the Board of Aldermen." Private corporations could profit handsomely from the corrupt award of city contracts and franchises. One firm netted a million dollars out of two trolley franchises bought with $50,000 distributed among the aldermen.[4]

As repeated scandals demonstrated the incapacity of the board to govern, it was gradually stripped of power. Most of it was conferred upon the state legislature, on the theory that it was wiser to have a partly corrupt rather than a completely corrupt body determine municipal policies. The remainder was largely diffused among executive organs—the mayor and semi-independent administrative departments. A body that had once wielded important powers, controlling the police force and serving as magistrates as well as legislators, was reduced to impotence. By 1897, when New York merged with neighboring communities, the aldermen did little more than grant permits for peanut stands and confirm the tax rate computed by the comptroller.[5]

[3] James Bryce, *The American Commonwealth* (London, 1889), I, 608; *Proportional Representation Review,* I, No. 1 (1893), 7; Ernest S. Griffith, *The Modern Development of City Government in the United Kingdom and the United States* (London, 1927), I, 110-11.

[4] Gustavus Myers, *The History of Tammany Hall* (New York, 1917), pp. 155-57, 167-71; M. R. Werner, *Tammany Hall* (New York, 1928), pp. 70-72, 107-8; William R. Riordan, *Plunkitt of Tammany Hall* (New York, 1948), p. 4; James Parton, "The Government of the City of New York," *North American Review,* CIII (1866), 447-49; Dennis T. Lynch, *"Boss" Tweed* (New York, 1927), p. 67 ff.

[5] *The Charter of the City of New York, with Notes Thereon: Also, A Treatise on the Powers and Duties of the Mayor, Aldermen and Assistant Aldermen, Pre-*

While its powers were being whittled away, the board slowly fell under the sway of Tammany Hall. Surprising as it may appear to those who knew the aldermen in later days, no city boss demanded fealty before the Civil War. In 1852 the body was an unbossed assemblage of conniving politicians, where a rank newcomer like William M. Tweed could become a ringleader. When he became boss, Tweed himself submitted to their extortionate demands for tribute (until he by-passed them with a charter transferring their authority to his cronies). "Honest" John Kelly, Tweed's successor, gave Tammany the rudiments of organization. "He found it a horde," declared a contemporary. "He left it an army." Yet Kelly never controlled the municipal legislature. The city's Democrats were split into rival factions, all "gnawing on the same bone of patronage," and a crude system of proportional representation helped elect members of all groups as well as Republicans. In 1884 the "Boodle Board" perpetrated one of the most brazen thefts in the City's history: selling a Broadway franchise for a song after a bribery fund had been distributed among the members. Twenty-two aldermen were indicted; some were imprisoned or escaped to Canada just ahead of the law. But no one suggested that Tammany was responsible—the aldermen had actually defied Boss Kelly and his chief lieutenant, Richard Croker.[6]

It was Croker who brought the Board of Aldermen under his sway. Ascending the throne in 1886, he soon crushed all opposing factions and established his rule over the entire Democratic organization. As Kelly's heir apparent, Croker was compelled to pay $180,000 for aldermanic confirmation of a single appointment; as one-man ruler of the city he subjected the aldermen

---

pared at the Request of the Common Council by Chancellor Kent, and Published at Their Direction (New York, 1854), p. 291 ff.; "Govt. of the City of N. Y.," *North Am. Rev.*, CIII, 454-55, Frank Goodnow, *City Government in the United States* (New York, 1910), pp. 144-45, 153.

[6] Lynch, *"Boss" Tweed*, pp. 277-78, 325 ff.; Theodore L. Stoddard, *Master of Manhattan: The Life of Richard Croker* (New York, 1931), p. 87; I. H. Phelps Stokes, *The Iconography of Manhattan Island* (New York, 1915-28), V, 1985-86; Mark D. Hirsch, *William C. Whitney: Modern Warwick* (New York, 1948), p. 213 ff.; *Final Report to the Special Committee of the Assembly Appointed to Investigate the Public Offices and Departments of the City of New York and of the Counties Thereof* (Albany, 1900), I, 489 (Hereafter called "Mazet Investigation").

to his unqualified control.[7] The City Fathers became "dummies" for the dominant political machine in the same sense as boards of directors serving as fronts for Wall Street operators. Croker confided to Lincoln Steffens that business men preferred to deal with one leader rather than a plethora of officials. Under boss rule mad scrambles for franchises were replaced by negotiations with the majority leader, who delivered the requisite votes to the successful bidder.[8]

Few men of substance and integrity could be persuaded to run for the office. Once individuals of dignity and influence, the City Fathers were now drawn from "barrooms, brothels, and political societies." Ward politics in this period was conducted in an atmosphere of booze. District politicians found it convenient to make their headquarters the saloon, the poor man's club; at the same time retail liquor dealers, who more often than not flouted Sunday closing laws, welcomed political protection. From mutual needs sprang an intimate affiliation between the saloon and local politics. Many district leaders were rum-sellers, and in the typical Board of Aldermen half the members were saloon-keepers, most of the remainder wardheelers.[9]

Primary contests and conventions were usually held in rum-shops, the centers of neighborhood political life. (About three-fourths of all aldermanic conventions in 1884 were held in saloons or next door to them.) Such gatherings were no place for molly-coddles. Political leaders found it advantageous to employ gangsters to intimidate opponents, and respectable citizens who attended were constrained to silence at the risk of being thrown

[7] Alfred R. Conkling, an alderman in 1888, asserted that the Board began to take orders from Croker that year. All dissident factions save the County Democracy had been exterminated in 1887, and in 1888 they, too, were routed. Alfred R. Conkling, *City Government in the United States* (New York, 1899), pp. 48-49; Stoddard, *Master of Manhattan*, pp. 88, 93.

[8] Werner, *Tammany Hall*, pp. 315 ff.; Harold Zink, *City Bosses in the United States* (Durham, 1930), p. 140; Lincoln Steffens, *Autobiography* (New York, 1931), pp. 233-36; *Testimony Taken before the New York Senate Committee on Cities* (Albany, 1891), I, 484-87, 550-58 (Hereafter called "Fassett Committee Hearings").

[9] Werner, *op. cit.*, p. 69; Theodore Roosevelt, *New York* (New York, 1903), pp. 218-20; "Fassett Committee Hearings," I, 474; Albert J. Kennedy, "The Saloon in Retrospect and Prospect," *Survey Graphic*, XXII (1933), 205; Harold J. Jonas, "An Alderman in New York City, 1887-8 As Seen in His Journal," *New York History*, XXIX (1948), 188.

down stairs or pitched out of windows. "Personal courage, physical as well as moral," explained Theodore Roosevelt, "was a prime requisite for political workers, and pugilistic ability was a capital asset in the political game." All Tammany leaders in this period—Tweed, Kelly, and Croker—were handy with their fists; Tweed and Croker had been gang leaders. A former police chief found every branch of city government infested with ruffians and thieves, and his professional eye spotted plug-uglies and thugs among the aldermen. An investigation revealed that one legislator was a "fence." Another, an ex-convict, was elected before he had outgrown his prison haircut. The notorious Five Points district, which harbored criminals of every description, was regularly represented by members of the underworld or their allies. One ex-alderman believed that legislators' seats were occupied by the lowest type of political hack. "The very name alderman is repugnant to an honest man," he declared.[10]

Across the river, the City of Brooklyn's Board of Aldermen displayed the same squalid pattern of rapacity. In their checkered history the Brooklyn legislators demonstrated an aversion to granting franchises to corporations that failed to proffer boodle, a magnificent disregard for the taxpayers' interests, and a perennial propensity for dubious appropriations. The Governor once charged that the lawmakers had ignored the "most fundamental safeguards for economy and honesty," and a newspaper intimated that the city was safe against looting only when they were on vacation. Dominated like their Manhattan counterparts by saloonkeepers and politicians of low estate, they, too, were subjected to charges of fraud and corruption, and, when scandals broke out, indictments for dishonesty.[11]

Popular distrust of the Brooklyn aldermen led to a similar transfer of authority to the State Legislature and municipal

[10] William M. Ivins, *Machine Politics and Money in Elections in New York City* (New York, 1887), pp. 20-21; Theodore Roosevelt, *Essays on Practical Politics* (New York, 1888), pp. 63, 71; George W. Walling, *Recollections of a New York Chief of Police* (New York, 1887), pp. 598, 605; Herbert Asbury, *The Gangs of New York* (New York, 1937), pp. 269, 277; Theodore Roosevelt, *American Ideas and Other Essays* (New York, 1900), p. 86; Conkling, *City Govt. in the U.S.*, pp. 8, 47; "Fassett Committee Hearings," I, 483.

[11] Harold C. Syrett, *The City of Brooklyn* (New York, 1944), pp. 31-32, 143-45, 205 ff; Conkling, *op. cit.*, pp. 113-14.

executive department. Brooklyn, in fact, pioneered in the strong mayor plan of government, and the "Brooklyn plan," which created an independent executive at the expense of the legislature, was imitated in every section of the country. When Brooklyn and New York were merged, the Brooklyn model was followed, making the Mayor of Greater New York an administrator second in importance only to the President of the United States.[12]

GREATER NEW YORK'S FIRST CHARTER

From these unpromising antecedents a new legislative body emerged in 1898, when the cities of New York and Brooklyn were consolidated with Long Island City, Richmond, and other outlying sections, to become a five-boroughed metropolis. Almost immediately, however, the new government proved unworkable.

Part of the difficulty lay in the charter itself—a document drafted with appalling speed and passed by the legislature after perfunctory consideration. Technically it was not even a charter but an ill-digested mass. Its one redeeming feature was the inclusion of the Consolidation Act of 1882, a first-rate codification of the laws pertaining to the old City of New York. Since 1882, however, hundreds of special acts and general laws affecting the city's government and administration had been placed on the statute books. Nor were there any recent law codes for the municipalities and corporations with which New York was merged, only a series of statutes scattered over dozens of legislative sessions. All these were re-enacted and loosely combined in the Greater City charter. Some authorities predicted this confused instrument would plunge the new metropolis into legal chaos.[13]

The most involved sections of the charter related to the legislative authority. Working on the principle that municipal poli-

[12] Goodnow, *City Govt. in the U. S.*, p. 153; Patton, *Battle for Municipal Reform*, p. 67; Mark Ash, *The Greater New York Charter as Enacted in 1897* (Albany, 1897), Introductory, cxv.

[13] James W. Pryor, "The Greater New York Charter," *Annals of the Academy of Political and Social Science*, X (1897), 23-28, 32; Arthur W. Macmahon, *The Statutory Sources of New York City Government* (New York, 1923), pp. 15-17; Lawrence A. Tanzer, *The New York City Charter* (New York, 1937), pp. 16-17, 476-77.

cies should be determined locally rather than at Albany, the commission which drafted the document endeavored to restore important powers to the local legislature. In the light of the recurring scandals in the Board of Aldermen during the latter half of the nineteenth century, however, it was considered wise to place a variety of checks and safeguards against extravagance and corruption in the exercise of these powers. Most local ordinances could be initiated only by the administrative departments whose work they affected, and the Municipal Assembly could merely ratify or reject their proposals without amendment. The annual budget originated in another deliberative body, the Board of Estimate and Apportionment. Important public works could not be approved without the prior recommendation of a Board of Public Improvements. An additional complication arose out of the fact that the Municipal Assembly was bicameral (a Board of Aldermen and a Council). This merely lengthened the time required for passage of legislation and increased the opportunities for holdups. It was scarcely necessary to have a double check, for neither house shaped public policy.[14]

Tammany Hall, the Manhattan Democratic machine, could have solved the charter difficulties created by these checks and safeguards in its own fashion, had it completely dominated the legislative branch. The Tammany formula was simplicity itself—to secure a unified municipal policy by compelling both the city administration and the city legislature to take orders from the Hall. During this brief period (1898-1901) it did control all administrative appointments. Many heads of departments were powerful district leaders, and no one familiar with the tradition of the Hall could expect mere legislators to challenge these party chieftains. Hence aldermen seeking an intelligent basis for voting on measures originating in these departments and requesting information from the Tammany commissioners were unceremoniously rebuffed. One lawmaker who inquired about a bond issue was told he could wait "till hell froze over"

[14] Ash, *Greater N. Y. Charter*, Introd., cxxxvi-cxxxix; Frank J. Goodnow, "The Charter of the City of New York," *Political Science Quarterly*, XVII (1902), 6-7.

before a statement would be forthcoming. What the organization demanded was prompt and blind obedience to administration proposals.[15]

Among the legislators the Democratic majority readily acquiesced. Alderman Thomas F. Foley, later mentor to Alfred E. Smith, explained to an investigating committee that an organization man was not expected to entertain personal opinions about bills drafted by the party boses. "I believe in leaving it to those who are a little above me in matters of that kind," stated Martin Engel, an East side district leader.[16]

But assent was not always automatic. Historians have depicted the first four years of Tammany's administration of Greater New York as an "orgy of corruption." There was a little knot of Citizens Union aldermen, seated in the first election under the new charter, who regarded the legislature as the only check upon "improvident, corrupt, or oppressive exercise of power" within the municipal government. With the two Republicans in the chamber they formed a solid opposition bloc. From time to time they were joined by the fourteen Brooklyn Democrats. This group's insurgency grew out of different motives. They claimed that after their borough was consolidated into the Greater City it was shabbily treated in the allocation of public improvements. "We have not received anything for Brooklyn," declared one alderman. "Brooklyn was the bride. We were seduced." Again, no love was lost between "Willoughby Street," headquarters of Brooklyn Boss McLaughlin, and Tammany Hall. Tammany was never reluctant to turn its power over the city administration to political advantage. "Borough leaders had to go to the National Democratic Club and practically kiss Boss Croker's hand in order to get patronage," recalled a politico many years later. The Brooklyn contingent in the Board of Aldermen retaliated by repeatedly exploiting local

[15] *Investigation of Offices and Departments of the City of New York by a Special Committee of the Assembly: Report of Counsel* (1899), 7-8; *Mazet Investigation,* II, 2225-26, 2243-45; Philemon T. Sherman, *Inside the Machine: Two Years in the Board of Aldermen,* 1898-1899 (New York, 1901), pp. 37-41.

[16] "Mazet Investigation," II, 2269-72.

issues to block essential measures until brought to terms by Tammany's control over patronage.[17]

When the Citizens Union minority came across a dubious or extravagant proposal and the department from which it emanated persistently refused any explanation, they held it up to "starve out" the offending department. Often they were supported by the Brooklyn Democrats. It was particularly easy to "hang up" financial measures, for they required the consent of three fourths of *all* members elected to each house. But assembling 45 out of 60 aldermen was difficult. Subways had not yet been built, and the trip from outlying sections was a real hardship. Meetings were dull, the calendar was filled with trifles, non-legislative duties were onerous, the salary meagre. Hence the legislators skipped meetings on the slightest pretext. It was not difficult for a cohesive minority to keep suspicious financial proposals in a state of suspended animation.[18]

Boss Croker countered by summoning the Tammany Executive Committee and admonishing the district leaders to instruct the legislators they sponsored to attend sessions. No Democratic alderman would dream of voting against an organization-sponsored bill, and, barring defections among the Brooklyn contingent, the Democratic majority of 47 out of 60 was sufficient to break the opposition blockade.[19]

Matters came to a head when the Municipal Assembly held up a bond issue for the construction of a Hall of Records in order to investigate rumors of irregularities in the contract. At this point, the administration moved in to destroy the legislators' will to resist, once and for all. When the contractor applied to the courts for a writ of mandamus ordering the lawmakers to vote for the bond issue, the Corporation Counsel (who is supposed to protect the interests of city officials) not only failed to contest the motion, but also concealed it from the Municipal

[17] *Ibid.*, II, 2198-99, 2208-9, 2231-35, 2238-43; Cleveland Rodgers and Rebecca B. Rankin, *New York: The World's Capital City* (New York, 1948), p. 98; Sherman, *Inside the Machine*, pp. 23-24; *Minutes of Meeting of New York City Charter Commission*, July 24, 1934.

[18] "Mazet Investigation," II, 2210-14, 2243; Sherman, *op. cit.*, pp. 36-41.

[19] "Mazet Investigation," I, 332-35; *New York Herald*, January 10, 1899.

Assembly until their meeting time. It fell on both houses like a bombshell. Ultimately the bond issue passed, but an effort was made to apply legal sanctions against the members who opposed it. Once again the Corporation Counsel worked hand in glove with the prosecution rather than the lawmakers, his presumed clients. To the shocked aldermen, it now appeared as if the administration could compel them to perform any act it desired. One wrote that the stratagem crushed the Municipal Assembly's spirit, "shattered the last remnants of its power in financial matters, and left it but the cash register of the Comptroller." Its usefulness was at an end.[20]

By imposing its will upon the city legislature, Tammany had temporarily overcome the delays and obstructions inherent in the municipal charter. But only a thoroughgoing revision of the instrument itself could eliminate its intrinsic defects. The very first session of the Municipal Assembly had demonstrated that the existence of two houses and rigid requirements for approval of financial measures multiplied opportunities for obstruction, while scattered legislative authority led to frequent snarling of the city government. Administrators could initiate legislation, but the aldermen had no means of compelling them to furnish essential information about their proposals.[21]

To remedy these defects, a Charter Revision Commission appointed by Governor Theodore Roosevelt endeavored to streamline legislative procedure. In the charter of 1901 the bicameral Municipal Assembly gave way to a single-chambered Board of Aldermen. To make it the real director of local policy, the Commission centered the city's entire ordinance-making power in this body. Deprived of power to frame ordinances, city commissioners were partially compensated by a voice on proposals affecting their departments—they gained floor privileges in the Board of Aldermen. The aldermen, in turn, were empowered to summon department heads and interrogate them on

[20] "Mazet Investigation," II, 2215-18, 2236-38; Sherman, *op. cit.*, pp. 41-46; Letter of Alderman Sherman to *New York Daily Tribune*, July 28, 1899.

[21] *Report of the Charter Revision Commission to the Governor of the State of New York* (New York, 1900), p. 5 ff.

the affairs of their departments. Protracted holdups of bond issues by small minorities were precluded by requiring a simple majority of all members; failure to act within six weeks would be equivalent to approval.[22]

The Brooklyn aldermen, it will be recalled, had been stirred to revolt over the issue of local improvements. To protect Brooklyn's interests as well as those of the other outlying boroughs, the authority of borough presidents and local improvement boards was increased. The borough presidents gained seats in the Board of Aldermen and Board of Estimate as well as new administrative powers. The improvement boards, comprising aldermen from adjacent districts, together with their borough presidents, could initiate local improvements, subject to approval by the Board of Estimate. The new charter was designed to create a government responsive to local needs and capable of functioning without repeated deadlocks.[23]

The city legislature had gained a modicum of its powers; but the Charter Commission could not restore its reputation. As long as it remained the "Board of Aldermen" its unsavory repu-

22 *Ibid.*, p 4 ff; Goodnow, "Charter of City of N. Y.," *Political Science Quarterly*, XVII, 7-12; Henry J. Lee (ed.) *The Charter of the City of New York, Chapter 466, Laws of 1901, with Amendments to May 1, 1930.* Hereafter all references to the charter which governed the actions of the Board of Aldermen will cite the aforementioned volume and Francis Savona, *Amendments to the Eagle Library Edition of the Charter of the City of New York from May 1, 1930, to the Close of the Extraordinary Session of the 1934 State Legislature* (Brooklyn, 1934).

23 Goodnow, "Charter of City of N. Y.," *Pol. Sci. Quart.*, XVII, 14-20; *The Outlook*, CXV (1900), 200; *Charter of 1901*, Secs. 18, 226, 425-37. Governor Alfred E. Smith later asserted that the borough governments were designed not to safeguard genuine local needs, but to build the power of the county machines outside Manhattan. "The origin of borough government in this city had nothing to do with genuine local sentiment," he declared. "Its origin was purely political. It was part of the price paid to powerful borough political leaders when the City Charter was revised in 1901" (*New York Times*, August 7, 1934). The Charter Revision Commission, however, really believed it was necessary to strengthen the borough governments in the interests of their communities. Mr. W. W. Niles, Counsel to the Commission, wrote: "I drafted the chapter relating to borough government and gave the borough presidents a seat and a voice in the Board of Estimate . . . This was necessary at the time as the boroughs were faring badly under the centralized local government . . . The boroughs were sadly in need of local improvements and couldn't get them." (Quoted by Peter Grimm, testfying before the Charter Revision Commission, June 11, 1935.) In this instance it would appear that Governor Smith confused the causes with the results.

tation clung to it. "One of the greatest disadvantages and obstacles which your predecessor . . . met with," wrote Mayor La Guardia to its successor, "was not whether it was good, bad or indifferent in the year 1934, but that at its beginning and inception it was vicious, cruel, and dishonest." Not until it was renamed the City Council did the odium disappear.[24]

[24] *Proceedings of the Council of the City of New York, 1938*, I, 15.

2. AN INEFFECTIVE LEGISLATURE, 1902–1937

If only the Board of Aldermen would function! No one tried to prod it into action but me. . . . It was exactly like punching a stuffed bag. No comeback. No debate. No defense. No anything but a stencilled routine.—ALDERMAN RUTH PRATT [1]

THE NEW CHARTER failed to breathe life into the Board of Aldermen. From the very beginning the new body proved ineffective. Scarcely five years after it first convened, a commission reported that it had "signally failed" in the making of general ordinances—one of the principal reasons for its existence.[2]

Few of its enactments were of general interest. During the 1918 session, for example, the legislative mill ground out 541 measures. Yet only three were of popular concern: an ordinance regulating theatre ticket speculators, one requiring owners of abutting property to keep sidewalks in repair, and a third prohibiting the Red Flag at assemblies (a reflection of the current apprehension about radicals). Just one ordinance passed in 1919 was popular in nature—permission for ball clubs to play Sunday baseball.[3]

1 *New York Evening World,* March 29, 1929.

2 *Report of the Charter Revision Commission of 1907 to the Governor of the State of New York, November 30, 1907,* p. 32.

3 Perhaps the most careful analysis of the work of the board was made by the Citizens Union in a study of the 1918 session. Of the 541 measures passed in that year, 465 covered the following subjects: 171 permitted purchase by heads of departments without public letting; 79 requested the Board of Estimate to authorize the issue of special revenue bonds; 112, made jointly with the Board of Estimate, established, abolished, or changed the qualifications of city employees; 62 were drafts on the city treasury for minor contingent expenses; 41 appointed commissioners of deeds. The remaining 76 were miscellaneous items, as follows: 4 granted leaves of absence to city employees; 18 were concerned

None of the boards which convened in the next two decades could boast a more constructive record. The aldermen managed to dispose of a large number of items, but they busied themselves with routine and petty matters. A member of the Corporation Counsel's office assigned to help draft their bills noted that virtually all were trivial, almost irrelevant to the work of a city legislature. The City Fathers named and renamed streets and parks, designated play streets, permitted rifle clubs to discharge small arms, and made recommendations to Congress and foreign governments. And, of course, each alderman saw to those minor local matters affecting his own constituents—the matter dearest of all to his heart.[4]

POWERS OF THE BOARD OF ALDERMEN

The board's futility could be explained partly by the meagerness of its powers. The grant of authority made to it would appear quite sweeping. Upon it were conferred all unassigned powers in the charter, and there devolved upon the aldermen all authority formerly wielded by the common councils of Brooklyn, Long Island City, and the various communities incorporated into Greater New York by consolidation. The charter specifically centered upon the board the legislative power of the city of New York and the aldermen alone could pass ordinances.[5]

Yet the board did not possess sufficient authority to make it a vigorous legislative body. Even after the 1901 charter was adopted, malfeasance by members led to further divestiture of power. Early in the present century the Pennsylvania Railroad sought a franchise for a terminal in Manhattan. For several

---

with the renaming and redistricting of streets; 8 were administrative and concerned with the publication of the aldermanic manual, display of the aldermanic flag, etc.; 6 dealt with memorials, holidays, etc.; 8 were war measures; one enacted the annual tax levy and another the annual budget appropriation; 21 amended in a minor way the Code of Ordinances. *The Searchlight*, IX, No. 1 (1919), 9-10. (*The Searchlight* is the official organ of the Citizens Union.)

[4] *The Searchlight*, XIII, No. 1 (1923), 6-7; *Those Aldermen*, City Affairs Committee Bulletin, January, 1933; testimony of Bernard S. Deutsch, President of Board of Aldermen, before Charter Revision Commission, May 2, 1936; interview with the Hon. Newbold Morris, August 8, 1947.

[5] Charter, Secs. 1, 4, 17, 41, 44.

years the aldermen withheld consent until a certain trucking company was awarded a lucrative contract. It later was disclosed that shares in the corporation were held by the alderman from the home district of Charles F. Murphy, leader of Tammany Hall, and by Mr. Murphy's brother. As a result of this holdup and incidents of a similar nature, the state legislature in 1905 virtually stripped the aldermen of power to grant franchises and vested it in the Board of Estimate and Apportionment. From this time on the Board of Estimate was the most powerful governing body in the city.[6]

A number of powers were exercised concurrently by the aldermen with the Board of Estimate, but in all of these the Board of Aldermen merely echoed the actions of its sister body. Easily the most important was its role in the determination of the annual budget. Here was the aldermen's one power of prime importance; yet their influence in budget-making was infinitesimal. This was due to a number of reasons:

For one, the board had no power to increase or insert new items. It could only reduce or eliminate the appropriations submitted by the Board of Estimate. Some items, moreover, were specifically exempted by the charter from any aldermanic action (namely, sums fixed by state law and entries set aside for payment of interest and principal of the city's debt). Again, they hesitated to make budget cuts for fear of antagonizing their constituents. Reductions made by the Board of Estimate were scattered throughout the entire budget, but because of the more limited number that could be made by the aldermen, they were all the more conspicuous. Moreover, the philosophy of the aldermen impelled them always to pass appropriations, never to vote taxes.[7]

For another reason, the board was limited to a maximum of twenty days for the investigation of a budget which sometimes

[6] Charles M. Stebbins, *Tammany Hall* (Brooklyn, 1921), pp. 74-76; G. M. Myers, *History of Tammany Hall* (New York, 1922), pp. 95-102, 301-2, 309-12; Stokes, *Iconography of Manhattan Island*, V, 2060; Charter, Secs. 72 and 75 as amended by L. 1905, C. 629; sec. 73 as amended by L. 1934, C. 8; sec. 74 as amended by L. 1914, C. 467.

[7] Sec. 226, as amended by L. 1917, C. 258 and Local Laws Nos. 11 and 15 of 1933.

amounted to more than $600,000,000. More than one Finance Committee pointed out that no adequate study of the budget was possible in the limited time spent on it by the aldermen. The fault was not entirely theirs, for they had no information until the work was done. During the actual period of preparation, which began in August, the board did not meet; [8] yet, for a genuine familiarity with the document it was necessary to study it in meticulous detail during August and early September, when the heads of the city departments testified at hearings. When the board resumed sessions in the fall the budget was already crystallized.[9]

For a third reason, the aldermen lacked expert assistance in reviewing the budget. "Without any staff, bureau, or in fact a single individual to aid in the work," reported one Finance Committee, "it is manifestly impossible to examine minutely into every corner of the budget." The budget of the nation's largest city was so vast and complicated that without adequate investigatory staffs the aldermen could make no intelligent criticism. A little might be gleaned from interested citizens who attended public hearings of the Finance Committee, but the taxpayers who were present usually were not intimately acquainted with the document. Some deemed the aldermen themselves incapable of understanding it. "Of the fifty-eight Tammany Hall aldermen in 1928," declared one observer, "it is doubtful if five could, if they would, read an annual report of services obtained from tax money." Whatever their capacities, the aldermen made little pretense of studying the budget. In 1926 a freshman alderman (Ruth Pratt) was appalled by their indifference and nonchalance. Few took the trouble even to scan the totals. When Alderman Pratt inquired of her colleagues how they proposed to digest so vast a body of statistics, they reassured her: "Don't fret about it. . . . They had a lot of experts go over this budget. We needn't bother about it. Why worry?" Lacking adequate analysis of

[8] The aldermen's summer recess in 1936, for example, lasted from July 7 to September 24, and in 1937 the board did not convene from July 20 to September 20.

[9] Testimony of Kenneth Dayton, Assistant to the President of the Board of Aldermen, before Charter Commission, March 5, 1935; *Report of the N. Y. Charter Commission to the Legislature*, March 5, 1923, pp. 162-63.

the budgetary estimates, the majority of aldermen voted for the annual budget without comprehension, without challenge, without concern.[10]

Finally, the mayor could veto all budget cuts made by the aldermen. This authority was wielded for political purposes. When the mayor was of an opposing political party he was almost certain to restore cuts made by the aldermen. The sole exception occurred in 1917, when Mayor Mitchel allowed them to stand. He had already been voted out of office and he permitted the incoming Democrats to assume responsibility for the reductions they had made through the Board of Aldermen. For obvious reasons a mayor of the same political persuasion as the aldermen was likely to employ his veto powers more sparingly. Just how much of the aldermen's budget cuts were restored by various mayors between 1902 and 1937 is indicated in table 1.[11] The aldermen could pass amendments to the budgets over the mayor's veto by a three-quarters vote. This was attempted several times, but it never succeeded.[12] On such occasions the mayor was in a far better position to discuss the budget intelligently than the aldermen. Aided by his staff agencies he could controvert their every argument. Where economy was proposed he could marshall facts to point out that budget cuts would impede city administration by crippling the work of a department. If the aldermen attempted to eliminate a position, he could point out that a department would be improperly manned or that the position had actually saved the city more than the cost of the job.[13]

[10] Testimony of Rufus McGahen, Director of the Budget, before Charter Commission, February 28, 1935; William H. Allen, *Al Smith's Tammany Hall* (New York, 1928), p. 289; *Joint Legislative Committee to Investigate the Affairs of the City of New York: Transcripts of Hearings* (1932), pp. 9889-90 (hereafter referred to as "Seabury Minutes"); Ruth Pratt, "Men Are Bad Housekeepers," *Harpers Magazine*, CLIV (1927), 684, 688.

[11] Lahee, *New York City Budget*, pp. 75-76; *City of New York: Budgets for 1921, 1922, 1924, 1933, 1934, passim.*

[12] Lahee, *New York City Budget*, pp. 76-77.

[13] See veto message of Mayor Mitchel in *Proceedings of Board of Aldermen, 1915*, IV, 633 ff.; see also message of Mayor La Guardia in *Proceedings of Board of Aldermen and Municipal Assembly, Aldermanic Branch, 1934*, II, 819-26.

Table 1. MAYORS' VETOES OF ALDERMANIC BUDGET CUTS

OPPOSING PARTY CONTROLS BOARD OF ALDERMEN

Year of Action	*Maj. Party in Ald.*	*Mayor and Party*	*Aldermanic Reduction*	*Amount Vetoed*	*Percentage Vetoed*
1906	Rep—Fus	McClellan —Dem	$ 259,700	$259,700	100.00
1912	Rep—Fus	Gaynor —Dem	583,525	247,720	42.45
1916	Dem	Mitchel —Fus	120,420	119,540	99.27
1917	Dem	Mitchel —Fus	1,854,004	...	...
1934	Dem	La Guardia—Fus	131,366	122,866	93.5
Total			$2,949,015	$749,826	...
Average			589,803	149,965	25.4
Median			259,700	122,866	93.5

ALDERMEN AND MAYOR OF SAME PARTY

Year of Action	*Maj. Party in Ald.*	*Mayor*	*Aldermanic Reduction*	*Amount Vetoed*	*Percentage Vetoed*
1909	Dem	McClellan	$ 2,000	...	...
1910	Dem	Gaynor	111,500	...	...
1911	Dem	Gaynor	8,151,930	$ 31,500	0.39
1914	Rep—Fus	Mitchel	408,700	165,200	40.42
1915	Rep—Fus	Mitchel	90,760	90,760	100.00
1920	Dem	Hylan	42,260	...	...
1921	Dem	Hylan	278,104	...	...
1923	Dem	Hylan	231,790	...	...
1932	Dem	McKee	585,028	585,028	100.00
1933	Dem	O'Brien	3,604,264	39,395	1.09
Total			$13,506,336	$911,883	...
Average			1,350,634	91,188	6.75
Median			254,947	15,750	.020

Source: See n. 11.

For these reasons the influence of the Board of Aldermen on the annual budget was pitifully small. Over a period of thirty-six years the average reduction amounted to less than one seventh of one per cent. If the mayor's vetoes were taken into account, the effective reductions were even smaller. The budget reductions made by the aldermen are indicated in Table 2.[14]

A minority member once offered a cogent summary of the board's role in budget-making:

> The participation of the Board of Aldermen of this city in the making of the annual budget is very much in the nature of a farce, and not even an amusing farce. . . . It would be impossible to find anywhere else in the world a representative body nominally vested with legislative authority on behalf of more than five millions of people, which, in the first place has so little power over the public purse strings, or which, in the second place, shows so little disposition to use the limited power that it has. . . . Even within the narrow limits prescribed by the charter, the Board of Aldermen could exercise a certain beneficial influence on the city government, if its members were less inclined to save trouble for themselves by leaving all responsibility to the men higher up.[15]

A number of administrative powers were shared with the Board of Estimate. Among them the fixing of salaries of municipal officers and employees clearly paralleled the authority of the aldermen on the budget.[16] Here, too, the aldermen could reduce but not increase the recommendations of the Board of Estimate. Again, the mayor could veto their decisions, subject to overriding by a three-quarters vote of the aldermen. In concurrence with the Board of Estimate the aldermen also approved the issuing of special revenue bonds (short-term notes) to provide funds for unusual, emergency, or deficiency operations. Finally, the two boards could jointly authorize the issuance of corporate stock (long-term notes) for public improvements.[17]

[14] *Proc. of Bd. of Ald., 1902-5, passim*; Herbert H. Lehman (chairman), *The Finances and Financial Administration of New York City* (New York, 1928), p. 256; *Fiscal Facts Concerning the City of New York* (New York, 1940), p. 26.

[15] *Proc. of Bd. of Ald.*, 1918, IV, 641-42.

[16] Day laborers and the teaching and supervisory staff of the Board of Education were exempted from their jurisdiction.

[17] Charter, Sec. 56, as amended by Local Laws Nos. 1 and 2, 1925; Sec. 187, as amended by L. 1933, C. 29; Sec. 188, as amended by L. 1931, C. 284; Sec. 169, as amended by L. 1934, C. 90.

Table 2. BUDGET CUTS MADE BY ALDERMEN

Year of Cut	*Year of Budget*	*Total Tentative Budget (in Thousands of Dollars)*	*Proposed Reduction (in Thousands of Dollars)*	*Reduction After Veto (in Thousands of Dollars)*	*Percentage of Total Budget Effectively Reduced*
1902	1903	$ 97,119	...	...	...
1903	1904	106,674	...	...	...
1904	1905	110,525	...	...	...
1905	1906	116,805	...	...	...
1906	1907	130,422	$ 260	...	...
1907	1908	140,572	...	...	...
1908	1909	156,545	...	...	...
1909	1910	163,130	2	$ 2	0.0012
1910	1911	174,079	112	112	0.06
1911	1912	189,211	8,151	8,120	4.3
1912	1913	193,047	584	336	0.18
1913	1914	192,996	...	...	...
1914	1915	199,233	409	244	0.12
1915	1916	212,956	91	...	...
1916	1917	211,115	120	1	0.0004
1917	1918	238,663	1,854	1,854	0.778
1918	1919	248,025	...	...	...
1919	1920	273,689	...	...	...
1920	1921	345,572	42	42	0.01
1921	1922	350,602	278	278	0.08
1922	1923	353,351	...	...	...
1923	1924	375,468	232	232	0.06
1924	1925	399,619	...	...	...
1925	1926	437,000	...	...	...
1926	1927	474,893	...	...	...
1927	1928	512,529	...	...	...
1928	1929	538,929	...	...	...
1929	1930	569,769	...	...	...
1930	1931	620,840	...	...	...
1931	1932	631,366	...	...	...
1932	1933	518,428	585	...	...
1933	1934	551,048	3,604	3,564	0.65
1934	1935	553,433	131	9	0.0016
1935	1936	552,042	...	...	...
1936	1937	562,999	...	...	...
1937	1938	589,981	...	...	...
Total		$12,092,675	$16,455	$14,794	
Percentage of Total		...	0.136	0.122	

Source: See n. 14.

In these administrative transactions the Board of Aldermen usually gave their assent almost automatically. The dominant organization saw to that. "We are rubber stamps for the Board of Estimate," complained a Republican in 1926. Essentially, the aldermanic vote on any financial item was an observance performed solely to comply with the requirements of the city charter.[18]

On the other hand, an appropriation originating in the Board of Aldermen received short shrift if it was not welcome to the Board of Estimate. "We may deliberate for days on a subject and finally pass it," explained an alderman. "Then if it doesn't meet the approval of the members of the Board of Estimate we were merely wasting out time, for theirs is the real power, as every alderman knows." [19]

How far the financial powers of the aldermen had atrophied was demonstrated in the fixing of the tax rate. The charter required the Board of Aldermen to receive the assessment rolls containing the assessed valuation of taxable property from the Board of Taxes and Assessments by March 1 and to establish the tax rate by dividing the assessed valuation into the sum to be raised by taxes. The last figure was submitted by the comptroller. This procedure became no more than a *pro forma* performance. Since the budget and tax limits were known, the tax rate was set automatically. In practice the tax rate was set in the comptroller's office and printed copies of the aldermanic Finance Committee's report were placed in the hands of its members less than half an hour before they were expected to sign it. The board's ratification then became a mere formality.[20]

18 *New York Evening Post,* June 4, 1926; *Report to the Legislature of the Joint Legislative Committee to Investigate the Affairs of the City of New York,* December 28, 1932, pp. 6-7 (hereafter cited as "Hofstadter Committee Report").

19 *New York Evening Post,* June 4, 1926.

20 Sec. 900, as amended by L. 1914, C. 451; Sec. 907 and 910 as amended by L. 1933, C. 469; Sec. 908; Sec. 909 as amended by Local Law No. 16 of 1926; Sec. 911, as amended by L. 1934, C. 152; Sec. 912; testimony of Kenneth Dayton before Charter Commission, March 5, 1935; testimony of Mayor La Guardia before Charter Commission, May 9, 1935; *Memorandum Prepared for Charter Revision Commission,* August 8, 1934 (see *New York City Charter Revision Commission Documents,* Vol. II, Kent Hall, Columbia University); Joseph D. McGoldrick, "Our City Councils: New York—The Eclipse of the Aldermen," *National Municipal Review,* XIV (1925), 365.

In theory the aldermen possessed sole legislative power in the city; in practice law-making authority was shared with other agencies. The Board of Health was granted virtual autonomy in the enactment of health laws by its right to prepare the Sanitary Code, and the courts were required to take judicial notice of its actions. Several commissioners obviously possessed more expert knowledge concerning areas of the city administration under their jurisdiction than the aldermen, and in practice they were permitted to draw up the ordinances affecting matters under their control. Ordinances relating to traffic rules, for example, were invariably passed in the form requested by the police commissioner. The usage was known as "propriety," and an alderman who desired to introduce an ordinance creating a play street in his district would first make a preliminary visit to the police commissioner to secure his blessing for the proposal. Resolutions concerning local improvements in the several sections of the city could be initiated by twenty-five local boards of improvements. By charter provision or by custom, the law-making authority of the city, theoretically concentrated wholly in the Board of Aldermen, was actually dispersed among a number of municipal bodies.[21]

What powers were actually exercised by the aldermen? Within set limits they could enact ordinances, subject to a veto by the mayor, which they could override by a two-thirds vote. The board changed the names of streets and numbers of buildings, appointed commissioners of deeds, regulated theatres, shooting galleries, and billiard parlors, authorized displays and parades, permitted churches to build vaults without fee, regulated the licensing of junk dealers and pawnbrokers, and made minor changes in its annual revision of the codes of ordinances. Heads of city departments who found it expedient to purchase in excess of $1,000 without public letting of contracts were required to obtain the consent of the board. Enjoined to see to the faithful

[21] Sec. 17, as amended by L. 1905, C. 629; Sec. 1168; Sec. 1172, as amended by L. 1904, C. 628; Sec. 50, as amended by L. 1916, C. 592; Sec. 407, as amended by L. 1904, C. 602 and C. 628; Secs. 425–427; Sec. 428, as amended by L. 1926, C. 520; *Synopsis of the Greater New York Charter* (New York, 1921), pp. 27-30.

execution of laws and ordinances, the board could appoint a special committee to report on matters which dealt with the "orderly and economical administration of the affairs of the city government," a power that was exercised but rarely, and then usually for political motives.[22]

THE USE OF ALDERMANIC POWER

Trifling as these powers appear, lack of authority does not entirely explain the legislature's barren record. Competent witnesses—presiding officers and legislative leaders—testified that the house made ridiculously slight use of the authority lodged in it.[23]

Occasionally, however, a Board of Aldermen demonstrated that it had a scope for vigorous action if it chose to employ these powers. Such a body convened in 1912. After a police lieutenant was prosecuted for instigating the murder of a notorious gambler, Herman Rosenthal, the aldermen responded to widespread public indignation and conducted an investigation of the police department and its administration of vice conditions in the city. When a retired proprietress of a disorderly house named Mary Goode volunteered to testify, a sensation was created. Hearings were crowded with spectators, and every paper in the city found space for Mme. Goode's comprehensive picture of the operations of the "Vice Trust." The committee delivered a scathing indictment of Police Commissioner Waldo and elements in his department that had consummated an alliance with commercialized vice. A series of reforms were recommended for the department and most were adopted. These revelations did more than embarrass the incumbent mayor; they became a campaign issue in the municipal election of 1913. They were instrumental in turning out the Democratic administration and install-

[22] Sec. 43, as amended by L. 1905, C. 629; Sec. 50, as amended by L. 1916, C. 592; Sec. 51, as amended by Local Law No. 33, 1933; Sec. 54; Sec. 58, as amended by L. 1917, C. 610.

[23] Testimony of former President George McAneny before Charter Commission, June 4, 1935; of President Deutsch, May 2, 1935; of former Minority Leader Joseph Clark Baldwin, May 23, 1935.

ing John Purroy Mitchel as Fusion mayor; they helped elect the last Fusion majority to sit in the Board of Aldermen.[24]

The Fusion Board which was elected for the 1914-1915 sessions was unique. Perhaps it was the only Board of Aldermen which made ample use of its powers to perform constructive work. During this period a code of ordinances and building code were drawn up, the procedure of meetings and committees reformed, and opportunities for petty graft among the aldermen diminished. This body actually took pride in its achievements. "The board has ceased being an assemblage of petty politicians chiefly interested in patronage and graft," stated a contemporary editorial, "and has become a city legislature of character and intelligence." [25]

When seven Socialists were elected to the Board in 1917, they became an energetic and ambitious minority which made strenuous efforts to goad the majority into activity. In their efforts to make an impresive showing, the Socialists ran an aldermanic research bureau at their own expense, filled the galleries with their own followers, and attempted to put life and meaning into the legislature's deliberations. The machine Democrats were visibly perturbed, but with less than 10 per cent of the seats the Socialists were almost completely stymied. B. Charney Vladeck, a Socialist leader, found the only way to get his bills passed was to have a friendly Democrat sponsor them. (Peter J. McGuinness, the famous Brooklyn alderman, once made Vladeck this offer: "Cheeney, if you got something you want to slip through here, just give it to me, old pal. I'll make it Irish for you.") Eventually the Socialists came to the reluctant conclusion that

[24] Henry H. Curran, *Pillar to Post* (New York, 1941), pp. 118, 150 ff.; Pringle, "Wet Hope; Profile of Henry Hastings Curran," *The New Yorker*, VI, No. 17 (1940), 22-25; Alva Johnson, "Courtroom Warrior: Profile of Emory R. Buckner," *The New Yorker*, VIII, No. 4 (1942), 20-23; Stephen Wise, *Challenging Years* (New York, 1949), pp. 12-14; *Report of the Special Committee of the Board of Aldermen of the City of New York Appointed August 5, 1912, to Investigate the Police Department* (New York, 1913), pp. 1-39; *Report of the Committee on the Board of Aldermen, 1912-1913* (New York: Citizens Union, 1913), pp. 4, 8-13.

[25] Curran, *Pillar to Post*, pp. 177-87, 193; *Record of the Work of the Board of Aldermen, January 1, 1914, to July 6, 1915* (New York, 1915), *passim*; *The Searchlight*, V, No. 4 (1915), 7-8.

it was well-nigh impossible to secure any real reform through the Board of Aldermen. As they viewed its morbid condition, they concluded that its weakness lay partly in the body's limited powers and partly in the fact that it was in the grip of a powerful political machine.[26]

ONE-PARTY RULE

The most active sessions were those in which the majorities enjoyed the smallest margins; those in which overwhelming majorities held sway tended to be the most inert. By and large, the bodies that convened between 1902 and 1921 tended to fall into the first category. In this period the average size of the majority was less than 60 per cent, as Table 3 indicates.[27]

Table 3. PARTY REPRESENTATION IN THE BOARD OF ALDERMEN, 1902–1921

Sessions	*Number of Democrats*	*Number of Republicans*	*Others*	*Majority Percentage*
1902–3	36	37	0	51
1904–5	51	22	0	70
1906–7	26	41	6	56
1908–9	48	24	1	66
1910–11	40	33	0	55
1912–13	35	38	0	52
1914–15	32	40	1	55
1916–17	53	20	0	73
1918–19	45	15	7	67
1920–21	35	25	7	52

This period encompassed the most productive era in the body's history—the time of the police investigation, a new code of ordinances, a new building code, and internal reform of the legislature. This all occurred when minority and majority were almost evenly matched (1912-15). Even though the Republicans and

[26] Clark Evans and Charles Solomon, *The Socialists in the New York City Board of Aldermen* (New York, 1918), p. 37; *The Searchlight*, VIII, No. 1 (1918), 7; Richard H. Rovere, "The Big Hello: Profile of Peter J. McGuinness," *The New Yorker*, XX, No. 48 (1946), 34.

[27] *Proportional Representation Review*, No. 24 (October, 1922), pp. 65-67; *Annual Reports of the Board of Elections of the City of New York for the Years 1918-1935, passim.*

Socialists were unable to carry out their legislative programs from 1918 to 1921, their presence in sizable numbers acted as a wholesome influence upon the majority. Some regarded the efforts of the Socialists in particular as mere obstruction; others believed they made the Board of Aldermen an open forum for full and critical discussion of municipal affairs. Some years later, Acting Mayor McKee recalled that in this period vigorous and vociferous minorities, whether Republican or Socialist, had proved deterrents to wrongdoing on the part of their majority colleagues.[28]

After 1921, the Republicans dwindled in numbers and the Socialists disappeared altogether. As Table 4 indicates, in one session a single Republican sat among sixty-four Democrats.

Table 4. PARTY REPRESENTATION IN THE BOARD OF ALDERMEN, 1922–1937

Sessions	*Number of Democrats*	*Number of Republicans*	*Others*	*Majority Percentage*
1922–23	52	12	1	80
1924–25	57	8	0	88
1926–27	62	3	0	95
1928–29	58	7	0	89
1930–31	61	4	0	94
1932–33	64	1	0	98
1934–35	49	16	0	75
1936–37	62	3	0	95
Total	465	54	1	89.4 (Average)

This period marked a rapid decline of the city legislature; it was soon eclipsed by the municipal executive branch and the Board of Estimate and Apportionment. In 1923 the Citizens Union reported that the Board had reached a "new low in impotence and uselessness," its chief purpose being to grant "automatic consent to such measures as still required the approval of the city legislature." Meetings lapsed into cut-and-dried affairs, often lasting a bare twenty minutes. "The defunct Board of

[28] McGoldrick, "Eclipse of the Aldermen," *Nat. Mun. Rev.*, XIV, 367; *The Searchlight*, XIII, No. 3 (1933), 5; Norman Thomas and Paul Blanshard, *What's the Matter with New York* (New York, 1932), p. 20; "Seabury Minutes," p. 10493.

Aldermen might have been called a municipal lodging house," wrote an authority soon after its demise, "a place for a weekly nap at the city's expense." [29]

Not until a Fusion administration gained office in 1934 did the moribund Board of Aldermen revive. A drastic change took place in the first La Guardia regime (1934-37). Meetings eventually lasted hours instead of twenty minutes, and committees were conscientiously attended. The aldermen probably spent more time on their work during the board's last four years than in the previous ten. Yet they failed to make a more impressive showing than their predecessors. They continued to permit the discharge of small arms, to designate street numbers, and to increase the waiting period before a secondhand dealer might sell his articles. There were two notable exceptions—an income tax law and a sales tax. The latter, incidentally, became a model for other cities. But both originated with the city administration and the aldermen merely accepted the mayor's recommendations.[30]

In the light of these facts, many ascribed the futility of the board in its last two decades to the lack of a minority large enough to command the respect of the majority. When the opposition groups were unable to exercise a vigilant and active-minded criticism, it became possible for the party in power to put through the legislature hastily conceived or one-sided measures. Others went further and insisted that the absence of a legislative minority vigorous enough to check the dominant political organization was partly responsible for the scandalous conditions in the city government exposed in a series of investigations in the early thirties. "There are few factors so stimulating to sound administration as an active minority," asserted a legislative committee. "Adequate minority representation is

[29] *The Searchlight*, XIII, No. 3 (1923), 5; Eleanor C. Tanzer, "The First P. R. Council," *The Searchlight*, XXIX, No. 1 (1939), 3.

[30] Testimony of Kenneth Dayton before Charter Revision Commission, March 5, 1935; Rebecca Rankin (ed.), *New York Advancing: 1934-1935* (New York, 1936), pp. 137-39; *Municipal Assembly Record*, XI, No. 10 (1937), 3, 14; Interview with the Hon. Morton Baum, May 28, 1948.

probably the best insurance . . . against waste, inefficiency, and corruption." [31]

CALIBER AND OUTLOOK OF THE ALDERMEN

The board's sterile record reflected the quality of its membership. "Men of capacity and high character," noted the Charter Commission of 1907, found their way into the body "as occasional exceptions, not as a rule." The Citizens Union regarded the aldermen of 1912-13 as "totally unfit to hold any important position in the public service." Yet they were an improvement over their immediate predecessors! [32] In 1919 the City Fathers were censured in the following terms:

> The present status of the personnel of the Board is very low. There are not more than fifteen, at the most twenty, members out of the whole sixty-seven whom the average man would entrust with an ordinary business transaction. There are many who are downright ignorant, and with very few exceptions the remainder is of a mediocre order, without either the ability or the desire to tackle their jobs seriously—lazy, superficial, and unwilling to make the effort to investigate the facts or even to familiarize themselves with the ordinances under consideration.[33]

Of far different stripe, however, were the presidents of the Board of Aldermen. They were usually men of repute, even of distinction. Three were later elected mayor—George B. McClellan, son of the Civil War general, John Purroy Mitchel, and Fiorello H. La Guardia. Probably the most illustrious president of the board was Alfred E. Smith, who occupied the office at the time he was first elected Governor in 1918.[34]

[31] "Seabury Minutes," p. 10484; *Report of Charter Commission of 1923*, p. 15; *Charter Revision for the City of New York: A Plan Prepared by the Division of Research in Public Administration, Department of Government, Washington Square College, New York University* (New York, 1934), pp. 8-9; "Hofstadter Committee Report," p. 11.

[32] *Report of the Charter Revision Commission of 1907*, p. 33; *Report of the Committee on the Board of Aldermen of the Citizens Union for the 1912-1913 Term* (New York, 1913), p. 4.

[33] *The Searchlight,* IX, No. 1 (1919), 10.

[34] Milton Mackaye, "Out of the Past: Profile of George Brinton McClellan," *The New Yorker*, VIII, No. 15 (1932), 21-25; Henry F. Pringle, "The Italian Table D'Hote: Profile of Fiorello H. La Guardia," *The New Yorker*, V, No. 28 (1929),

The vast difference in stature between presidents and members elected to the board may be explained in part by the nature of the ballot. The three most conspicuous candidates in municipal elections were those elected on a city-wide ticket—mayor, comptroller, and president of the Board of Aldermen. For these offices the political leaders carefully selected men of some eminence. But the ballot was a lengthy one. In 1933, for example, the voters of Manhattan were asked to elect twenty officials, and the alderman was at the bottom of the list. How the average citizen reacted to this array of candidates may be judged from the admission of President Woodrow Wilson that he voted intelligently only for those at the head of the ticket and from the confession of President Eliot of Harvard that he habitually voted blindly. "A majority of the voters, having little opportunity for knowing the personal qualifications of the obscure condidates," wrote Judge Seabury of the New York City elections, "vote blindly under the emblem of their party and elect the hand-picked candidate of the bosses." Indeed, many expressed no preference at all for the minor offices. In 1933, for example, the vote for the aldermen was more than 14 per cent smaller than that cast for mayor. Under these conditions, political leaders could nominate and "get by" with compliant machine candidates, regardless of their qualifications.[35]

These leaders wanted docility, not statesmanship. There were a handful of intelligent and public-spirited members in every session, but a reliable observer once described the greater part as the "left-overs of the district clubs." One ungenerous critic excoriated the body as "an anteroom for Tammany spoilsmen, a gathering place for second-rate gentlemen who cannot get their feet into the main trough." [36]

22-25. In later years Governor Smith was taken to task for failing to reform the Board of Aldermen during his year as presiding officer and for leaving it "as futile and blind as he found it." Allen, *Al Smith's Tammany Hall*, p. 137.

[35] Richard S. Childs, *The Short Ballot: A Movement to Simplify Politics* (New York, 1930), p. 4; George H. Hallett, *Proportional Representation—The Key to Democracy* (New York, 1940), p. 148; *Annual Report of Board of Elections for 1933, passim.*

[36] Joseph D. McGoldrick, "The Board of Estimate and Apportionment of New York City," *National Municipal Review*, XVIII (1929), 140; radio address of Executive Director of City Affairs Committee over Station WEVD, July 11,

Political leaders were not interested in candidates who would display energy and initiative in solving the city's problems. They preferred nonentities who would confine their efforts to scurrying about to assist their constituents with their troubles. Indeed, few aldermen had the perspective that would enable them to envisage legislation from a broad municipal viewpoint. Almost invariably they were men who had grown up in their districts and were chosen from its party workers. They were expected to be local representatives rather than city officials, and rarely did they conceive any duties beyond their responsibilities to the people of their districts. If an alderman ever took the trouble to examine a particular bill, it would be for its effects upon particular groups among his constituents. When the results were unfavorable he would vote against the proposal, even if he recognized that it would serve the best interests of the city at large. Most of the business transacted in the board, however, concerned local matters. By a custom called "privilege," the aldermen deferred to the decisions of individual members in matters relating to their respective neighborhoods. With their attention focussed on the needs of their own districts, few among the aldermen possessed an outlook broad enough to encompass the entire city.[37]

AN APATHETIC ELECTORATE

Theodore Roosevelt once remarked that the citizens of New York might become interested in the qualifications or conduct of the mayor, but never in those of the aldermen. Few knew the name of their alderman, fewer still the powers of the board. On one occasion a Democratic alderman sought to dampen the ardor of the zealous Socialists by admonishing them: "These Socialists

1933. In an interview on March 4, 1947, Joseph Clark Baldwin, who served as minority leader in the Board of Aldermen from 1930 until 1934 and who also was elected to the State Senate, City Council, and national House of Representatives, observed that any legislature will contain a number of "spineless goops" and that the Board of Aldermen was not exceptional in this regard.

[37] Margaret I. Tanzer, "Aldermen Cannot Say 'No,'" *The Searchlight*, XXI, No. 1 (1931), 10; testimony of President Deutsch before Charter Revision Commission, May 2, 1935.

have just got in and they think it's something great to be an alderman. We older men know better. Why, Mr. President, a hundred thousand persons pass through City Hall Park every day and I want to assure my Socialist friends that not one per cent of those people know that such a thing as the Board of Aldermen is in existence." That might have been an exaggeration. Yet even Henry H. Curran, lawyer, ex-reporter on the *Tribune,* and active member of a district club, confessed that he began his six-year term in the Board with almost no knowledge of the aldermen themselves. But ignorance of them was general—"to most people they were no more than a name." [38]

A SUBSERVIENT HOUSE

Assured that the public would take little interest in the proceedings of the board, the leaders of the dominant political party found it easy to manage its subservient membership. "They say the members of the Board of Aldermen are rubber stamps," asserted the Borough President of Queens, "because if they don't do what they are told, they are put out." [39] A penetrating analysis of the operation of the Board was made by the Citizens Union in 1911:

> The large powers conferred by the Greater New York Charter upon the Board of Aldermen are not commonly understood because many of them are seldom exercised. Many others when exercised are used for the sole purpose of securing patronage for the district organizations of the political parties, or to gain partisan advantages. . . . The Board of Aldermen serves rather as an adjunct to the political organizations than as a branch of the city government.[40]

The activities of the board can be understood only in terms of its subordination to the city's political organization. From 1918 until 1934 the aldermen supinely accepted the orders of

[38] Theodore Roosevelt, *Autobiography,* p. 82; Evans and Solomon, *Socialists in the N. Y. C. Bd. of Ald.,* p. 1; Curran, *Pillar to Post,* p. 127.

[39] Samuel Seabury, *Final Report to the Members of the Joint Legislative Committee to Investigate the Administration of the Various Departments of the Government of the City of New York,* December 27, 1932, p. 19; "Seabury Minutes," p. 10485.

[40] *Report of the Committee on the Board of Aldermen of the Citizens Union for the 1910-1911 Term* (New York, 1911), p. 3.

the Democratic bosses, the mayor, and the Board of Estimate. It was a period of complete and uninterrupted Democratic control over virtually all branches of the city government—the mayor's office and the administrative departments, the Board of Estimate and Apportionment, and most of the county and borough governments. In this scheme of things the Board of Aldermen became a mere cog in the party machine, its chief function being to ratify those decisions of the party chiefs which required the sanction of the board in conformity with the city charter. "We aldermen are just a small part of the big machine that turns out legislation by the yard at the will of Tammany Hall," complained a Republican alderman in 1926.[41] Overwhelming Democratic majorities, especially after 1921, made the task relatively simple. During this sixteen-year period the board went through the motions of conducting business in a constitutional manner; in reality it was a travesty of a legislative body.

With the advent of a Fusion mayor and Board of Estimate in 1934, as we have said, the board took a new lease on life. But their failure to enact important reforms requested by the administration, their attack on the mayor's budget, and an investigation of the relief situation revealed that their purpose was to harass and bedevil the Fusion executive rather than to carry out a constructive program. Mayor La Guardia, in turn, vetoed 106 of the 438 ordinances sent him by the Board of Aldermen during his first year in office.[42]

INVESTIGATIONS AS POLITICAL WEAPONS

It was only when the mayor belonged to one party and the majority in the board to another that the governing body displayed a semblance of vitality. No Board of Aldermen ever instituted an investigation without a political motive. When Alderman Curran inquired into police inefficiency in 1912, he boasted of performing constructive work where groups like the

[41] *New York Evening Post*, June 4, 1926.

[42] Statement of Paul J. Kern, law secretary to the Mayor, before the Charter Revision Commission, March 5, 1935; statement of Kenneth Dayton, March 5, 1935.

Lexow Committee of 1894 and the Mazet Committee of 1899 had built "bonfires of sensational exposure" but presented no remedy. There is little doubt that a clean-up of the department was overdue; yet it is worth noting that Alderman Curran's investigation was launched when a Fusion majority in the Board of Aldermen confronted a Democratic mayor. What is more, the report of the investigating committee was presented shortly before a municipal election, and public reprobation of police corruption subsequently gave a powerful impetus to a reform movement. Tammany was swept out of office, and Fusion gained control of the city government.[43]

For a brief interval Fusion controlled both the city administration and the Board of Aldermen (1914-15); then followed a long era of Democratic hegemony over all important areas of municipal government (1918-33). As long as the same party dominated the administrative and legislative branches, no major aldermanic investigation was undertaken. Indeed, relations with Democratic commissioners in the twenties were most cordial, for their party confreres in the Board of Aldermen regarded the city departments as legitimate sources of patronage and small favors for their constituents. Hence, efforts on the part of the Republican minority to summon the commissioners for questioning or to investigate their departments for inefficiency were promptly tabled without debate. In 1923, the Democrats conceived the happy idea of omitting such resolutions from the printed minutes.[44]

Only once in this era did an alderman seem to initiate an investigation. In 1927 it was revealed that a sewer ring had mulcted home owners in Queens of millions of dollars for defective pipes. In newspaper accounts it was George U. Harvey, elected as Republican alderman from the borough, who led the fight against the extortionate sewer assessments and filed with

[43] Curran, *Pillar to Post, passim*; *Report of Comm. on Bd. of Ald. of the Citizens Union for the 1912-13 Term*, pp. 8-13; Edward J. Flynn, *You're the Boss* (New York, 1947), pp. 7-8.

[44] *The Searchlight*, XIII, No. 3 (1923), 5-6; Emanuel H. Lavine, *"Gimme": Or How Politicians Get Rich* (New York, 1931), pp. 30-33; *New York Times*, Feb. 15, 1931; *Proc. of Bd. of Ald. and Mun. Assem., Aldermanic Branch, 1931*, I, 634-35.

Governor Smith charges against President Maurice E. Connolly which eventually landed that administrator in prison. To some he was the "Fighting Alderman," and Harvey-for-Governor clubs sprang up all over Long Island. Others called the episode a "curious story of manufactured public opinion." Actually the "Fighting Alderman" knew little about sewer pipes; he merely served as a mouthpiece for metropolitan newspapers which found it expedient to have a public official make charges on the basis of evidence which they themselves had dug out. Not only did reporters compose his public statements, but also they sometimes neglected to explain them to Harvey, the "terror of sewer malefactors," until after they were published.[45]

In the ensuing five years a whole battery of inquiries was instituted into municipal affairs. Magistrates retired or were removed, and no less a figure than a Tammany mayor resigned under fire. As counsel to a legislative committee, Judge Seabury uncovered "graft and crookedness of every description and in every phase of the city government."[46] But other than answering subpoenas to appear at hearings, the aldermen took no official cognizance of the proceedings. Reform groups reproached them for failure to set in motion exposés of their own, but the sixty-odd Democratic aldermen gave no heed, for they were not disposed to terminate their political careers abruptly. Even when the Republican minority leader, Joseph Clark Baldwin, demanded an investigation of the city's administration, he found it more effective to send a public letter to Governor Roosevelt rather than to sponsor a resolution in the Board of Alder-

[45] Milton Mackaye, *The Tin Box Parade* (New York, 1934), pp. 178-80; Thomas and Blanshard, *What's the Matter with New York*, pp. 198-99, 336; Richard F. Warner, "On the Up: Profile of George Upton Harvey," *The New Yorker*, III, No. 30 (1927), 19-22. The columns of the *New York Evening Post* of December 6, 8, 13, 14, 15, 16, 20, 21, and 27, 1927, clearly demonstrate the spadework of a staff of reporters. In 1931 Harvey himself, as President of the Borough of Queens, became involved in activities which Governor Roosevelt censured as "incompatible with the ideals of official conduct." He had borrowed considerable sums of money from concerns doing business with the borough and lent his name to a stock promotion scheme of a "highly suspicious nature," after accepting five hundred shares as a gift. When the Governor rebuked him but permitted him to remain in office, a *New York Times* editorial (August 5, 1931) stated that he had "saved his skin but lost . . . his good repute as a public officer."

[46] Richard Welling, *As the Twig Is Bent* (New York, 1942), p. 85.

men. That approach had been attempted several months before, when Baldwin had introduced a resolution calling for a legislative investigation of the magistrates' courts. It was speedily filed with the board's Committee on State Legislation, where it was buried forever.[47]

When a Fusion administration took office in 1934, however, the Democratic majority in the Board of Aldermen found the time ripe for an investigation of the administration's relief program. This undertaking was denounced by a civic organization as a "political circus . . . engineered and conducted by the Tammany-controlled Board of Aldermen" for no purpose other than discrediting the city administration.[48] Fortunately, perhaps, the investigation had little effect on municipal politics; but it did enrich the American language. When a work-relief teacher testified he was giving instruction in "boondoggling," the conservative press picked up the expression and used it frequently to ridicule work-relief projects.[49]

THE BUDGET AS A POLITICAL WEAPON

Decisions on the annual budget were also made for political rather than fiscal considerations. When the executive and legislative branch were both dominated by the same party the aldermen usually accepted the budget as presented.[50] On a number of occasions during the 1920's minor alterations were made in the budget, but these occurred with the prior knowledge and consent

47 City Affairs Committee Press Release, December 23, 1932; Geoffrey T. Hellman, "The Festive Touch: Profile of Joseph Clark Baldwin, III," *The New Yorker*, XIX, No. 2 (1943), 30; *New York Times*, January 15, 1930, August 22 and 23, 1930.

48 *The Relief Situation and the Aldermanic Investigation*, City Affairs Committee Bulletin, April, 1935.

49 John D. Millett, *The Works Progress Administration in New York City* (Chicago, 1938), p. 22; Frederick Lewis Allen, *Since Yesterday* (New York, 1940), p. 177. The term was not listed in the 1931 edition of H. L. Mencken's, *The American Language*. It first appeared in the 1945 edition (pp. 303, 511).

50 Seventy per cent of the budgets presented by Boards of Estimate controlled by the same party that had a majority in the Board of Aldermen were adopted as submitted. *Proc. of Bd. of Ald., 1902-19, passim*; *City of New York: Budgets for 1921-1933, 1937, 1938, passim*; Lahee, *New York City Budget*, pp. 74-76.

of the administration and were essentially final proofreadings to correct clerical errors and other small discrepancies that had been overlooked in the Board of Estimate.[51]

During the twenties, in fact, the Board of Aldermen gave up all pretense at independent consideration of the budget. Until 1934 it followed the ritual set forth in the charter for the exercise of its financial powers, but few aldermen ever attempted to participate actively in the proceedings. In all this time the board was geared to the machine which dominated the city's political life. If the budget adopted in 1932 was typical, then the county leaders were consulted in the initial stages of budget preparation.[52] After preliminary estimates had been formulated by the commissioners of the administrative departments, they were turned over to the Board of Estimate, which adopted the tentative budget. Under Mayors Hylan, Walker, and O'Brien, not only were the members of the Board of Estimate of the same political persuasion as the majority, but also they towered over the aldermen in power and prestige. Hence the legislators offered little criticism and no effective opposition to the Board of Estimate's budget. After 1918, Finance Committee reports were prepared by a clerk, and committee members hardly glanced at it. To be sure, the Republican minority usually brought in a report for reduction of the budget, but they could not hope to influence the immense Democratic majorities. Indeed, some Democrats believed their periodic but futile protests were merely for the record. Reports of the Finance Committee were adopted as a matter of course, most aldermen voting without troubling to look inside the cover of the document. The board was permitted twenty days in which to consider the budget, but often the deliberations lasted only twenty minutes.[53]

[51] *New York Times*, December 6, 1921; *The Searchlight*, XIII, No. 3 (1923), 5.

[52] Comptroller Charles W. Berry testified under examination by Judge Seabury that he had discussed the budget with Tammany Leader John F. Curry and other county leaders. His personal preference for reductions in the budget had been overruled by the county leaders, he stated. "Seabury Minutes," pp. 10577-85 and *New York Times*, December 8, 1932.

[53] "Seabury Minutes," pp. 9888-89, 9896-98; Lehman, *Finances and Financial Administration of New York City*, p. 256; press release of City Affairs Committee, July 12, 1933.

But when the aldermen faced a hostile Board of Estimate and Apportionment, they suddenly became aware of their financial authority. Then the budget was held up for trading purposes, or to annoy the enemy. There were nine years in which opposing parties controlled the two houses. In seven of those nine years the aldermen cut the budget.[54] In 1934, for example, the Democratic Finance Committee struck out of the Fusion budget such essentials as health and hospital services. Apparently little effort had been made by the committee to ascertain precisely what they were eliminating. "Actually they were not cutting hospitals," observed the aldermanic whip some years later. "They were cutting La Guardia." [55]

Even a mayor of the same party could be taught a lesson. In 1910, Mayor William J. Gaynor served notice on Tammany leaders that the "seat of the government was at City Hall, not at Fourteenth Street." A Democrat himself, Gaynor nevertheless appointed only one Tammany district leader as head of an administrative department. The anti-Tammany commissioners attempted to resist the demands of Democratic district leaders to use their departments for patronage and favor, but unhappily they were required by the charter to appear before the aldermen when they found it necessary to request special revenue bonds for expenses not covered in the annual budget or to secure authorization for contracts over $1,000 without public letting. On such occasions they were made painfully aware of the error of their ways.[56] A member of the board in 1911 has described the proceedings:

[54] Eight of those nine years were 1906, 1907, 1910, 1911, 1916, 1917, 1934, and 1935. The ninth was 1912, when the Republican-Fusion forces had an ostensible majority in both houses. In the Board of Aldermen, however, the Democrats won control both in the Finance Committee and on the floor of the chamber. Then they were able to run the Board of Aldermen to their own satisfaction. In every one of those nine years, except 1907 and 1935, the aldermen cut the budget as it came from the Board of Estimate. Lahee, *New York City Budget*, pp. 74-76; *Report of Committee on Bd. of Ald. of Cit. Un. for 1912-1913 Term*, p. 8; *Proc. of Bd. of Ald., 1917*, IV, 668 ff.; *City of New York: Budget for 1935*, pp. 359-67.

[55] Testimony of Mayor La Guardia before Charter Revision Committee, May 9, 1935; interview with the Hon. Murray Stand, June 13, 1947.

[56] *Report of Comm. on Bd. of Ald. of Cit. Un. for 1910-11 Term*, pp. 4-7; Louis Heaton Pink, *Gaynor: The Tammany Mayor Who Swallowed the Tiger* (New York, 1931), pp. 143-46. At that time the headquarters of Tammany Hall was on Fourteenth Street.

> The slight financial powers possessed by the aldermen were exercised . . . with an eye to a proper reciprocity on the part of the city department that wanted the money. If the commissioner had been good to the alderman in giving them odd jobs for their constituents . . . then the aldermen would be good to the commissioner and vote for the city money he wanted. . . . The question was not so much the merit of the commissioner's request as it was his treatment of the aldermen when they "went to the front" for . . . little accommodations and adjustments for citizens. . . . If their bestowal upon the aldermen had been generous enough to give an atmosphere of benediction, then there was no debate and all were happy. If the degree of bestowal had been a little pinched, however, there would be debate. Searching questions would be asked of the commissioner, who was there in person to defend and promote his application. The city fathers would for a moment become the stern watch-dogs of a hard-pressed treasury. "Efficiency and economy" would be dwelt upon. When a word from the commissioner, withering under the interrogation, gave sign of a light dawning upon him, then happiness would reappear and the money would be voted.[57]

When Fusion obtained a majority in the Board of Aldermen (1914), steps were taken to end the financial tilting with commissioners, especially when Fusion controlled both the administration and legislature. And during sixteen years of Democratic hegemony over all branches of the city government (1918-33), there was complete harmony with commissioners. Members might miss the "Ciceronian invective" directed at heads of departments who had not "come across" with favors and jobs, but during the Hylan, Walker, and O'Brien regimes aldermen and commissioners were on the friendliest of terms. For in soliciting small benefits for their constituents, the aldermen usually received a cordial welcome in the city departments. The aldermen most often acted on behalf of the political leaders of their respective districts, and these powerful politicians often held commissionerships themselves or exerted a potent influence in the city departments in which they served. Hence a brisk trading in favors took place among district leaders, with the aldermen often acting as intermediaries.[58]

[57] Curran, *Pillar to Post,* pp. 131-32.

[58] Curran, *Pillar to Post,* p. 147; *Report of Comm. on Bd. of Ald. of Cit. Un. for 1914-15 Term,* p. 12; McGoldrick, "Eclipse of the Aldermen," *Nat. Mun. Rev.,* XIV, 365-66; "Hofstadter Committee Report," p. 6.

There was power, then, in the old Board of Aldermen, if only the lawmakers had the will to use it. When the mayor or Board of Estimate were of the same political persuasion, it became a mere organ of registration for the will of the regnant party, unless His Honor did not see eye to eye with the party managers. Only when the administration or the second house was controlled by the opposing party were its financial authority and power to investigate employed, and then solely as partisan weapons. But no one seriously expected the aldermen to grapple with the city's major problems.

3. HOME RULE, 1924–1937

A city is not a province to be administered by some outside authority, but a government.—HORACE DEMING [1]

UNTIL 1924 New York was not a self-governing community. The city legislature could exercise no authority whatever without a grant of power from the state. And from the state legislature at Albany flowed a continuous stream of special or local laws. Charter-revising legislation was enacted in such numbers that New York's charter became a "thing of shreds and patches." In 1921 a charter revision commission published a volume of digests of special laws of the legislature pertaining to New York City which filled 1300 pages in fine print. Nor did the state legislature confine itself to delimiting the powers of the municipal government. A large proportion of its time was spent in passing special legislation dealing in minute detail with the organization and operation of city governments. One local law increased the space in New York City's Hall of Records to be allotted to the Register and Commissioner of Records from 10,000 to 40,000 feet. Another abolished the grade of doorman in the New York Police Department.[2]

For two generations various officials and official bodies in the state condemned the recourse of individuals to the state legislature for special bills as a serious abuse. The New York Charter Revision Commission of 1907, for example, scored the "frequent legislative interventions which have practically destroyed all self-government, created more local mischief than they have

[1] *The Government of American Cities* (New York, 1909), p. 153.

[2] *Report of Chart. Rev. Comm. of 1907*, p. 11; *Home Rule for New York City* (New York, 1916), unpaged; Joseph D. McGoldrick, "Home Rule in New York State," *American Political Science Review*, XIX (1925), 695.

remedied, and grown to be prolific of abuse and corruption" in successive legislatures. The movement for Home Rule really gained momentum after 1910. Reform of this type was particularly desired by the administration of Mayor John Purroy Mitchel (1914-1917), who demanded that New York City frame its own charter and keep it in force "without the meddlesome interference from any accidental state legislature which might wish to intervene on matters of local concern or pass special acts at the behest of special interests." In 1915 the State Constitutional Convention adopted a Home Rule amendment, but the entire constitution was rejected at the polls. The following year a group of civic organizations drafted an amendment at a meeting called by a conference of mayors and other city officials and introduced it into the state legislature every year thereafter until the 1922-23 sessions. In those years, with the approval of Charles F. Murphy, leader of Tammany Hall, a constitutional amendment instituting home rule was passed, and in 1924 an Enabling Act followed.[3]

For decades the Board of Aldermen had been gradually divested of its more important powers. Home Rule reversed this movement, conferring upon the board greater authority than it had ever possessed since the consolidation of the city. The state legislature was now prohibited from passing special or local acts relating to the "property, affairs, or government of cities" and the power transferred to the cities themselves.[4]

Following the mandate of the Home Rule Law there was established, in May 1924, a "Municipal Assembly." It was a two-chambered body in which the Board of Estimate and Appor-

[3] *Rep. of Chart. Rev. Comm. of 1907*, p. 16; John Purroy Mitchel, *The City and State Constitution* (New York, 1914), p. 10; *New York City Government Functions and Problems* (New York, 1938), pp. 21-26; *Address of Mayor John P. Mitchel to Academy of Political Science*, Nov. 19, 1914 (Files of Municipal Reference Library).

[4] *State Constitution*, Art. XII, Secs. 2, 3. The phrase, "property, affairs, or government of cities," which had been part of the State Constitution since 1895, had applied to measures of local concern enacted by the State Legislature. It was deliberately retained by the framers of the amendment in order to avoid litigation over interpretation of language as far as possible. The words had been interpreted by the courts on a number of occasions. *Home Rule For Cities* (New York, 1924), p. 14.

tionment acted as the upper branch, the Board of Aldermen the lower. In addition to its ordinance-making powers, the Board of Aldermen, when meeting as the Aldermanic Branch of the Municipal Assembly, now gained the right to pass local laws relating to "property, affairs, or government" of the city. A local law could originate in either branch, and after receiving an affirmative majority in both houses, and the approval of the mayor, would become law.[5]

Along with their added duties the aldermen also received a salary increase. Their annual income was raised from $3,000 to $5,000 a year on the theory that a higher type of legislator would be attracted to the position. Needless to say, none of the incumbents who were reëlected for the 1924 sessions expressed resentment at the implied slur upon their capacities.

From this time on the Board of Aldermen led a double life. It convened Tuesday afternoon as the Aldermanic Branch of the Municipal Assembly, the president of the board acting as chairman. Immediately thereafter it adjourned to meet again as the Board of Aldermen. The same personnel played the same roles in their dual capacity, save the president of the board and the five borough presidents. They had voting rights in the Board of Aldermen, but since they could vote for local laws in the Board of Estimate and Apportionment Branch, their votes were not recorded in the adoption of local laws in the Aldermanic Branch of the Municipal Assembly.[6]

The local legislature at last seemed free from the domination

[5] Except in cases where the mayor certified that immediate passage was urgently necessary it was required that a pending bill be considered for at least seven days, exclusive of Sundays. Upon the mayor's certification the time minimum was waived, but an affirmative vote of two-thirds the voting power of each branch was required. Before final passage of any local law the mayor was required to hold a public hearing. Approval of the mayor was necessary for its enactment, unless the two branches of the assembly passed it over his veto by two-thirds of their voting strength. (In its reconsideration of the Board of Estimate and Apportionment, however, the mayor was not entitled to a vote.) Should the mayor disregard a bill for thirty days it would be adopted as if he had signed it. *City Home Rule Law*, L. 1924, C. 363, Sec. 10, as amended by L. 1928, C. 671; Sec. 11, as amended by L. 1928, C. 678 and C. 670 and L. 1929, C. 646; Secs. 13 and 14, as amended by L. 1928, C. 672.

[6] Rules of the Municipal Assembly, Aldermanic Branch, No. 21. *Manual of the Board of Aldermen: 1936-1937* (New York, 1936), p. 76. They were included in the roll call.

of state politics. But to those who had expected an active and independent body the Municipal Assembly was a sore disappointment. By 1924 the Board of Aldermen was considered as important to the city's government as a "fifth wheel." Its performance as the lower branch of the city's home rule legislature brought about no change in its reputation. Scheduled as fifteen minute sessions, the meetings of the Aldermanic Branch usually lasted ten. Most of the time was spent on the invocation and roll call. Normally the recommendations of the Committee on Local Laws were accepted without comment, consideration, or dissenting vote.[7]

In the days before Home Rule, nearly one-third of the laws passed by the state legislature were local laws. Hence a flood of legislation was expected in the Municipal Assembly, to which the power had been transferred. The results, however, were meager and insignificant. In its first decade the Municipal Assembly passed an average of less than twenty local laws, and of these, about a third were initiated in the Aldermanic Branch. With few exceptions, the local laws were of little importance; many were of a trifling nature.[8]

The first La Guardia administration (1934-1937) brought a renaissance of activities. Both branches initiated and passed more legislation in this period than in the entire preceding decade.[9] Yet few significant measures emerged from the Aldermanic

[7] Joseph D. McGoldrick, "New York City's Municipal Assembly," *Weekly News*, IV, No. 3 (April 17, 1925) (A publication of the New York League of Women Voters); *The Searchlight*, XVII, No. 2 (1927), 14. In the last term of the board, the Aldermanic Branch of the Municipal Assembly was scheduled to meet at 2:00 P.M., the Board of Aldermen at 2:15 P.M. *Manual of the Board of Aldermen: 1936-1937*, pp. 3, 30, 31.

[8] *The Searchlight*, XV, No. 1 (1925), 5, 7; Russel Forbes, "The Municipal Assembly: New York's Home Rule Legislature," *National Municipal Review*, XVIII (1929), 632-34; Joseph D. McGoldrick, "Home Rule Thus Far," *Weekly News*, IV, No. 6 (May, 1925).

[9] The following chart illustrates the increased activity during the four years:

	1924-1933	*1934-1937*
Bills Introduced Into Aldermanic Branch	606	1092
Local Laws Passed by Municipal Assembly	198	205
Local Laws Originating in Aldermanic Branch	75	82
Resolutions Introduced in Aldermanic Branch	5	11
Resolutions Passed in Aldermanic Branch	1	9

Sources: *Mun. Ass. Rec.*, Vols. I-XIII (1925-1937), *passim*; Joseph L. Weiner, "Municipal Home Rule in New York," *Columbia Law Review*, XXXVII (1937), 581.

Branch. In 1934, for example, only two of the local laws originating in that body were of general importance—one imposing an income tax, the other creating a city sales tax. The latter, moreover, really originated with the city administration. It was introduced by a Republican member, and the Democratic leaders approved only after informal conferences in the mayor's office and a personal plea by Mayor La Guardia in the Aldermanic Chambers.[10]

The aldermen never forgot that they were district political workers, and at all times there were introduced into the Municipal Assembly hosts of special bills to meet the needs of a single person or of a limited group. During the 1930's two species of this type grew highly popular in the Aldermanic Branch—reinstatement and reassessment bills. The former attempted to restore individuals who had been in the employ of the city to their old positions, regardless of civil service regulations. The latter were framed to relieve a community of paying all or part of its share of a special assessment for a local improvement by shifting the burden from the locality to the borough or city. Both were designed to give the incumbent alderman a political advantage in his district at election time for favors bestowed upon small groups of voters. Most of the bills introduced into the Aldermanic Branch during this period were in one of these two categories, and in each session there were aldermen whose contributions to the Committee on Local Laws were of this type exclusively. Table 5 indicates how this practice grew, and Table 6 shows the number and proportion of successful bills of this type.[11]

Fusion might gain the city administration in 1933, but during the entire fourteen years in which the Board of Aldermen Branch of the Municipal Assembly functioned, the Democrats carried a safe majority of its members. Hence it served as a reliable defender of party interests. No legislation that met with the disapproval of the party leaders was ever enacted. A case in

[10] *Mun. Ass. Rec.*, X, No. 10 (1934), 3, 15, 19; *Proc. of Bd. of Ald. and Mun. Ass., Ald. Br., 1934*, II, 731; Interview with the Hon. Murray W. Stand, June 13, 1947.

[11] *The Searchlight*, XVII, No. 2, 15; *Mun. Ass. Rec.*, VI-XIII, *passim.*

Table 5. PROPORTION OF REINSTATEMENT AND REASSESSMENT BILLS INTRODUCED INTO MUNICIPAL ASSEMBLY, ALDERMANIC BRANCH

Year	*Number of Bills Introduced*	*Number of Reinstatement Bills*	*Percentage of Bills Introduced*	*Number of Reassessment Bills*	*Percentage of Bills Introduced*	*Combined Percentage*
1930	49	2	4.1	4	8.2	12.3
1931	49	2	4.1	7	14.3	18.4
1932	46	5	10.9	14	30.4	41.3
1933	89	10	11.2	36	40.4	51.6
1934	184	70	38.0	27	14.7	52.7
1935	248	121	48.8	34	13.7	62.5
1936	234	80	34.2	53	22.6	56.8
1937	426	143	33.6	64	15.0	48.6
Total	1,325	433	32.7 [a]	239	18.0 [a]	50.7

Source: See n. 11.

[a] Percentage of all bills introduced.

Table 6. PROPORTION OF REINSTATEMENT AND REASSESSMENT LAWS AMONG LOCAL LAWS PASSED BY MUNICIPAL ASSEMBLY, ALDERMANIC BRANCH

Year	*Local Laws Originating in Aldermanic Branch*	*Reinstatement Laws*	*Reassessment Laws*	*Combined Percentage of Total*
1930	9	1	2	33.3
1931	6	0	2	33.3
1932	4	0	1	25.0
1933	8	0	3	37.5
1934	18	0	5	27.8
1935	6	2	0	33.3
1936	23	0	9	39.1
1937	35	2	27	82.9
Total	109	5	49	49.5 [a]

Source: See n. 11.

[a] Percentage of all local laws passed.

point was its refusal to eliminate performance bonds. These securities were required of contractors performing work for the city as a guarantee that their projects would be fulfilled. Since the same protection could be afforded by withholding a portion of the payment until the work was completed, the underwriting of these bonds was considered a needless expense. The practice was legitimate, but an investigation disclosed that most of the commissions were drawn by such firms as the John F. Curry Agency, Inc., or Herbert J. McCooey, and Charles F. Murphy, Jr., Inc. Needless to say, the aldermen would not deprive the families of eminent political leaders of a lucrative source of income. Bills to eliminate the bonds or reduce the fees, introduced at the behest of the Fusion administration, were simply buried in committee.[12]

Even more significant was the successful resistance of the Aldermanic Branch to county reform. In 1935 the electorate had voted in favor of a constitutional amendment permitting the Municipal Assembly to abolish or consolidate county offices. The proponents of county reorganization insisted that these positions were "as useful as a vermiform appendix," for their functions were often duplicated by city and borough positions. But they offered much in the way of patronage to sustain party fortunes. Many district leaders were lodged in these berths. Affirming that the county reorganization amendment was permissive and not mandatory, the Democrats determined to maintain these jobs at all costs. Resolutions were adopted in 1936 for consideration of the question by a Joint Committee on County Consolidation of the two houses of the Municipal Assembly, but in that year not a single meeting was held. In August, 1937, with a municipal campaign approaching, identical bills to effect minor county changes were introduced by the leaders of both houses. This was mere shadow boxing, however, for the measures were never reported out of committee. To the very end the Aldermanic Branch successfully defied all efforts to dislodge county office holders.[13]

[12] Blanshard, *Investigating City Govt. in the La Guardia Administration*, pp. 107-09; *Mun. Ass. Rec.*, XII, No. 10, 18, 21, 26; *ibid.*, XIII, No. 8, 25, 45.

[13] *Mun. Ass. Rec.*, XII, Nos. 2, 10, 22; *ibid.*, XIII, Nos. 8, 2, 16, 17, 37, 39; Blanshard, *op. cit.*, pp. 8-9, 28; *The County Reorganization Amendment: A*

When the Home Rule Amendment was adopted, there was some hope that their newly granted powers would inspire the aldermen to take the leadership in the Municipal Assembly. Since the members of the Board of Estimate were burdened with important and demanding administrative responsibilities, the Board of Aldermen had an opportunity to become a real legislative body by sponsoring important local laws, with the Board of Estimate confining itself to passing on bills initiated in the lower chamber. These expectations were never realized. In ability, prestige, and party standing, the members of the Board of Estimate continued to tower over the aldermen. Most of the constructive measures enacted by the Municipal Assembly originated in the upper house, and on the average, a bill introduced into the Board of Estimate Branch had more than four times the chance for final passage as a measure initiated in the Aldermanic Branch. As long as a single party maintained majorities in both branches, the Board of Estimate expected and obtained prompt acquiescence from the aldermen. Home rule failed to convert the Board of Aldermen from a "political luxury" to a "municipal necessity." "For all we accomplished," stated one alderman, "we might as well have stayed at home." [14]

One reason for the board's persistent truckling to both political machine and upper house of the home rule legislature lay in the character of its membership. While the Home Rule amendment was still in the discussion stages there were grave misgivings about enlarging the Board of Aldermen's powers, since the city had been so "unfortunate" in the selection of representatives to

---

Challenge to Democracy, City Affairs Committee Bulletin, September, 1940, pp. 2-4; *The City Affairs Committee vs. Tammany: A Review and a Challenge*, City Affairs Committee Bulletin, September, 1941, p. 4; interview with the Hon. Murray W. Stand, June 13, 1947.

[14] McGoldrick, "N. Y. City's Mun. Ass.," *Weekly News*, IV, No. 3; Testimony of Kenneth Dayton before Charter Rev. Comm., March 5, 1935; *The Searchlight*, XIX (1929), 10; *New York Evening Post*, June 4, 1926. The following table indicates the comparative success of bills introduced and passed in the two houses of the Municipal Assembly:

	Aldermanic	*Bd. of Est.*	*Totals*
Number of Bills Introduced	1,698	652	2,350
Bills That Became Local Laws	157	247	404
Percentage of Bills Passed	9.2	37.9	. . .

Source: *Mun. Ass. Rec.*, I-XIII, *passim*.

that body. To these apprehensions the Citizens Union replied that the "fear that the city will suffer more at the hands of the aldermen than at the hands of the legislature is undoubtedly due to a closer view of the local than of the state body." [15] No one could construe this opinion as a compliment either to the state legislature or to the Board of Aldermen; and the Citizens Union was far from complacent about the members of either group. "Able as the leaders [of the board] are," it pointed out when the Home Rule Law went into effect, "they will have difficulty in finding enough intelligence in their membership to make possible a delegation of the constructive work that must be done." Hence the Citizens Union undertook a vigorous campaign in 1923 to persuade party leaders to nominate "real law makers" instead of "rubber stamps." The results obtained were hardly gratifying, for about ninety per cent of the incumbents were renominated and only a few more were defeated at the polls. Some authorities believed that unless a substantial improvement were to take place in the character of the board, the local law-making process would break down under the strain. That this anticipated collapse never occurred was due to the simple fact that the board never began to take advantage of its home rule powers. Despite a turnover of two-thirds of its personnel, no discernible improvement took place within the next decade. In the municipal election of 1933 the Citizens Union considered 64 out of 65 aldermen unfit for re-election, some because of their limited capabilities, others for their disregard of the public interest.[16]

The disappointing record of the Municipal Assembly was not entirely due to the incapacity of the aldermen. The power granted to cities under the Home Rule Act proved more restricted than municipal authorities had hoped. In the words of a justice of the Appellate Division:

Neither the Constitution of New York nor the City Home Rule Law confers . . . blanket powers upon the cities of this state. The local laws must touch a city in its property, affairs, or government, but this alone

[15] *Rep. of Comm. on Bd. of Ald. of the Cit. Un. for the 1912-13 Term*, p. 17.

[16] *Cit. Un. Comm. on Bd. of Ald. for 1914-1915 Term*, p. 15; *The Searchlight*, XIII, No. 2 (1923), 1; *ibid.*, XIII, No. 3, 9, 13; *ibid.*, XXIII, No. 2 (1933), 20; *Annual Reports of Bd. of Elects. of City of N. Y. for 1921, 1923, 1933, passim.*

will not support them. There is yet another restriction. They must touch the city's property, affairs, or government in one or more of certain ways.[17]

Under the Enabling Act a series of restraints were placed on city legislatures on subjects considered matters of state concern.[18] The state legislature was now barred from passing local laws, but not all of the authority it had once exercised was transferred to the cities. Hence there existed a gap, termed by some a "No Man's Land." [19] Some authorities believed that the Home Rule Amendment had not bestowed an effective grant of powers upon the cities of the state.[20]

17 *Clark v. La Guardia*, 245 A. D. 325.

18 Local legislatures were prohibited from passing local laws which:

a. Removed or raised limitations of indebtedness or raised the amount that could be collected in taxes in one year.

b. Removed restrictions on issuing bonds or other evidences of debt.

c. Affected maintenance, support, or administration of the educational system or teachers' pensions or retirement systems.

d. Changed the number or term of office of a county board of supervisors.

e. Affected the labor law or workmen's compensation law.

f. Changed any provisions of the tenement house law.

g. Restricted the powers of the State Comptroller to examine municipal accounts.

h. Affected laws regulating or eliminating railroad crossings.

i. Applied to property, affairs, or government of counties.

L. 1924, C. 363, Sec. 21.

19 The allocation of powers to be exercised by city and state was not precisely defined in either the Home Rule Amendment or the Enabling Act of 1924. The latter appeared to limit the scope of local laws to five subjects in the following language: "The local legislative body of a city shall have power to adopt and amend local laws in relation to property, affairs, or government of the city relating to the powers, duties, qualifications, number, mode of selection and removal, terms of office and compensation of all officers and employees of the city, the transaction of its business, the incurring of its obligations, the presentation, ascertainment, and discharge of claims against it, the acquisition, care, management and use of its streets and property, the wages or salaries, the hours of work or labor, and the protection, welfare and safety of persons employed by any contractor or subcontractor performing work, labor or services for it, the government and regulation of the conduct of its inhabitants, and the protection of their property, safety or health." L. 1924, C. 363, Art. II, Sec. 11.

In 1928 and 1929 the scope of home rule was broadened by substituting for the phrase "power to adopt and amend local laws relating to the property, affairs, or government of the city" the expression, "power to adopt and amend local laws including but not limited to the property, affairs, or government of the city." L. 1928, C. 670 and L. 1929, C. 646. See Also *N. Y. C. Govt. Functions and Problems*, pp. 50-52; Joseph D. McGoldrick, "What Home Rule Includes," *Weekly News*, IV, No. 2 (April 10, 1925).

20 *N. Y. C. Govt. Functions and Problems*, p. 59.

It remained for the courts to indicate the boundaries within the twilight zone, between distinctly state matters and distinctly city functions. In general, the courts placed a strict construction upon the local laws passed by the Municipal Assembly. Indeed, six of the first ten measures passed by the city's home rule legislature in 1925 were set aside by the courts.[21] In the case of *Browne v. the City of New York* (1925),[22] four local laws which attempted to create a municipal bus system were invalidated on the grounds that neither the Home Rule Amendment nor the enabling act authorized cities to establish such businesses, and that the city was not privileged to confer that power upon itself by local law.[23] The following year, in the case of *Schieffelin v. Berry,*[24] the courts held that a local law which sought to reduce the retirement age of beneficiaries of the city pension system was contrary to the city charter since it affected the rights of county and judicial employees. Control over the affairs of government of counties was specifically forbidden to local legislatures under the Enabling Act.[25] In 1927, a taxpayer's suit successfully challenged the right of the city to increase the salaries of municipal court justices. The courts ruled, in *Schieffelin v. Leary,*[26] that since such salaries were fixed by state law, the city could not make a grant of authority to the Municipal Assembly by a local law authorizing that body to legislate on the justices' salaries. Undoubtedly the early setbacks that local legislation met in the courts helped create a cautious policy in the enactment of home rule laws.[27]

[21] Only two local laws were passed in 1924, the first year the Municipal Assembly functioned.

[22] 241 N. Y. 96, 149 N. E. 211.

[23] After the 1928 amendment had amplified the Home Rule Law, municipal bus operation was again attempted and again ruled to be outside the scope of "property, affairs, or government of cities," in *Clark v. La Guardia*, 245 App. Div. 325, 281 N. Y. Supp. 54 (1935).

[24] 217 N. Y. App. Div. 451, 216 N. Y. Supp. 367 (1926), (First Dept.) aff'd 243 N. Y. 603, 154 N. E. 623.

[25] L. 1924, C. 363, Sec. 21, Par. 9.

[26] 219 N. Y. App. Div. 660, 220 N. Y. Supp. 587 (1927).

[27] *The Searchlight*, XVII, No. 2 (1927), 5. For digests of the invalidated laws vid. *Mun. Ass. Rec.*, I, No. 6, unpaged.

On the other hand the courts tended towards a liberal construction of the state's powers to pass special laws. Under the Home Rule Act, the legislature could enact general laws, applying ostensibly alike to all cities, or special laws, after an emergency message from the Governor and a two-thirds vote of both houses. This legislation withstood litigation more successfully than the city's local laws. From 1924 through 1937, the years in which the Board of Aldermen were a branch of the Municipal Assembly, only two special laws of the state legislature were invalidated on the ground that they contravened the Home Rule Amendment.[28] In the leading case on home rule, *Adler v. Deegan*,[29] the State Multiple Dwelling Act of 1929, applying exclusively to tenements in New York City, was held to be a state concern, since it dealt with hygienic conditions in the city. Likewise adjudged to be a state concern were the boundary line between New York City and the town of Hempstead (*City of New York v. Village of Lawrence*) [30] and the granting of franchises (*City of New York v. Fifth Avenue Coach Co.*).[31]

Home Rule did not end state intervention in municipal politics. Before the passage of the Home Rule Amendment, authorities had pointed out that state interference was not altogether unwelcome to city administrators, for sometimes it afforded an excuse or justification for unwise actions at home. "Albany interference has been made a scapegoat for . . . shortcomings in home control over home work," stated one authority. There had always been a safeguard against up-state domination in the form of a "suspensory" veto. The mayor could disapprove a special bill concerning the conduct of the city, and unless the legislature repassed it, his veto killed the measure. Yet with few exceptions, special laws affecting New York City had passed at

[28] *Matter of Mayor, etc. of N. Y. (Elm St.)*, 246 N. Y. 72, 158 N. E. 24 (1927) and *Matter of Osborne v. Cohen*, 272 N. Y. 55, 4 N. E. (2nd Series) 289 (1936). The latter provided for a three-platoon system for firemen in those cities having a population of more than 1,000,000. Subsequent to the decision the act was repassed as an emergency measure after a Governor's message and a two-thirds vote of the Legislature. *N. Y. C. Govt. Functions and Problems*, pp. 58-59.

[29] 251 N. Y. 467, 167 N. E. 705 (1929).

[30] 250 N. Y. 429, 165 N. E. 836 (1929).

[31] 237 App. Div. 383, 262 N. Y. Supp. 228 (1933).

New York's request, with New York votes, and with the mayor's signature.[32]

After Home Rule went into effect the annual torrent of local bills in the state legislature was reduced to a trickle, although not entirely eliminated. Special laws continued to pass under the emergency message and two-thirds rule. Following a precedent established by Governor Alfred E. Smith, such messages were issued only at the request of the administration of the city affected. On the other hand, they were considered courtesies, and no effort was made to test the emergency. Hence the messages were delivered whenever requested. In time more and more appeals for emergency messages reached Albany. In his annual message to the legislature in 1936, Governor Lehman expressed concern over the rapidly growing trend towards enacting legislation of this type. Unfortunately, once a local law of this nature was passed by the state legislature, the city could not contravene the special act by legislation of its own.[33]

Some of the laws were introduced because there was a question of whether they were in the range of municipal competence; but the bulk could have been enacted by local legislatures. It was tempting, however, for city officials to "pass the buck" to Albany, especially since little difficulty was encountered in obtaining the requisite two-thirds majority for measures passed under the emergency message provision. An anti-Tammany writer called the practice a Tammany trick to give politicians an alibi for raising salaries of political favorites, for imposing new tax burdens, or for refusing to eliminate unnecessary positions from the budget. Voters could be informed by politicos, "There is nothing we wouldn't do for you if we could, but the blankety-blank state legislature has tied our hands with all these mandatory laws."

[32] *Rep. of N. Y. Chart. Comm., 1923,* 6; *N. Y. C. Govt. Functions and Problems,* p. 21; *Speech of Mayor John P. Mitchel,* April 12, 1915 (Typewritten copy in files of Mun. Ref. Library).

[33] *The Searchlight,* XV, No. 1 (1925), 7, 13; *ibid.,* XVIII, No. 1 (1928), 6-7; *ibid.,* XXII, No. 1 (1932), 3-4; State Constitution, Art. XII, Secs. 2, 3; Joseph D. McGoldrick, "What Home Rule Means Today," *National Municipal Review,* XXI (1932), 671; *Excerpts from the Annual Message of Governor Herbert H. Lehman to the State Legislature,* January 1, 1936 (*Documents of Chart. Rev. Comm.,* Vol. VIII).

Seen in this light, special laws passed by the Legislature were "Tammany rackets, engineered by Tammany for Tammany." But a Fusion mayor did not discard the strategy. Facing an overwhelming majority in the Aldermanic Branch of the Municipal Assembly during his first four years in office, Mayor La Guardia found it expedient to detour the aldermen and appeal to the State Legislature.[34]

At Albany the city administration often vied with its employees in appeals to the legislature. Representatives of school teachers' organizations had a legitimate motive, for education is primarily a state function, but policemen and firemen had grounds for believing they would fare better at the hands of state senators and assemblymen than at City Hall. The state legislators would reap the credit; the city would be compelled to administer the laws and foot the bills. Sometimes a mayor who anticipated opposition from local taxpayers would himself suggest that the city employees apply at Albany.[35]

Whatever the reasons, a greater share of legislation affecting the city originated in Albany than in the Aldermanic Branch of the Municipal Assembly. From 1935 through 1937, 64 local laws were initiated in the Aldermanic Branch and 84 in the state legislature under the emergency message rule alone. Home Rule had failed to provide a brake on legislative intrusion into the affairs of the city.[36]

If the aldermen resented state legislation on local matters, they left little evidence of it. Some efforts were made by the minority leader in 1936 to arouse them from their complacency, but without notable success.[37] The situation harmonized well with their philosophy of taking the safest course and doing nothing.

[34] James E. Finegan, *Tammany at Bay* (New York, 1933), pp. 50, 63, 76, 88-89, 182-83, 226-27; *New York Times*, July 11, 1934.

[35] Belle Zeller, *Pressure Politics in New York* (New York, 1937), pp. 200-3; Warren Moscow, *Politics in the Empire State* (New York, 1948), p. 221.

[36] *Problems Relating to Home Rule and Local Government* (Albany, 1938), pp. 264-67; *Mun. Ass. Rec.*, XI-XIII, *passim*; Joseph L. Weiner, "Municipal Home Rule in New York," *Columbia Law Review*, XXXVII (1937), 578-79.

[37] *Proc. of Bd. of Ald. and Mun. Ass., Ald. Br., 1936*, I, 8-9.

4. A MUNICIPAL LODGINGHOUSE

The defunct Board of Aldermen might have been called a municipal lodginghouse, a place for a weekly nap at the city's expense. —The Searchlight, October, 1939

A New Yorker was showing the sights to his friend from out of town. As they entered the aldermanic chamber, while the meeting was going on, the stranger stared in amazement. "Are these the aldermen?" he asked. "They are." "But they're all fast asleep—oughtn't we do something about it?" "Leave them be, leave them be," counselled the New Yorker. "While they sleep, the city's safe."—HENRY H. CURRAN, *Former Majority Leader of the Board of Aldermen*

MEMBERSHIP

AT MEETINGS of both the Board of Aldermen and the Aldermanic Branch of the Municipal Assembly the president of the board acted as chairman, and in his absence the vice chairman presided. Occasionally the president was prevented from fulfilling this duty when he acted for the mayor, for the charter directed that in the absence of the mayor, or when the mayor's office was vacant, the president of the board would become acting mayor. In this capacity he usually attracted little attention, for the acting mayor could sign or disapprove ordinances or resolutions only after he had served for at least nine days, nor could he exercise his powers of appointment or removal until at least thirty days had elapsed. Most acting mayors contented themselves with ceremonial public appearances, but Joseph V. McKee was a conspicuous exception. The resignation of Mayor Walker placed him in the mayor's office for the last four months of 1932, during a critical period in municipal affairs. Previously the frequent absences of Jimmy Walker had made him acting mayor for a longer period than any other aldermanic president.[1]

The president of the board also exercised congeries of duties, including ex officio membership on all aldermanic committees and such miscellaneous functions as membership on the Sinking Fund Commission, the Armory Board, and the boards of trustees of the New York Public Library and the Queens Borough Public Library. Even so, the position of president was not so trying as to prevent his serving as a free lance elsewhere. Fiorello H. La Guardia, elected to the office shortly after World War I, found time and energy to join a crusade against daylight saving time, to canvass the city with feminists, and to carry on a transatlantic dispute with the Italian premier, Vittorio Emanuele Orlando. Not all presidents sought the glare of publicity during their incumbency. When the business office of the president was taken over by the first President of the City Council in 1938, he found it necessary to rearrange his office, for his predecessor had set up a Manhattan branch of his Queens real estate business in one corner of the room.[2] Hence presidents of the board found little reason to be other than regular and prompt in their attendance.[3]

Aldermen were elected to the board for two-year terms from single-member districts. The charter required only that they be citizens and residents of the city, but custom dictated that they reside in their own districts. Aldermen were removable by a two-thirds vote of all members and vacancies filled by a majority

[1] Charter, Secs. 18, 23; Rules of the Board of Aldermen, Chapters II, III, printed in *Manual of Board of Aldermen: 1936-1937* (New York, 1936), pp. 3-4; Henry F. Pringle, "Bringing up the City Fathers: Profile of Joseph Vincent McKee," *The New Yorker*, III, No. 30 (1927), 20.

[2] Charter, Secs. 204, 1565; Rules of Bd. of Ald., Ch. VIII, in *Man. of Bd. of Ald: 1936-37*, 7; Richard H. Rovere, "Good Citizen: Profile of Newbold Morris," *The New Yorker*, XX, No. 37 (1944), 31; Radio Address of Raymond V. Ingersoll, Borough President of Brooklyn, over Station WHN, Dec. 21, 1935. (*N. Y. C. Chart. Rev. Comm. Documents*, Vol. VIII).

[3] In 1936 Acting President Timothy J. Sullivan attended all but six meetings, when Majority Leader Stand presided. *Proc. of Bd. of Ald. and Mun. Ass., Ald. Br., 1936, passim.*

vote of all members, with the proviso that the person so elected be of the same political party as his predecessor.[4]

Unlike the cabinet members in the national government, the heads of the municipal administrative departments were entitled to seats in the legislature. Space was reserved for them in the front part of the aldermanic chamber. Although they had no right to vote, they were entitled to participate in the discussions. This provision was placed in the charter in 1901 to compensate the commissioners for the loss of their right to initiate ordinances for their respective departments, a privilege granted them in the Charter of 1897. They could also be required to attend meetings and answer questions relating to the affairs of their departments by members of the board. When members of their own political party controlled the board, however, the commissioners were carefully protected by their party colleagues in the board from embarrassing interrogation by minority members. Heads of departments rarely attended meetings.[5]

At the time Greater New York was created, the Irish comprised the largest nationality group in the city, and with their special talents for political association, they took the lead not only in the Board of Aldermen, but in all phases of municipal politics. A generation of immigration from all parts of Europe, however, introduced new population elements seeking recognition and political office. But most Tammany leaders remained Irish, and to the end the Board of Aldermen contained a preponderance of Irish names. Yet in the last board, alongside of Timothy J. Sullivan, John J. Mahoney, and Patrick McCann, there sat a cross-section of a metropolitan city. Newbold Morris, descendant of a signer of the Declaration of Independence, served with representatives of the Italian, German, and Jewish ele-

[4] Charter, Secs. 18, 20, 27. Where a seat was filled by the selection of the Aldermen, an election in the district was required at the next annual election.

[5] Charter, Sec. 25; Goodnow, "The Charter of the City of N. Y.," *Pol. Sci. Qu.*, XVII, 8. In 1931 Minority Leader Baldwin attempted to summon the Hospitals Commissioner, Dr. J. G. William Greef, for questioning about alleged irregularities in his department. His efforts obtained some newspaper publicity, but in the board parliamentary procedure was effectively employed by members of the majority to silence him. *New York Times*, February 15, 1931; *Proc. of Bd. of Ald. and Mun. Ass., Ald. Br., 1931*, I, 634-35.

ments—Baldassare Lamberta and Pasquale Fiorella, Schwab and Haas, Moses and Fassler.[6]

Only three women ever acted as members of the board. Easily the most distinguished was Mrs. Ruth Pratt, who represented the "Silk Stocking" Fifteenth District from 1926 until 1929. During her first term her colleagues were aghast at the presence of a woman to inhibit their masculine practices, but they became reconciled to her attendance. When she retired to become a member of Congress, Peter J. McGuinness, her opponent in a number of tiffs, made an effusive farewell speech. Mrs. Ebba M. Winslow was later chosen to fill out the term of a Queens member who had been elected borough president in 1928, and Mrs. Mary E. Mahoney served out the remaining portion of her husband's term when he died in office in 1936. Neither was as active or aggressive as Mrs. Pratt, who had employed a staff to assist her in legislative work.[7]

With successive reapportionments the membership in the board was gradually reduced from 73 to 65. From 1921 until the last meeting in 1937 the number of members elected to the board remained fixed at 65. In addition there were the five borough presidents or their deputies, who sat in the front row and "got in everyone's way," as Mayor La Guardia recalled, twenty years after his presidency.[8] This was considered by many too cumbersome. The Charter Revision Commission of 1935 found that almost universally the civic organizations and individuals who offered recommendations believed the Board of Aldermen too large and unwieldy for effective work. The constructive suggestions proposed a body ranging in numbers from eleven to thirty-five.

6 Roy V. Peel, *The Political Clubs of New York City* (New York, 1935), pp. 1, 52, 252-67, 272-4, 287-90, 306-7, 315; *New York Times*, January 10, 1947.

7 Mrs. Pratt introduced thirty bills and two resolutions into the Municipal Assembly (none of which passed) and the other ladies initiated none. *Mun. Ass. Rec.*, III, No. 10; V, No. 10; XIII, No. 8, *passim*; *New York Evening Post*, June 4, 1926; *The Searchlight*, XIX, No. 3, 11; Interview with the Hon. Newbold Morris, August 8, 1947.

8 Message of Mayor La Guardia, January 1, 1940. *Proc. of Council of City of N. Y., 1940*, I, 16.

MODES OF PROCEDURE

One of the most encouraging aspects of the board's activities was the gradual improvement in the conduct of meetings. In March, 1911, Henry H. Curran, just appointed to the body, slipped into the rear of the aldermanic chamber at City Hall and viewed the proceedings with quiet disapproval:

It looked mostly like fat men and tobacco smoke, with a rabble of favor-seekers and two-by-four politicians wandering about at will. It sounded mostly like general conversation, oblivious of the proceedings that were going on. It smelled of garlic and bad cigars. The portrait of George Washington looked around the dark panels and disorderly inmates with quiet disdain. It was the old Board of Aldermen as it used to be.[9]

Much of the confusion came from hordes of favor-seekers who crowded the chamber. A keeper of a little street stand selling soda-water and newspapers was required to obtain the consent of the alderman of the district before a license would be issued by the Bureau of Licenses. It was hardly a legislative function, but it increased the power of each alderman in granting or denying political favors. Many suspected that the practice involved considerable petty graft. Filled with standkeeper-petitioners, the aldermanic meetings looked like a "cross between a stock exchange and a bargain sale in hand-me-downs." Not until the board of 1914 transferred its license-granting powers to the city's executive departments and excluded non-members from the floor, was the conduct of meetings brought up to a reasonable standard of dignity. Appearances also were improved at this time by the installation of new Windsor chairs, which seemed almost "spirituelle" beside the old "revolving fortresses" which had contained the shanks of the aldermen for many years. Even a three-hundred-pound legislator who split his chair at the first sitting had a wider, reinforced Windsor piece especially made for him—"still spirituelle." Promoted to majority leader, Alderman Curran now observed with pleasure that "instead of looking like Paddy's market it looked and acted like a legislature."[10]

[9] Curran, *Pillar to Post*, p. 126.

[10] Curran, *op. cit.*, pp. 130-33, 177, 182-86; *Rep. of Comm. on Bd. of Ald. for 1914-15 Term*, pp. 3-5; *The Searchlight*, IX, No. 6, 13. Taken out of the hands of the aldermen, the licensing of news-stands blossomed into a big business. Two decades later an investigation directed by the Commissioner of Accounts

The transformation was not complete, however, for a decade later *The New Yorker* could still report that the meetings were one of the "laughs of the town." During the early twenties the board was noted for its rough-house manners, and sessions were sometimes marred by personal encounters. On one occasion a burly Republican came to blows with Democratic Vice-Chairman Kenneally during a meeting. Vice Chairman Collins (1922-25) set the example for the Democratic majority by his efforts to browbeat Republicans on the floor of the chamber and his provocative language from the rostrum when presiding. Epithets and personal abuse greeted minority speakers. But Joseph V. McKee, inaugurated as president in 1926, was determined to elevate the dignity of the body. His first innovation was to open the metings with a prayer for divine guidance, an invited clergyman delivering the invocation. Henry F. Pringle of *The New Yorker* wrote sarcastically: "A chance visitor now receives the impression that these are godly men, not ex-saloonkeepers, who are prayerful that their labors shall redound to the advancement of the city." McKee brought a copy of Robert's Rules of Order to the board and insisted on parliamentary etiquette. He put an end to the hooting and yelling at members of the infinitesimal Republican minority when they attempted to speak, and footstampings and cat-calls gave way to petitions for recognition from the chair. In deference to Mrs. Ruth Pratt, newly elected from the "Silk Stocking" district, the members' language was bowdlerized and the custom of floor-spitting discontinued. Toward Mrs. Pratt, McKee was the soul of gallantry. When the Republicans increased their representation from three to seven, Peter J. McGuinness, a Brooklyn district leader and Chairman of the Seating Committee, attempted to reduce the effectiveness of the minority by scattering the members about the aldermanic

---

revealed the existence of a flourishing "racket" in this sphere. Nominally newsstand licenses were granted by the City License Department for a $5 fee. In practice news-stands were purchased for sums ranging from $1,000 to $18,000 through "fixers," who retained a substantial portion of the purchase price. It was estimated that the graft netted the procurers $500,000 annually, the transactions taking place with the endorsement of the local district leaders, whose permission was necessary for the transfers. Blanshard, *Invest. City Govt. in La Guardia Admin.*, pp. 35-41; Ellis Chadbourne, *New York Blazes the Way*, Municipal Affairs Pamphlets, No. 1 (New York: Citizen's Movement, 1934), 12-13.

chamber. Mrs. Pratt appealed to President McKee, however, and he directed that the Republican delegation be allotted seats together, near the front of the chamber. The Social Registerite had balked the plebian Greenpointer.[11]

Under McKee's guidance the aldermen became reconciled to the proprieties of parliamentary procedure, and debate, when there was any, became gentlemanly and courteous. To be sure, no one could ever mistake the Board of Aldermen for the House of Lords. One observer in the nineteen thirties compared the appearance of the aldermen to the figures in the Nast cartoons portraying the Tweed Ring. But the legislators were captivated by parliamentary rules, and meetings were conducted with touches of dignity and courtliness. When a member exceeded the time allotted him by the cloture rules, another would inevitably obtain the floor and promptly yield his own five minutes to his "distinguished colleague." [12]

In the minds of aldermanic floor leaders party discipline loomed large, for theirs was the responsibility of welding their partisans into a cohesive unit. Republican leaders were always beset by greater problems than their Democratic counterparts. Only four times in this century did their party win majorities in the board, and always it was the result of amalgamation with aldermen of varied political complexion—Democrats, Progressives, and assorted independents. These Fusion coalitions could not be held together by party discipline. Fusion Leader Henry Curran found that keeping his majority in line during the 1914-1915 sessions required conferences, social functions, and legerdemain. With the connivance of his good friend, Minority Leader Frank L. Dowling, Curran staged a series of verbal encounters at meetings, and the two leaders "laid on lustily." After great efforts, Curran manged to establish control, despite complaints

[11] *New York Evening World*, February 16, 1923; *World*, January 13, 1926; *New York Times*, January 13, 1926, December 21, 1927; Pringle, "Bringing up the City Fathers," *The New Yorker*, III, No. 30, 19-22; *The Searchlight*, XIII, No. 3, 6.

[12] S. J. Woolf, "Lone Republican among Our Aldermen," *New York Times Magazine*, June 25, 1933; Rovere, "Good Citizen," *The New Yorker*, XX, No. 38 (1944), 31; interview with the Hon. Newbold Morris, Aug. 8, 1947.

that he and Dowling were "running the whole board." Other Fusion majorities, however, crumbled. Floor Leader Ralph Folks discovered within the first two months of the 1912 sessions that enough members of his slender Fusion majority had been weaned away by the Democrats to leave his group in a "hopeless shadowland," unable to carry on any constructive program. When votes on decisive measures were taken, the errant Fusion legislators either voted with Tammany "with an explanation" or missed the roll call entirely by remaining in a telephone booth outside the aldermanic chambers. The Democrats were able to wrest control from uneasy Fusion majorities by maintaining firm discipline among their own cohorts and by winning over individual Fusionites. Alluring promises of patronage were held out, and on one occasion Mayor Seth Low publicly charged that the Democrats were tendering bribes to Fusion aldermen.[13]

Nor were the meager Republican minorities of the twenties and thirties noted for their cohesiveness. More often than not Republicans would vote with the majority or refrain from voting. In 1924 the seven Republicans cast their ballots as a unit in opposition to Democratic proposals on only three occasions. Sometimes the minority leader would find himself almost alone—even when he had as many as a half dozen party associates. There seemed to be little reason for holding the party together, for the overwhelming Democratic majorities made opposition appear futile.[14]

One explanation for the ineffectiveness of the Republican minority during this period lay in the unaggressive character of the Republican city organization, which was then hardly noted for determined opposition to its party rivals in power. To Democratic Boss Flynn of the Bronx it appeared that the Republican Party was "content to sit patiently for a decade or more, waiting for unorganized citizens clamoring for change to

[13] Curran, *op. cit.*, pp. 146-47, 176-77, 182-84, 256; *Rep. of Comm. on Bd. of Ald. of Cit. Un. for 1912-13 Term*, p. 5; *Rep. of Comm. on Bd. of Ald. of Cit. Un. for 1914-1915 Term*, p. 14; Interview with Justice Henry H. Curran, Jan. 24, 1947; *New York Times*, January 4, January 7, 1902; *Proc. of Bd. of Ald., 1902*, I, 11-12.

[14] *The Searchlight*, XIII, No. 3, 6; McGoldrick, "Eclipse of the Aldermen," *Nat. Mun. Rev.*, XIV, 367; Interview with Joseph Clark Baldwin, March 4, 1947.

come to it for the machinery needed to win elections." An anti-Tammany Democrat went further, and charged that Tammany wielded "strong influence, if not practical control" over the Republican Party in the city. Republican district leaders were variously described as "Tammany's poor relations" and allies who "lived on the crumbs that fell from Tammany's table." Republican aldermen could derive scant encouragement from the fact that their party made no bid for the urban vote.[15]

Little difficulty was experienced by Democratic floor leaders in maintaining party control, for theirs was a thoroughly disciplined band of followers. In 1926 a Republican alderman wrote:

> Tammany is built upon discipline—discipline from the top to the bottom, like an army. The leader of Tammany Hall has as much authority over the rank and file of the party as Von Hindenburg had over the German soldiers. . . . If a mere brave should set himself up to criticize his leader he would find himself out of politics before he could blink an eye. The result is that our city government under Tammany waits for Tammany.[16]

As a consequence the decisions of the Democratic leaders were accepted in the board without question, often without understanding. " 'It's orders'—that is enough for Tammany, and Tammany rules the Board, 67 votes to 3," asserted the same Republican legislator.[17] "Aldermanic decisions had regularly been made in advance by the Tammany and other Democratic organization leaders," stated an authority some years later. "And the sessions of the board had been mere perfunctory ratifications." [18]

When a new member began his career as alderman, he was instructed by the district leader who had nominated him to follow the party leaders in the board. Invariably he did. Some might comment adversely about a pending measure in committee or in the cloakroom, but on the floor of the aldermanic chamber

[15] Flynn, *You're the Boss*, p. 140; Finegan, *Tammany at Bay*, pp. 79-80; *Seabury Minutes*, p. 10435; Woolf, "Lone Rep. Among Our Ald.," *New York Times Mag.*, June 25, 1933.

[16] *New York Evening Post*, June 4, 1926.

[17] *Ibid.* Mrs. Pratt was including the votes of the five borough presidents.

[18] Hallett, *Prop. Rep.—The Key to Democ.*, p. 151.

personal feelings would give way to party discipline and criticism would vanish. Occasionally a legislator might object to a measure which would affect the interests of his constituents unfavorably, but as a rule the majority followed its leaders with "harmonious and sheep-like acquiescence." [19]

The Democratic leaders did not find it necessary to hold periodic caucuses of party members in the board or to issue instructions on pending legislation. Their followers simply watched the moves of the floor leaders and responded accordingly. If a member entered the aldermanic chamber late and was in doubt about the party attitude on the business under consideration, he would take his cues from the party leader or whip, one of whom would close the debate with a summary of reasons for adopting or rejecting the proposal. On bills of trivial importance some personal discretion would be permitted, but on measures of any consequence strict adherence to the party line was required.

Party control was facilitated during the presidency of Joseph V. McKee by the shrinking size of the Republican minority and by the adoption of the short roll call.[20] The latter involved calling out nine names instead of seventy—the first and last names in the alphabet, majority and minority leaders, and the five borough presidents. Then votes were counted in accord with party members present. In theory a full roll call could be taken at the request of any two members, but overwhelming Democratic majorities would make this procedure a futile gesture. On the other hand, the short roll call permitted a member to sleep through the proceedings, if he cared to, with the assurance that his vote would always be properly registered with those of his party colleagues. The practice also permitted measures to be

[19] Tanzer, "Aldermen Cannot Say 'No'," *The Searchlight*, XXI, No. 1, 8, 10; Woolf, "Lone Rep. Among Ald.," *N. Y. Times Mag.*, June 25, 1933; Testimony of Kenneth Dayton before Chart. Rev. Comm., March 5, 1925. In his experience of 16 years in the Board of Aldermen (1922-37), most of which were spent as Democratic whip, Murray W. Stand always saw the members of the majority stand by their leaders on the floor. He himself had defied Mayor Hylan, however, on an issue in which he felt the welfare of his district was at stake. Interview with the Hon. Murray W. Stand, June 13, 1947.

[20] During the years in which McKee presided over the Board the Republicans elected 3 aldermen for the 1926-27 sessions, 7 for 1928-1929, 4 for 1930-1931, and 1 for 1932-33.

sped through the board without waste of time, and usually without study or comprehension on the part of the great majority. "I am sometimes astonished at the nonchalant way we have of tossing off ordinances and appropriations as mere routine matters," wrote an alderman the year McKee took office. "Ordinances are passed or beaten; money is appropriated or held up without anyone bothering to find out why." Not infrequently an alderman would be uncertain about just what had been enacted. But if he were sufficiently interested he could always consult the *City Record* the next day to find out.[21]

The Democratic leaders varied greatly in ability and fitness for legislative office. During his later years of power, Charles F. Murphy, leader of Tammany Hall (1902-1924) was convinced that capable and conscientious men should be selected for important public offices. At the time of Mr. Murphy's death, the majority leader in the board was William T. Collins, who had earned an accolade from the Citizens Union as the "ablest member of the Majority." During the administration of James J. Walker, however, incompetent officials appeared in every branch of the city's government. At the outset of the Walker regime the choice for majority leader fell upon a politician who had used his position in the board to put through an unsavory financial deal and who had been condemned by the Citizens Union as an "inarticulate, incompetent machine politician" with no qualifications for work in a legislative body. Among all Democratic leaders of the board the common denominator was the favor of the party leaders. During the first eight years that the board functioned under the Charter of 1901 the Democratic forces were managed by Timothy P. Sullivan. "Little Tim," as he was popularly called, was cousin and right hand man to "Big Tim" Sullivan, overlord of the Bowery. In the closing sessions of the board in 1937 the Democratic majority leader was Timothy J. Sullivan, a Yorkville district leader. Both Sullivans, and all aldermanic leaders who ever controlled the Democratic aldermen, invariably possessed the full confidence of the Democratic bosses. It was

[21] Rule 40, *Manual of Bd. of Ald. 1936-1937*, p. 14; Katherine MacKenzie, "A Portrait of the New York Alderman," *N. Y. Times Mag.*, January 28, 1934; *New York Times*, January 13, 1926; *New York Evening Post*, June 4, 1926.

the majority leader who relayed the decisions of the county chiefs to the Democratic members and ensured their enforcement. Dennis J. Mahon, majority leader in 1933, was described by the Citizens Union as an "ideal lieutenant of Tammany Hall, adept in executing Tammany orders and enacting them into law." [22]

For sixteen years (1918-1933) the Democrats dominated all branches of the city government, but their political competitors still retained a voice in the Board of Aldermen.[23] Here the Democrats sought to reduce their rivals to impotence, especially in the early years of this era, when they were pressed by sizeable and active minorities. Cloture rules were stiffened—speakers were permitted five minutes for debate, rather than ten, as in previous sessions. The rules were also amended to require objections from at least three aldermen in place of the single objection usual in parliamentary bodies to prevent immediate consideration of a newly introduced measure. Occasionally steamroller methods were employed when a vote was taken on the previous question before the debate on the business under consideration could really get under way.[24]

As the Republican delegations dwindled in numbers the Democrats often could afford a more tolerant attitude. Mrs. Ruth Pratt, who served in the board from 1926 until 1929, praised the majority for treating her with the utmost courtesy and permitting her to exercise her "woman's prerogative" to say whatever she believed. But they rarely went so far as to act on her advice. Early in her aldermanic career she attempted to secure the appointment of more tenement house inspectors. A committee hearing was scheduled to consider the proposal, but only Mrs. Pratt attended—no notices had been issued. At the next meeting of the board she attempted to obtain the floor to demand the

[22] Flynn, *op. cit.*, pp. 62-63, 139-40; *The Searchlight*, IX, No. 5 (1919), 19; *ibid.*, XI, No. 5 (1921), 19; *ibid.*, XIII, No. 4, (1923), 17, 19; *ibid.*, XV, No. 5 (1925), 18; *Facts versus Flourishes and Ruffles* (New York, 1921), pp. 5-6; Zink, *City Bosses in the U. S.*, pp. 89, 165.

[23] Although the Democrats did not always retain unanimous control in the Board of Estimate, the Republicans were always hopelessly outvoted in that body.

[24] Cf. Rules of the Board of Aldermen, Nos. 9 and 10 in *Manual of the Board of Aldermen: 1918-1919* (New York, 1919), p. 5 and *Manual of the Board of Aldermen: 1920-1921* (New York, 1920), 4; *The Searchlight*, XIII, No. 3, 6.

committee report, only to be ruled out of order. "Of course you weren't out of order," President McKee assured her, "but what did you expect?" Ultimately she obtained passage by removing her name from the resolution and letting a Democrat take credit for it.[25]

For two years the entire minority was concentrated in her successor, Joseph Clark Baldwin. Usually he was permitted to speak, although it was a solitary voice in the wilderness. But on occasion parliamentary tactics were employed like a radio dial to shut off his rhetoric on short notice. Sometimes he was informed that he was out of order; at other times his proposals were tabled; and often he found that none among the sixty-four Democrats would second his motions. Baldwin received tremendous publicity, but in the Board of Aldermen he could accomplish little or nothing. A Republican who hoped to achieve much in the board in those days was sanguine indeed. Newbold Morris, who succeeded Baldwin as representative from the fifteenth district, brought with him a brief case filled with bills whose purpose was to end a variety of abuses. In four years only one of his proposals passed—a measure giving city employees a holiday with pay on St. Patrick's day. Sometimes he was allowed to read a proposal from the floor, but more often the chair ruled him out of order. Few of the measures he sponsored ever came to a vote, and attempts to bring the others out of committee proved futile. Appeals to the chairman of the committee in which his bills had reposed for months were politely shrugged off, and motions to discharge them were promptly tabled. All his efforts were in vain, as Newbold Morris struggled against an "avalanche of 62 votes and a gavel." On the whole, however, the Democrats could afford to be patient with the minority, for their insuperable majority enabled them to flatten opposition with the "smooth, ponderous efficiency of a road roller." [26]

[25] Pratt, "Men are Bad Housekeepers," *Harpers Mag.*, CLIV, 682; *New York Evening Post*, June 4, 1926; *New York World*, May 11, 1926.

[26] Woolf, "Lone Rep. Among Our Ald.," *N. Y. Times Mag.*, June 25, 1933; *The New Yorker*, VIII, No. 5 (1932), 14-15; Rovere, "Good Citizen," *The New Yorker*, XX, No. 38, 30-31; *Mun. Ass. Rec.*, XI, No. 10, 15; XII, No. 10, 13; XIII, No. 8, 21; broadcast by Newbold Morris over Radio Station WNBC, October 2, 1947; interview with the Hon. Jos. Clark Baldwin, March 4, 1947; interview with the Hon. Newbold Morris, Aug. 8, 1947.

Most aldermen, however, were concerned neither with constructive legislation nor serious debate. A new member once related how he was indoctrinated by a veteran of the body with the aldermanic spirit:

Toward the end of that first meeting . . . I asked the alderman next to me what I might do to be a good alderman.

"You want a straight tip?" he inquired kindly.

"Yes."

"Just don't do anything. It's safer. . . . And keep your mouth shut—sometimes if you're silent they think it's knowledge—and you don't get committed." [27]

For the most part the aldermen adhered faithfully to the rule. Perhaps they were playing safe. One authority suggested that it was a "general lack of information." Whatever the reasons, only a handful of members ventured to address the assemblage as often as once a year. Easily the most voluble member of the board was Peter J. McGuinness, the sage of Greenpoint. For more than thirteen years McGuinness attended every meeting and almost always had something to say.[28]

Most of the business of the board was routine and the procedure was well adapted to disposing of a large volume of work. Once an item had emerged from committee it was almost invariably accepted, and many were voted unanimously. Some measures, as bond issues to be approved without a waiting period, required unanimous consent. In such cases log rolling might win the acquiescence of the minority, and little deals could be worked out to ensure passage of legislation favored by leaders of both parties. Occasionally there was a little flurry as the minority would oppose an ordinance, but party discipline and the prodigious Democratic majorities would eventually dispose of the opposition.[29]

Conducted in a depressing, humdrum manner, with the clerk droning out routine business, the board's meetings were uninter-

[27] Curran, *op. cit.*, pp. 128-29.

[28] *Ibid.*, pp. 130, 133, 136, 145; McGoldrick, "Eclipse of the Aldermen," *Nat. Mun. Rev.*, XIV, 367; Rovere, "The Big Hello," *The New Yorker*, XXII, 29; Tanzer, "Aldermen Cannot Say 'No'," *The Searchlight*, XXI, No. 1, 10.

[29] *The Searchlight*, XIII, No. 3, 6-7; *ibid.*, XXI, No. 1, 8; McGoldrick, "Eclipse of the Aldermen," *Nat. Mun. Rev.*, XIV, 367; Charter, Sec. 48.

esting even to its own members. Joseph V. McKee, who presided over them from 1926 until 1933, described them during this period:

If you were in my place . . . in the Board of Aldermen, you would find that the meetings began at 1:30 or 2:00 o'clock every Tuesday. They last about twenty minutes. They are absolutely perfunctory. They are deadly in their monotony, and you will find that the average work done is either in agreeing in some action of the Board of Estimate, or time is given on calling the roll, or the naming of a public square, or whether or not a street should be dedicated to play use. . . . Once in a while you will have a real debate on a question of policy, such as a taxicab bill, or at times the budget . . . but on the average you will come away from the meeting feeling that that was an enormous waste of time, even the 20 or 35 minutes that might have been given up to the proceedings there.[30]

Fortunately, perhaps, the meetings were brief—usually no more than half an hour in duration. When there were interesting events at the Polo Grounds or Belmont Park they rarely lasted more than ten minutes, for what are season passes for if not to be used? Occasionally a member would be a bit careless about punctuality and attendance. During one term, the Citizens Union pointed out, an important member frequently came too late for meetings of the Municipal Assembly. Two aldermen became so incapacitated that for several years they scarcely attended a meeting and were otherwise unable to perform their duties. Despite their physical disqualifications, which virtually deprived their districts of any real representation, they were renominated and reëlected. But such cases were exceptional. As a rule members were regular and prompt in their attendance, for experience had taught politicians the wisdom of putting in an appearance at their official posts, however perfunctory the performance at their tasks.[31]

Republicans and reformers deplored the policies of the majority in the Board of Aldermen, but personal relations, even among political rivals, were most cordial. Minority Leader

[30] "Seabury Minutes," pp. 10490-91.

[31] *The Searchlight*, XIX, No. 4 (1929), 2; *ibid.*, XXI, No. 2 (1931), 16; *ibid.*, XXIII, No. 2 (1933), 21-22; *ibid.*, XXV, No. 2 (1935), 22, 24; Rovere, "Good Citizen," *The New Yorker*, XX, No. 38, 31; interview with the Hon. Newbold Morris, Aug. 8, 1947.

Baldwin believed that his opponents did not have the best interests of the city at heart, but personally they were "good fellows." "Of course the city would be in an awful mess by now if we'd let those fellows go on," remarked Newbold Morris, after he had become President of the City Council. "But just the same they are wonderful people. I guess part of me will always be an alderman." [32]

Although the leaders might fight along political lines during sessions, after adjournment hostilities were quickly forgotten. Henry H. Curran, Fusion leader from 1914 until 1917, and Frank L. Dowling, shepherd of the Democrats during those years, quarreled in the aldermanic chambers "like a couple of cats on the back fence," but in private they were best of friends. Joseph Clark Baldwin and Timothy J. Sullivan, minority and majority leaders in 1934, opposed each other vociferously in debates during meetings, but between sessions it was "Tim" and "Joe." [33]

As professional politicians, members of both parties cultivated ingratiating personalities. "They slap backs, pass out cigars, go to funerals, call strangers by their first names, have plenty of time to gossip," asserted an anti-Tammany Democrat. "They are expert glad-handers, mixers; they listen well, they are agreeable to meet." This brotherhood created a boisterously friendly body, noted for its "hail-fellow-well-met" attitude. "There is something very club-like about it," declared Mayor La Guardia. The social side was not neglected. In the tradition of district politicians, the aldermen turned out annually for a boat ride and clam bake, accompanied by hordes of friends and adherents. After the Board of Aldermen had given way to the City Council, President Newbold Morris invited his colleagues of the old board to a reunion, where the Association of Past Members of the Board of Aldermen was founded. By acclamation, the presi-

[32] Pratt, "Men Are Bad Housekeepers," *Harpers Mag.*, CLIV, 682; Woolf, "Lone Rep. Among Our Ald.," *N. Y. Times Mag.*, June 25, 1933; Rovere, "Good Citizen," *op. cit.*, 31. Many have commented on the friendly spirit that prevailed among the aldermen. "I made more good, warm friends among the Democratic Majority, and in shorter time, than in any group I ever met," remarked Lambert Fairchild, Republican alderman in 1934-35. Interview of October 12, 1947.

[33] Curran, *op. cit.*, pp. 182-84; *New York Times*, July 11, 1934.

dency went to Peter J. McGuinness, the statesman from Greenpoint.[34]

COMMITTEES AND STAFF

Like most modern legislative bodies, the Board of Aldermen found it advantageous to carry on its detailed or specialized work in committees. After Home Rule was established fourteen standing committees functioned, in varying degrees of activity; and from time to time committees were created for special purposes.[35]

With a great show of fairness, the leaders designated representatives from every borough and from both political parties for each committee. During the 1932–33 sessions, when Joseph Clark Baldwin was the sole Republican member, he was named to every committee, including those which met simultaneously. The president of the board and vice-president (majority leader) were ex-officio members of all committees, and the Citizens Union observer noted that the Democratic Party whip attended all public hearings and committee meetings, carefully following the proceedings. Before the first meeting of each legislative session the Democratic majority held its only caucus to nominate

[34] Finegan, *op. cit.*, p. 89; Testimony of Mayor La Guardia before Ch. Rev. Comm., May 7, 1936; *New York World*, June 9, 1922; *New York Times*, July 1, 1927; July 17, 1936; Rovere, "Good Citizen," *The New Yorker*, XX, No. 38, 34; Rovere, "The Big Hello," *The New Yorker*, XX, No. 21, 31.

[35] E. g., a Joint Committee on County Consolidation, including members of the Board of Estimate, was created in 1936, following the enactment of a constitutional amendment authorizing consolidation of county offices. The standing committees of the board during this period were as follows: Apportionment; Buildings, which considered ordinances and resolutions affecting the Building Code, construction, and elevators; Codification of Ordinances, which brought the Code of Ordinances up to date; General Welfare, which took up matters not clearly within the province of some other committee; Markets, which discussed the establishment and regulation of public markets; Privileges and Elections, which passed on election disputes; Public Letting, which scrutinized requests of Commissioners to make purchases over $1,000 without competitive bidding; Public Thoroughfares, which dealt with street problems; Rules, which handled questions of procedure; Salaries and Offices, which received matters sent by the Board of Estimate on offices and grades; State Legislation; Traffic; and Local Laws, to which were referred all bills originating in the Aldermanic Branch of the Municipal Assembly. *Manual of the Board of Aldermen, 1926-1927* (New York, 1926), pp. 28-29; *Manual of Bd. of Ald., 1936-1937*, pp. 29-30.

the chairman of the Finance Committee and the Committee on Rules. The latter appointed the remaining chairmen and committee members. Seniority and party favor were the criteria for candidates for the most desirable posts. Memberships on some committees were greatly prized for the powers and perquisites they yielded. It was not altogether personal profit, but patronage and favors for constituents that were at stake. Private firms, seeking amendments to the Code of Ordinances, cultivated good relations with members of the Committee on Codification of Ordinances, offering jobs for deserving watchmen or timekeepers. Other committee assignments also offered interesting possibilities of patronage for needy voters.[36]

Perhaps the most conspicuous was the Finance Committee, whose operations may serve to illustrate the functioning of the standing committees. Together with the majority and minority leaders its chairman was considered important enough to rate a salary $2,500 above the annual stipend of the other sixty-two aldermen and the services of an automobile and driver. In 1932 the chairman of the Finance Committee, Frank A. Cunningham, found himself in the limelight for an inglorious moment. Judge Seabury, counsel for a legislative inquiry into New York's government, sought to demonstrate that the principal political organization of the city had filled the municipal offices with incompetents. Cunningham, who served as Finance Chairman for eighteen years, became Judge Seabury's prize exhibit. Asked a few questions about city finances on the witness stand, the hapless legislator grew bewildered, and finally confessed he could pretend to no knowledge of fiscal affairs. "I am not a financial man," he pleaded. "I am a member of the Board of Aldermen." As Chairman of the Finance Committee, Cunningham was also an ex-officio member of the Sinking Fund Commission. But Cunningham merely "went along" with the others, supinely accepting the orders of the Comptroller. "I just attend meetings

[36] *The New Yorker*, VIII, No. 5, 15; *Man. of Bd. Ald: 1936-37*; pp. 7-8, 30; *The Searchlight*, XXV, No. 2 (1935), 22; Testimony of Kenneth Dayton before Ch. Rev. Comm., March 5, 1935; *New York Times*, December 28, 1927; Intervieew with the Hon. Newbold Morris, August 8, 1947.

and vote," he explained. "I have no other facilities. It is all done by the Comptroller." [37]

Regardless of the qualifications of the remaining members of the Finance Committee, for many years no genuine effort was made to study the annual budget. For an intimate grasp of the details it was necessary to follow the proceedings as the budget was taking form. Until 1933 this document was drawn up by the Board of Estimate and Apportionment on the basis of estimates submitted by heads of departments and hearings before that body. In 1927 a minority member of the Board of Aldermen attended every public hearing before the Board of Estimate in connection with the budget and never once saw a member of the aldermanic Finance Committee present. "Do they get their information in private, and from whom," chided Mrs. Pratt, "that they consider themselves qualified to analyze this budget and make intelligent exposition of it?" After 1933 the budget was framed by the Budget Bureau. During Mayor La Guardia's administration the members of the Finance Committee occasionally attended hearings, but they were hardly interested in finances. Their interrogation of department heads was part of a none-too-subtle game of bringing pressure to bear on reluctant administrators. Commissioners might be tempted to yield to their importunate demands for jobs and favors in their offices, lest their budgetary appropriations be slashed.[38]

When the proposed budget was submitted to the Board of Aldermen, it was turned over to the Finance Committee. In earlier years some attempts had been made to summon department heads for questioning, but after World War I the practice was discontinued. Usually a notice for a public hearing of " in-

[37] Seabury, *Final Report*, pp. 3-4; "Seabury Minutes," pp. 9986, 9893-9898; Finegan, *Tammany at Bay*, pp. 97, 170, 267; *The Searchlight*, XXIII, No. 2, 24. "The incompetence of this prominent alderman was not unique," asserted Judge Seabury some years later. "Like nearly all his associates, he was there as a convenient rubber-stamp for the one dominant machine." Address over Radio Station WNBC, October 8, 1947.

[38] Letter of Kenneth Dayton to Charter Revision Commission, May 3, 1935; Speech of Alderman Ruth Pratt in Board of Aldermen, December 5, 1927 (Release in Municipal Reference Library); Allen, *op. cit.*, p. 137; Testimony of Rufus E. McGahen, Director of the Budget, before Chart. Rev. Comm., Feb. 28, 1935; Interview with Mr. McGahen, October 28, 1947.

terested citizens " was sent out, but few responded.[39] The aldermen listened to speakers politely enough, if one overlooked their yawns. They regarded the proceedings as a "mandatory farce," one observer stated in 1927. "They never blinked an eye," he reported. "They showed no interest and less intelligence. Not one of them pretended to know or considered it his business to know. It was pitiful to see their ignorance and tragic to see their indifference." A member of the aldermanic minority who attended that very public hearing protested that the committee had done nothing, for little more was required of them on such occasions than a formal appearance. The committee members knew virtually nothing about the budget, and the recommendations of the majority were written for them by a committee clerk, just as their annual report on the fixing of the tax rate was prepared for them in the comptroller's office.[40] It was hardly necessary for committee members to do more than glance at the statement and sign. The Republican minority always brought in a report for the reduction of the budget, but invariably the majority report was adopted as presented.[41]

The committees varied considerably, both in qualifications of members and in importance of work. Occasionally a committee was headed by a capable member, conversant with the city's problems. Such were Walter R. Hart, of the Committee on Local Laws (1936–1937) and Francis D. McGarey, of the General Welfare Committee (1926–1931). But aptitude for legislative duties was hardly the principal test of fitness. An alderman who had demonstrated his party regularity over a period of time was considered a suitable choice for a chairmanship, especially if the county leaders had nodded in his direction. Just before James J. Molen succeeded McGarey as Chairman of the

39 E.g., in 1916 two persons attended; in 1927, three; and in 1930, no one.

40 Judge Seabury seemed under the impression that the report on the budget was written for the Finance Committee by the comptroller's office, but Chairman Cunningham insisted, in his testimony, that they were prepared by John T. Eagleton, a committee clerk.

41 Lahee, *The N. Y. C. Budget*, pp. 67-69; Speech of Mrs. Pratt, Dec. 5, 1927; *New York Times,* November 20, 1927, November 18, 1930; Allen, *op. cit.*, pp. 226-27; "Seabury Minutes, pp. 9889-9890, 9896-9898; McGoldrick, "Eclipse of the Aldermen," *Nat. Mun. Rev.*, XIV, No. 6, 365; *The Searchlight*, XXI, No. 1, 8.

important General Welfare Committee, the Citizens Union noted that he had "performed the difficult feat of remaining wholly useless as an alderman in spite of twenty-two years' experience." In the selection of aldermen to the more important posts, the Committee on Rules was guided by seniority. When Mrs. Pratt, the first woman elected to the board, took office, the League of Women Voters protested that she was assigned only to minor committees. "Appointments to really vital committees," explained President McKee, "are usually made from more experienced members." Along with the Finance Committee, the Committee on Public Letting was of considerable importance, for in every session a large proportion of the time of the board was taken up in granting permission to heads of departments to purchase supplies in excess of $1,000 without public advertisement. The Committees on General Welfare and on Local Laws presented frequent reports, but some committees led a shadowy life, scarcely existing save on paper.[42]

Aldermanic committees were rarely noted for the quality or quantity of their work. The charter of 1901 required that the board reduce the general ordinances to a code, but the work of codification was not begun until 1906. In that year a volume was published, but unfortunately no effort was made to systematize the laws. The result was a mere listing, in a melange which failed to distinguish between obsolete and partly superseded ordinances and those fully in force. As a consequence the code became an enigma to lawyers and laymen alike, and even to city magistrates. It was not until 1915 that the board attempted to revise the Code, eliminating contradictions and

[42] *The Searchlight*, XVII, No. 3, 20; Vol. XIX, No. 3, 9-11; Vol. XIX, No. 4, 24-26; Vol. XXI, No. 2, 22-24; Vol. XXIII, No. 2, 24-25; Vol. XXV, No. 2, 27; Interview with the Hon. Newbold Morris, August 8, 1947. During the year 1936 there were 33 meetings of the Board of Aldermen and 30 meetings of the Aldermanic Branch of the Municipal Assembly. The standing committees reported in that year, in descending order of frequency, as follows: Public Letting (18 times); General Welfare (15); Finance and Traffic (11 apiece); Rules and Public Thoroughfares (8 apiece); Salaries and Officers (6); State Legislation (3); Codification of Ordinances and Markets (1 apiece). The Committees on Apportionment, Buildings, and Privileges and Elections as well as the Joint Committee on County Consolidation presented no reports. *Proc. of Bd. of Ald. and Mun. Ass., Ald. Br.*, 1936, *passim.*

grouping the ordinances in a form readily available for reference and for future expansion and amendment. At that, it was not a real work of codification, for the legal experts who drafted the city's Administrative Code two decades later discovered that the committee had merely re-shuffled and listed the ordinances in a logical order. Thereafter an edition incorporating changes and amendments was published annually. In most years, however, the revisions in the code were scanty and trifling.[43]

The committees themselves were not always to blame for delays in effecting results, for they were compelled to function under orders. Important Democratic committee chairmen sometimes exerted no more influence on the course of pending legislation than the negligible Republican minority. The revision of the Building Code, one of the most significant pieces of municipal legislation in the nineteen thirties, offers an interesting case study.

Since the Board of Aldermen lacked expert assistance and was not altogether reliable in excluding political favoritism, in 1927 Mayor Walker requested the Merchants' Association to draw up a modern version to replace the obsolete code. Competent architects, engineers, and experts in the building industry were employed, at a private cost of $60,000, and by January, 1931, their draft was ready. Mayor Walker offered to put it through the board under his sanction, but the association preferred to see it pass without pressure. Actively interested in the project, Chairman Edward J. Sullivan, of the Committee on Buildings, studied the code, conducted hearings, and was prepared to report, when word came that Tammany Hall disapproved. Mayor Walker was gone, and appeals to Tammany Leader James J. Dooling—even the intervention of Alfred E. Smith—were fruitless. After six years the revised code still reposed in committee. Until con-

[43] Charter, Sec. 57; George McAneny, *The City Charter*. One of a collection of addresses at lecture-conferences. Published in *The Government of the City of New York* (New York: New York State Constitutional Convention, 1915), 221; Curran, *op. cit.*, p. 184; *Rep. of Comm. on Bd. of Ald. of Cit. Un. for 1914-15 Term*, pp. 5-6; *Record of Work of Bd. of Ald., Jan. 1, 1914 to July 6, 1915*, p. 3; *The Searchlight*, XIII, No. 3, 6-7; IX, No. 6, 13; Interview with William S. Lebwohl, Asst. Corp. Counsel, Nov. 12, 1947.

struction companies knew which code would apply, building activity was suspended, and two hundred thousand workmen in the building trades were unemployed. At this juncture the City Club endeavored to obtain results by impressing Chairman Sullivan with the necessity for action. Sullivan candidly wrote that he had not yet received the proper instructions to report the code out of committee, for the county leaders were wintering in Florida. Whereupon the President of the City Club replied:

> We have a great idea to suggest to you and your fellow-members. Take a long breath and pass the code anyway! Just as if you were grown men! Just as if the Capitol of the city were located at City Hall! Just as if you were paid $5,000 a year for taking such responsibilities! Just as if you had minds! Just as if you had guts! For as long as you do not shake yourselves free, we the citizens are not free but victims of an invisible government with unknown motives of its own.

Eventually the party leaders reached an understanding about the contents of the code and the committee made its report. The code passed unanimously.[44]

The committee system served to maintain ironclad party control. Each year a great number of measures were introduced and referred to the appropriate committee, where they were carefully winnowed by the party leaders in the board and the greater part laid over, or "filed." An alderman who was intent upon seeing a bill through did well to consult the majority leader or whip, since his support would ensure passage. But when the aldermanic leaders had determined to pigeonhole a measure it was futile to contest them, for "any person so rash as to disturb the peace by moving to discharge a committee was silenced by a blow on the head in the form of a motion to table." [45] Committee reports were rarely challenged and almost never disapproved. "The board might as well set up an automaton to receive and

[44] *The Searchlight*, XXI, No. 2, 19; Vol. XXIII, No. 2, 20; Vol. XXV, No. 2, 22; Finegan, *op. cit.*, p. 191; Testimony of Kenneth S. Dayton before Charter Revision Commission, March 5, 1935; *New York Times*, March 18, 1937; Speech of Richard S. Childs over Radio Station WJZ, August 10, 1947; Interview with Dr. George H. McCaffrey, Director of Research, Commerce and Industry Association of New York (formerly Merchants Association), October 30, 1947.

[45] Tanzer, "The First P. R. Council," *The Searchlight*, XXIX, No. 1, 3.

approve committee reports," a Citizens Union observer once stated.[46]

The serious issues in the board were usually threshed out in committee rather than in plenary sessions. During the early twenties, when their numbers still gave them some perceptible influence, the Republican minority sought to obtain their ends in committee meetings, but their efforts were not attended with notable success. In later years the tiny minority normally limited their efforts to public hearings, when the presence of press representatives made the proceedings a sounding board for their views.[47]

Although the committees faithfully followed the prescribed forms, they did not often lend themselves to the transaction of serious business. Some led a nebulous existence; others included numbers of aldermen who were inclined to be less than regular in attendance. Rarely was there a thorough airing of issues. Meetings were conducted in a careless, hasty fashion, and even serious-minded aldermen found some difficulty in following the proceedings. "Committees sprint through legislation so quickly that it is impossible for anyone to be really aware of what is being accomplished, either in the affirmative or in the negative," complained a Republican in 1926. The Board of Estimate was periodically invaded by delegations of hundreds of citizens, carrying badges and banners, and their spokesmen pled their cause with eloquence and fervor. The attendance of civic organizations at aldermanic hearings, however, was meagre and perfunctory. "Past experience as a close observer and as an elected representative of the people has taught me the futility of a public hearing before the members of a committee whose minds are absolutely foreclosed and who have not the slightest intention of paying any heed to the suggestions made," declared a minority member. "Why on earth should anyone attend these meetings?"

[46] Test. of Kenneth Dayton, March 5, 1935; *The Searchlight*, VIII, No. 2 (1918), 15; Interview with the Hon. Newbold Morris, August 8, 1947. As an alderman Mr. Morris habitually referred his proposals to Minority Leader Thomas J. Curran, but the small size of the Republican-Fusion delegation made this procedure a joke.

[47] Test. of Kenneth Dayton; *The Searchlight*, XIII, No. 3, 5-6; Interview with the Hon. Lambert Fairchild, October 12, 1947.

In some quarters it was believed more effective to gain the ears of the party chieftains.[48]

The Board had within its gift a number of legislative appointments free from Civil Service regulations—Commissioners of Deeds, members of the Board of Elections, and the City Clerk and his staff, amounting to sixty in 1935. So tempting an opportunity to strengthen the political machine with patronage was not overlooked, for many of the positions made few demands on the time and energy of party workers. They were parcelled out to loyal adherents nominated by the county leaders, the election by the board being purely a formality.[49]

One of the Democratic county leaders insisted that in Mayor La Guardia's administration his office-holders were just as carefully selected for partisan purposes as those of any Tammany mayor. When Bernard S. Deutsch became Fusion president of the board in 1934, the entire Democratic secretarial staff of thirteen men, with a payroll well above $50,000, fell under the axe. Conversely, when Deutsch died the following year and the office was taken over by the Tammany vice-president of the board, the Democrats again made a clean sweep of the jobholders.[50]

The political favorites on the staff of the president of the board were hardly pressed to devote their full energies to their official tasks. It was not only political work that occupied their spare time, but unusual opportunities for personal profit. President McKee's chief staff adviser, whose duties included the inspection of school sites, was suspended for exploiting advance information on the purchase of property by the Board of Education. His investments in land later taken by the city for schools had yielded handsome profits. A real estate partner of another examiner in McKee's office was also involved in the purchase of sites later acquired by the city. McKee himself was

48 *The Searchlight*, XIX, No. 2, 10-11; *New York Evening Post*, June 4, 1926; Speech of Mrs. Pratt, December 5, 1927; McGoldrick, "Eclipse of Ald.," *Nat. Mun. Rev.*, XIV, No. 6, 363-64.

49 Charter, Secs. 27, 32, 33; Sec. 28, as amended by L. 1905, C. 629; Sec. 31, as amended by L. 1920, C. 733; Sec. 58, as amended by L. 1917, C. 610; Laws of 1922, C. 588, Sec. 30; Testimony of Kenneth Dayton.

50 Flynn, *op. cit.*, 141; *New York Times*, December 30, 1933, November 22, 1934, December 31, 1934.

criticized for accepting lucrative receiverships during his incumbency. There were those who believed that some of the profits were passed along, in part at least, to others in the dominant political organization.[51]

Yet the staff of the president of the Board of Aldermen, like those of the other members of the Board of Estimate, performed its functions with commendable proficiency. In the Board of Aldermen, however, the expert assistance that is so essential to a modern legislative body was sadly lacking. The sergeants-at-arms, chauffeurs, and clerks on the payroll of the board were selected by the county leaders from district political workers. Legislative facilities for fact-finding and for drafting of legislation were virtually nonexistent, and those aldermen who took their duties seriously enough to seek assistance relied upon the unofficial aid of the staff of the president of the board. After the Home Rule Law went into effect there was created a legal department, including a Commissioner of Bill Drafting, at a salary of $10,000 a year, and a staff of three assistants, to aid members of both houses of the Municipal Assembly in drawing up local laws and resolutions. But the commissioner hardly permitted his legislative tasks to interfere with outside work. "Where is his office and when is he there?" sarcastically inquired a Republican alderman. "Can one drop in any time or must one make an appointment?" Many considered the unit as it operated an unnecessary expense, and in 1933 it was eliminated from the budget as an economy measure.[52]

The Board of Aldermen sorely needed the services of a conscientious bill-drafting corps, for few members were competent in that capacity. At one time the Citizens Union had waged a campaign to induce more lawyers to run for the board, but with little success. Many aldermen lacked polish in English composi-

[51] Finegan, *op. cit.*, pp. 125-27, 181, 264, 266-67. *New York Times*, May 1, May 8, May 19, May 20, July 10, 1931, April 16, July 3, 1932.

[52] McGoldrick, "Eclipse of Ald.," *Nat. Mun. Rev.*, XIV, 363; Testimony of Rufus McGahen before Charter Revision Commission, February 28, 1935; *Governmental Organization Within Greater New York* (New York: Institute of Public Administration, 1931), 6; Speech of Alderman Ruth Pratt, December 5, 1927; *New York Evening World*, December 2, 1926; *New York Times*, May 2, 1933, December 21, 1933.

tion, and the Board of Statutory Consolidation, which undertook to codify the enactments of the Board of Aldermen, found ordinance after ordinance "ambiguous, tautological, repetitious, inartificial, contradictory, and often ungrammatical." One local law was utterly incomprehensible, even to a battery of legal experts, and among crudely drafted bills, some contained sentences lacking in subjects or predicates, spotted with split infinitives or split verbs, or either over-punctuated or entirely lacking in punctuation.[53]

Committee clerks relieved aldermanic committees of the burden of drafting reports, but official papers were often handled quite irresponsibly. At one time the validity of a local law dealing with taxicab fares was contested in the courts, and the report of the committee, written by the clerk, was presented as an argument to invalidate the law. The report in question came as a startling surprise to the Corporation Counsel's assistant who was arguing the case; for he believed that the report that was incorporated in the bill as it was passed was not identical with the one he had seen in the committee room. A considerable degree of looseness and disorder characterized the disposition of official documents by the staff. From the time the board first began to function under the Charter of 1901, the city clerk handled the original ordinances. An engrossed copy of each ordinance was certified by the clerk and, upon approval, signed by the mayor. When the Board of Statutory Consolidation of 1936-37 found it necessary to sift the details of all ordinances and local laws enacted by the board as a preliminary to the preparation of the city's Administrative Code, they were considerably handicapped by the fact that the originals of many ordinances passed prior to 1916 were missing. No one knew whether they had been lost, burnt, or discarded as rubbish. A file copy of the city charter, certified by the Secretary of State, had also disappeared.[54]

[53] *The Searchlight*, XIII, No. 3, 13; *Report of the Board of Statutory Consolidation of the City of New York: The Administrative Code of the City of New York* (Albany, 1938), lxviii; Interview with Mr. William S. Lebwohl, Asst. Corp. Counsel, November 12, 1947; Interview with the Hon. Reuben Lazarus, Counsel and Executive Officer of the Board of Statutory Consolidation, March 27, 1947.

[54] *Municipal Reference Library Notes*, XIX, No. 14 (October 18, 1933), 75-76; *Proc. of Bd. of Ald., 1902*, I, 35; *Rep. of Bd. of Stat. Consol. of City of N. Y.*,

Occasionally the small patronage available to the Board of Aldermen became an issue. When the last Fusion majority ruled the board, a "marriage trust" scandal came to light. In the eighteen nineties a former dungeon in City Hall was converted into a marriage chapel and aldermen were authorized to officiate at the rites. Directly above the old jail the City Clerk issued licenses to marry, and runners whisked the licensed couples downstairs to the chapel, where a coterie of marrying aldermen performed hasty ceremonies. It was regarded as "the Sullivans' graft," for the business was controlled by "Dry Dollar" and "Little Tim" Sullivan, rulers of the Bowery and the East Side. Technically the annual take of $30,000 was "honest graft," but the team of aldermen, runners, interpreters for foreigners, and collectors who shared the proceeds paid no rent for the chapel. A Fusion-controlled Board of Aldermen ended the practice by transferring the functions to the City Clerk. Today the chapel serves as a storeroom for the major, and only the Cupid's bows, arrows, and outlines of hearts on the iron grill-work of interior windows remind the visitor of the romantic role the aldermen once played.[55]

During the municipal campaign of 1933 some political capital was made of the size of the staff which ministered to the Board of Aldermen. In 1930 ten assistant sergeants-at-arms had been assigned to guard a single entrance to the aldermanic chamber. Their services were required one day a week and the annual stipend was $2,280 a year. A steady barrage of criticism was di-

pp. xxxix-xliv, li, liii; Interview with the Hon. Reuben Lazarus, March 27, 1947. In justice to the staff of the Board of Aldermen, however, it must be noted that scholars studying the city's public records as late as 1928 reported that the archives of many offices and departments were being stored in inaccessible quarters, hopelessly scattered, or destroyed, either by deliberate intent or through neglect. Stokes, *Iconography of Manhattan Island,* VI, 181.

[55] Curran, *op. cit.,* pp. 178-81; Henry H. Curran, *John Citizen's Job* (New York, 1924), pp. 88-96; *Record of Work of Bd. of Ald., Jan. 1, 1914 to July 6, 1915,* p. 1. After the transfer of this "racket" from the Board of Aldermen's jurisdiction, the City Clerk's office inherited it. A district leader who worked as First Deputy Clerk deposited $384,788 in his 37 bank accounts between 1925 and 1931. Eventually he was indicted for income tax evasion. Samuel Seabury, *Intermediate Report to the Members of the Joint Legislative Committee to Investigate the Administration of the Government of the City of New York,* January 25, 1932, pp. 127, 188.

rected at the city administration for creating the sinecures, and in 1933 they were dropped from the budget. Thereafter direct patronage in the Board of Aldermen disappeared as a burning issue.[56]

[56] *New York Times*, August 23, 1930, September 16, 1933; Walter Davenport, "Tammany's Own," *Collier's*, XCI (March 4, 1933), 42; Finegan, *op. cit.*, pp. 97, 260; "Has Tammany Reformed?—One Year After the Seabury Inquiry," *City Affairs Committee Bulletin*, September, 1933, p. 2.

5. THE ALDERMAN AND HIS BAILIWICK

The Alderman is the political trolley that meets all trains. He acts as interpreter of his city's government to the individual citizen. He explains and disentangles. He is government itself. . . . The alderman is more than a tradition, less than a cartoon. He is an institution. In New York he is Father Knickerbocker himself, to nine families out of ten.—HENRY H. CURRAN, *Member of Board of Aldermen, 1911–1917* [1]

A REPUBLICAN MEMBER once suggested delegating the powers of the Board of Aldermen to the leader of Tammany Hall on the ground that the legislators were "mere automatons moved at the will of that powerful organization." The actual governing power of the city resided not in its elected officials, but in the dominant political organization. Lincoln Steffens had once termed it the "unofficial, irresponsible, invisible government" behind the legal or constitutional facade. Steffens regarded the aldermen as "dummies" in the same sense as the Board of Directors of great corporations, which often served as fronts for financial operators. The Board of Aldermen was only nominally a deliberative body. Except for a few brief intervals when Fusion majorities prevailed, its public sessions were conducted for the purpose of formally registering the decisions of the leaders of the dominant party.[2]

From 1904 until 1934 the Democratic Party controlled the mayor's office and the Board of Aldermen almost uninterruptedly. Tammany Hall, the New York County Democratic organization, was popularly believed to rule the Democratic Party

[1] Curran, *John Citizen's Job*, p. 197.

[2] *New York Evening Post*, June 4, 1926; Steffens, *Autobiography*, pp. 232-35, 237; Peel, *Pol. Clubs of N. Y. C.*, pp. 120, 122-23; Statement of Judge Samuel Seabury, *New York Times*, January 5, 1933.

of the entire city, but there was an individual political mechanism in each of its five counties.[3] "We have five Tammany Halls," declared former Mayor La Guardia. The original Tammany was the oldest of the organizations and until the death of Charles F. Murphy in 1924, its leader actually did dominate all five machines, treating the other county leaders as "hand-picked viceroys." That was exactly what they were, testified Boss Edward J. Flynn of the Bronx, himself a Murphy protege. During the administrations of Mayors Walker and O'Brien (1926-1933), however, Tammany strength declined. In the initial sessions of the board in 1934, the Bronx delegation, in coalition with dissident elements in Kings and New York Counties, administered a crushing defeat to the Tammany bloc's candidate for a vacancy. Today Tammany Hall is no more than one of the five Democratic machines of the city.[4]

Within each of the county organizations there always resided a large measure of autonomy. The county committees, elected by the enrolled party members in the primaries, nominally exercised great authority. Actually the membership was carefully selected from party members holding civil service exempt jobs to do the bidding of the party leaders, and their sole function was to ratify the decisions of the County Executive Committee.[5] Here lay the real power, for the district leaders and county leaders who comprised the Executive Committee exerted more influence over the city's government than the elected officeholders. For all practical purposes the Board of Aldermen had relinquished its authority to them.[6]

[3] The boundaries of the counties of New York City are identical with those of the boroughs. In the case of the Bronx, Queens, and Richmond, the names serve both territorial divisions. Manhattan, however, is known as New York County and Brooklyn as Kings County. The Post Office also recognizes Richmond as Staten Island.

[4] Roy V. Peel "The Political Machine of New York City," *American Political Science Review*, XXVII (1933), 611-13; Fiorello H. La Guardia, "Bosses are Bunk," *Atlantic Monthly*, CLXXX (1946), 22; Flynn, *You're the Boss*, pp. 7, 27-33, 48-49, 127, 129, 131.

[5] In 1935 the Department of Investigations and Accounts disclosed that 61% of the employees in the five county offices were members of the county committees.

[6] Flynn, *op. cit.*, pp. 219-21; Joseph D. McGoldrick, "The New Tammany," *The American Mercury*, XV (1928), 1-2; Letter of Councilman Stanley M. Isaacs to *New York Herald Tribune*, March 31, 1947.

The leader or boss[7] of each county attained his position by a majority vote of the Executive Committee. Richard Croker, Charles F. Murphy, George W. Olvany, and John F. Curry held this position at various times in Tammany Hall; Hugh McLaughlin, Patrick McCarren, and John H. McCooey in Brooklyn; and Edward J. Flynn in the Bronx. No county leader could play the absolute monarch, as Louis XIV at Versailles. Rather, like Hugh Capet, he was regarded by local party chieftains as merely the highest suzerain of the land—*primus inter pares.* Almost invariably he had risen from the ranks of the district leaders, and after his selection he usually retained his place among the city's seventy-six district leaders.[8]

Nor could any county leader hope to maintain his rule without the aid of the powerful district leaders. "My control is entirely dependent on this support," explained Bronx Leader Edward J. Flynn. "If a majority of the (Executive) Committee decided they no longer wanted me they could call a meeting tomorrow and supplant me." Indeed, district leaders were known successfully to defy the county leader. "Big Tim" Sullivan installed his friend, Thomas F. Foley, as leader of a district in lower Manhattan, despite the opposition of a Croker candidate. Tammany Leader Charles F. Murphy could not dislodge William S. Devery, a former police commissioner, whose candidacy he had challenged in a primary fight for a West Side district leader-

[7] The political chiefs preferred to call themselves "leaders"; their opponents usually referred to them as "bosses."

[8] The basic geographic unit of most political districts was the Assembly District, or A. D., derived from apportionment for the lower house of the State Legislature. During the nineteen twenties and thirties there were 62 representatives of New York City in the Assembly, but 76 district leaders. The apparent contradiction may be explained by multiple leaderships. With the loss of population, some of the older areas of the city, notably Manhattan, had undergone reductions in number of assembly districts, but their district leaders were unwilling to give up their positions. Each A. D. was normally entitled to one vote on the Executive Committee, usually shared between leader and (female) coleader. In Assembly Districts split into multiple leaderships, the vote was shared fractionally. After a legislative reapportionment in the forties, the third A. D. of Manhattan contained seven district leaders and seven co-leaders, each entitled to one-fourteenth of a vote on the Tammany Executive Committee. Peel, *Pol. Clubs of N. Y. C.*, pp. 57-60; McGoldrick, "The New Tammany," *Amer. Merc.*, XV, 2; Zink, *City Bosses in the U. S.*, pp. 96-193; *New York Times*, February 10, 1947.

ship. The Brooklyn McCooey machine supported James McQuade for the leadership of Greenpoint; yet Peter J. McGuinness vanquished McQuade and his cohorts in five successive primaries. McCooey was compelled to arrange for McQuade's formal surrender in 1932.[9]

In Queens the county leader's control was quite tenuous and revolts were common. In the last elections for the Board of Aldermen an independent Democrat successfully defied County Leader James C. Sheridan in his home district, and replaced the incumbent in the primaries.[10]

District leaders gained and retained their positions through success in the primary elections. Since it involved their political destinies, many leaders were more vitally interested in victory at the primaries than in the general elections. In any given year the great majority of nominations were not disputed, and some leaders were not challenged for decades.[11] When struggles for power did occur in the biennial elections, they were often fought with fratricidal bitterness, and resort to extra-legal methods was not unknown. As late as 1947, a police commissioner ordered the streets cleared before the primary voting time of all "criminals, thugs, gangsters, strong-arm men, and neighborhood thugs," as well as professional votegetters.[12]

Intimately linked with the fortunes of the district leader was the choice of a party candidate for alderman. Normally the party primaries were merely formal ratifications of the leaders'

[9] Flynn, *op. cit.*, p. 224; Werner, *Tammany Hall*, pp. 471-73, 487-91; Peel, *Pol. Clubs of N. Y. C.*, pp. 49-50; Rovere, "The Big Hello," *The New Yorker*, XXI, No. 49, 32-34.

[10] Peel, "Pol. Machine of N. Y. C.," *Am. Pol. Sci. Rev.*, XXVII, 614.

[11] In 1932 primary contests for all parties—Republican, Democratic, and Socialist—took place in less than 28% of the city's election districts. "Hofstadter Committee Report," p. 120.

[12] *New York Herald-Tribune*, July 29, 1947. Nominally the members of the county committee elected from a particular assembly district convened to select a leader and co-leader to represent them on the Executive Committee. In practice the incumbent district leader hand-picked the county committeemen from his district, himself included, and they in turn voted for him. If he were unable to marshal sufficient delegates to gain election to the Executive Committee, he was supplanted by a new district leader. Alfred E. Smith, *The Citizen and His Government* (New York, 1935), pp. 13-16; "Hofstadter Committee Report, pp. 120-21.

selections. In 1925, for example, only eighteen per cent of the aldermanic candidates were involved in primary contests. Occasionally the district leader put himself in nomination, and after the Seabury probe had exposed widespread corruption, a number of leaders were faced with revolts in which their malfeasance as aldermen was charged by the opposition. In one primary fight Alderman Patrick S. Dowd contested the leadership of Andrew B. Keating on the grounds that the district machine had attempted interference with his aldermanic duties. Generally the entire slate of the successful faction in a primary struggle triumphed, but sometimes an aldermanic candidate won out despite the defeat of his ticket.[13]

The official party organization, however, had little contact with the citizenry. The real strength of the party lay in the district leaders themselves, and through them the power of the machine was carried into every area of the city. For many it was the only point of contact with the government itself.

It was the unremitting labor of the district leader and his clubhouse coterie that fostered and sustained the machine and "delivered" solid blocs of votes. "We are in business 365 days a year," boasted local politicians. Party workers came into ceaseless contact with the wants and needs of residents of their neighborhoods, cementing acquaintances and winning the gratitude of voters.

"What tells in holdin' your grip on your district is to go right down among the poor families and help them in the different ways they need real help," asserted George Washington Plunkitt, a district leader at the turn of the century. District captains reported to the leader entreaties of every description—requests for jobs, appeals for promotion in the civil service, urgent calls for assisting youths involved in minor brushes with the law. Almost every night in the week the leader could be found in the district clubhouse, paying heed to the solicitations of anxious citizens.[14]

[13] E. g., in 1925 Alderman Dowd failed to wrest the leadership from Keating, but secured the Democratic nomination as alderman. *The Searchlight*, XV, No. 3 (1925), 9-11; Peel, *Pol. Clubs of N. Y. C.*, p. 285.

[14] Prior to assuming the reins at Tammany Hall Charles F. Murphy was leader of the "Gas House" district. It was his practice to make himself available every morning, betweeen 7:30 and 10, at a lampost on the northwest corner of Twen-

Six nights a week, from six in the evening until twelve-thirty or one in the morning, Peter J. McGuinness sat in the Greenpoint People's Regular Democratic Organization Clubhouse, interviewing his constituents. The "contracts," as the city's politicians termed their commissions, would be fulfilled in the morning. Of a forenoon, an active district leader might be found arranging with the head of a city department the transfer of a club member from night to day work, telephoning a public agency regarding a widow's pension, obtaining admission of a voter to a hospital, securing a license for a local resident to follow an occupation, obtaining an excuse from jury duty or adjustment of a minor violation for a business man, or aiding a young man who had fallen into the clutches of the law. "Murder, rape, and robbery with a gun I never touch," asserted McGuinness, the famed Greenpoint leader. "But something like housebreaking—what the hell, the first couple of times don't prove there's anything wrong with a boy." [15]

The popular bestowal of favors was not confined to little adjustments between individual and government. Democratic politicians who extolled their "daily fountain of benefits to the needy and helpless" were not boasting idly, for even a Republican alderman who consistently opposed their alleged derelictions in the board conceded their valuable aid to the distressed and unfortunate.[16] Destitute families were furnished with the means to survive—a scuttle of coal, a bottle of milk, medical aid, or cash; the unemployed were assisted in obtaining work with private corporations or governmental departments. Clubhouse lawyers proffered free legal guidance and political secretaries assisted unlettered shopkeepers in filling out statements. On the social side the clubs offered outings, picnics, clam-bakes, and

---

tieth Street and Second Ave. Myers, *Hist. of Tamanny Hall*, p. 303. Although he could usually be buttonholed in the street, the typical district chieftain made the political club his headquarters.

[15] Rovere, "The Big Hello," *The New Yorker*, XX, No. 48, 29, 34-38; William L. Riordan, *Plunkitt of Tammany Hall* (New York, 1948), pp. 36-37; McGoldrick, "The New Tammany," *Am. Merc.*, XV, 5; Peel, *Pol. Clubs of N. Y. C.*, pp. 65-66, 102.

[16] Pratt, "Men are Bad Housekeepers," *Harp. Mag.*, CLIV, 687.

celebrations. For the poor the clubhouse clique acted as social workers, job agents, attorneys, accountants and advisors.[17]

The influence of the district leaders was maintained through widespread distribution of favors. To "Big Tim" Sullivan and "Little Tim," leader of the Democratic forces in the Board of Aldermen until 1910, the "respect, the esteem, and the eternal allegiance of . . . the Bowery were indissolubly consecrated," their silver-tongued campaign manager announced; and at one time "Big Tim's" picture was displayed in almost every house in his district. In Greenpoint Peter J. McGuinness was hailed as a neighborhood idol, "him with a heart of gold, who'd do anything for ya, especially if you're in trouble." District leaders were known to dispense political bounty so lavishly that they died penniless; but their zeal for the poor reflected a "studied and self-seeking humanitarianism." As they conceived it, the performance of a favor involved a contractual relationship that required the voter to assign his franchise. Whether the beneficiary made promises to vote for the leader's candidates or not, it was generally understood that most votes were assigned on a *quid pro quo* basis. The alderman played a conspicuous role in the year-round campaign for votes, for he was a key worker in the district machine, and the bulk of his time was spent in dealing with the troubles of his constituents.[18]

The great strength of the district machines rested on patronage. "Favors are the milk," ruminated an alderman, "jobs the cream . . . The strongest oath of political allegiance is spelled j-o-b, job." No more reliable fighters for the organization could be found than those whose livelihood depended on it. "It isn't only the job that is given the political boss when he puts his man in," asserted former Mayor La Guardia. "The loyalty of that man goes to the boss . . . He owes his job to the boss, and

[17] Edwin P. Kilroe, Abraham Kaplan, and Joseph Johnson, *The Story of Tammany* (New York: Democratic Organization County Committee, 1924), p. 73; Curran, *John Citizen's Job*, pp. 224-25; Smith, *Citizen and His Govt.*, pp. 6-11; *Final Report of Samuel Seabury, Referee in the Matter of the Investigation of the Magistrates' Courts in the First Judicial Department* (New York, 1932), 34, 36.

[18] Zink, *City Bosses in the U. S.*, p. 90; Smith, *op. cit.*, pp. 11-12; Curran, *John Citizen's Job*, pp. 198-99; *New York Daily Tribune*, December 7, 1902; *New York World-Telegram*, August 18, 1931.

therefore he, in turn, must do the bidding of the boss." Once established in his position, the officeholder became a potential source of favors himself. Again, government supervisors winked at time taken off for day-to-day political tasks, and during campaigns unofficial furloughs of days or even weeks were possible.[19]

Throughout the city the center of political life in every neighborhood was the district club. The Democrats usually maintained at least one in every district. At its core was a group of political jobholders, variously estimated at 200 to 600 in number. "The machine always has enough hangers-on, jobholders, payroll leeches eating from the public trough," affirmed La Guardia, "who with their families maintain a solid phalanx to keep the political machine and the boss in power." [20]

Among this set, habitually derided by La Guardia as "clubhouse loafers," about twenty held positions drawing a good salary or entailing important responsibilities. Perhaps the least desirable was state assemblyman, for frequent absence from the city and low pay made it a lesser prize, save among aspiring young lawyers. The office of alderman was a more tempting plum, especially after 1934, when a Fusion administration had begun to starve the Democratic machine and jobs were scarce. The duties were not arduous—one meeting a week in cool weather, and possibly one additional afternoon set aside for a committee meeting—and the basic salary was $5,000 a year.[21]

In the municipal scale of political society the aldermen held the lowest rank. Judges of the municipal courts (where cases involving $1,000 or less were heard) and of the magistrates' courts (in which minor offenses were tried) were in a higher stratum. They were nominated at the behest of the district leader in recognition of party service. And just as the district leader

[19] Curran, *John Citizen's Job*, pp. 218-27; George Creel, "The Tammany Take," *Collier's*, CLI (1933), 32; La Guardia, "Bosses Are Bunk," *Atl. Monthly*, CLXXX, 23; Flynn, *You're the Boss*, p. 24.

[20] Finegan, *op. cit.*, p. 50; La Guardia, *op. cit.*, p. 22.

[21] After January 1, 1933 the salary of 62 aldermen was cut to $4,640, and the income of majority leader, minority leader, and chairman of the Finance Committee reduced from $7,500 to $6,890. The president of the board also suffered a reduction from $25,000 to $15,000. *Official Directory of the City of New York, 1937* (New York, 1937), pp. 48-49.

prided himself on "taking care of the boys" who frequented the clubhouses, so the county leaders ensured the district leaders' positions, usually in offices exempt from civil service examinations. Edward J. Flynn, Democratic leader of Bronx County for more than thirty years, attributed his successful career to his diligence in installing his district leaders and their families in public office. A few stood for election, but they were a distinct minority. Of the 58 Democratic district leaders who held public positions in 1925, only nine were elected, among them two aldermen. The remaining 49 were appointees, drawing a combined income of $339,330 a year. District leaders regarded their municipal jobs merely as a technical device to reward them for their services to society in the district clubs. "You got to make jobs like this so a political man can get his work done," explained Peter J. McGuinness. Rarely were they fitted into positions for which they possessed special aptitudes. John Theofel, county leader of Queens, drew $8,000 a year as chief clerk in his county's Surrogate's Court; but he admitted he did not even know the names of the departments over which he supposedly presided. As Commissioner of Records, Hyman Schorenstein was the nominal custodian of the official records of Kings County. Yet he was a complete illiterate, unable to spell his own name. After she had suffered a paralytic stroke, Helen F. McRedmond, a Bronx co-leader, not only continued on the city payroll, but after four years confined to her home received a pay rise from $3,100 to $4,260. Even a Tammany representative at the Seabury hearings announced: "I have seen commissioners come on this stand getting $10,000 and $15,000 a year; on the outside they could not make $1,500 a year. And they know no more about their departments than a boy on the street." [22]

Some who aspired to rise in the city's political hierarchy found the office of alderman one of the first on the road to political success. Richard Croker, who had begun his public career as two-fisted boss of a gang of repeaters in the "Gas House" dis-

[22] *New York Herald-Tribune*, December 26, 1937; *Magistrates' Courts Investigation*, pp. 14-15, 30-34, 244; Flynn, *You're the Boss*, 56-57, 224; La Guardia, *op. cit.*, p. 22; *The Searchlight*, XV, No. 1 (1925), 8-9; Rovere, "The Big Hello," *The New Yorker*, XX, No. 48, 36; Blanshard, *Investigating City Govt.*, pp. 8, 9, 17, 89-90; Seabury, *Final Report*, p. 3; Seabury, *Intermediate Report*, pp. 128-30.

trict, obtained successive jobs as attendant in a Municipal Court, engineer on a city steamer, and alderman. Thence he graduated to a position in the comptroller's office, city marshall, and coroner. Ultimately he succeeded "Honest" John Kelly as Tammany chief in 1886. George Washington Olvany, who followed Murphy as leader of Tammany Hall in 1924, gained a start in politics in the office of the Corporation Counsel. Then he was twice elected to the Board of Aldermen, serving on a committee which formulated a sadly defective code of ordinances. In later years he was promoted to deputy fire commissioner, sheriff's counsel, General Sessions judge, and chairman of the Executive Committee of Tammany Hall. The *New Yorker* paid him a handsome compliment when it related that in 1905 a man thrust his head into the aldermanic chamber and shouted, "Alderman, your saloon's on fire!" It was said that a moment later Olvany was the only alderman to remain seated as the members stampeded out.[23] A celebrated alumnus of the board was Thomas M. Farley, who created a sensation at the Seabury hearings in 1931. His incredible explanation of an accumulation of a quarter of a million dollars in bank deposits became a by-word in political circles—the magical "tin box." [24] Farley began his public career in the Board of Aldermen, to which he was elected four times. Despite an arrest and indictment for extortion during his first campaign, he was twice endorsed by the Citizens Union. In later years he rose to deputy clerk, county clerk, Sheriff of New York County—and district leader.[25]

Apprentice politicians sometimes found the office of alderman a training school in district politics, but not all members of the board were young and ambitious. In 1927 an alderman divided

[23] Unfortunately the anecdote has been told about other aldermen and other cities, and it must be considered apocryphal.

[24] Requested to explain bank deposits of $360,000 during a period in which his total accounted income did not exceed $90,000, Farley blandly replied that the had drawn the excess from a tin box, a "wonderful tin box." Seabury, *Second Intermediate Report*, Appendix No. 1, pp. 3-4.

[25] Lothrop Stoddard, *Master of Manhattan* (New York, 1937), *passim*; Zink, *op. cit.*, pp. 128-33, 165-68; Alva Johnston, "No More Lawyers: Profile of George Washington Olvany," *The New Yorker*, VII, No. 47 (1932), 22-25; Dennis T. Lynch, *Criminals and Politicians* (New York, 1932), pp. 189-90; *The Searchlight*, IX, No. 5, 19.

the membership into two broad classes—those on the way up the ladder of political success and the veterans of long and faithful party service. Of the 65 aldermen elected in 1931 campaign, 17 had passed their sixtieth year. There was even a city employee who became an alderman after he had retired and was drawing a pension from a municipal department. For some the board served as a political Snug Harbor. The turnover of aldermen was rather slow. In the 1932-33 sessions there were only thirteen freshman members; 34 of the 65 had been elected at least five times, and two had begun their twelfth two-year term. By 1937 Frank A. Cunningham and James J. Molen could each boast of 28 years in the Board.[26]

As a power who could "deliver" his neighborhood in the elections, the leader was privileged to select several candidates from his district, among them the alderman.[27] Occasionally the leader nominated himself, but district leaders were always a small minority in the board. Two were elected for the 1924-25 sessions, five for the 1932-33 term. The most conspicuous in the twenties was "Pete" McGuinness, but for years he was at odds with the Kings County organization, and appointive office was closed to him. After his reconciliation with County Leader McCooey, McGuinness retired from the Board to accept the more lucrative post of Assistant Superintendent of Public Works, and designated a successor who was thenceforth known as McGuinness' "own alderman." Between alderman and district leader the normal relationship was that of subordinate to political superior.[28]

[26] Pratt, "Men Are Bad Housekeepers," *Harp. Mag.*, CLIV, 683; *The Searchlight*, XXI, No. 2, 19-27; Testimony of Mayor La Guardia and statement of Mr. S. John Block, of the City Charter Revision Commission, May 9, 1935; *Reports of Comm. on Bd. of Ald. of Cit. Un., 1910-19, passim*; *Ann. Rep. of Bd. of Elects. of City of N. Y. for Years 1917-1935, passim.*

[27] "When it comes to selecting the organization candidates from his particular ward for the legislature or city council," wrote Frank R. Kent, "he (the district leader) is the absolute or sole dictator. He brings the candidates out. He puts them in the field. He is their creator and their sponsor ... What he does is to decide on his man, take him 'downtown', introduce him to the boss, and that is all there is to it." Frank R. Kent, *The Great Game of Politics* (New York, 1940), pp. 52-54.

[28] *The Searchlight*, XV, No. 1, 8-9; Vol. XXIII, No. 2, 26; Peel, *Pol. Clubs of N. Y. C.*, p. 285.

Sometimes the county organization would suggest a candidate for alderman and the district leader would exact a reciprocal favor. When the opposing party or rival faction was dangerously strong, the leader would find it expedient to choose a man of ability and integrity. In a safe district, however, the leader was free to pick his own creature—a reliable machine man.

In political circles it was axiomatic that a district leader would rather install an alderman than elect a president. The motive was obvious. Day and night, almost every day in the year, the leader was a "slave to his voters," on call at the clubhouse, at his office, or at home. To gain relief from his routine duties he customarily had one of the clubhouse habitues placed on the city payroll as alderman. Statesmanship was not required, for that harvested few votes. Public opinion permitting, the leader deliberately nominated a tool who could be broken at the slightest sign of independence. First and foremost the alderman was a "contact man," or runner employed in the execution of contracts.[29]

Aldermen were rarely more than deputies for their district leaders. Without orders from their political masters few would take a stand on any public question or exercise discretion in any but the most routine duties. That would be courting political suicide. Rumor had it that one district leader went so far as to collect in cash the salary of his alderman, who never attended meetings.[30]

The local Republican machine could match the Democratic neither in power nor prestige. It never won a mayoralty race or a majority in the Board of Aldermen after the consolidation of the city, save in combination with apostate Democrats and other minority groups. Like the Republican Party in the deep South, it was sustained largely by patronage from Washington, with

[29] Smith, *op. cit.*, p. 9; Flynn, *You're the Boss*, p. 60; *Report of Chart. Rev. Comm. of 1909*, p. 127; *Hofstadter Committee Report*, p. 6; *The Searchlight*, XIX, No. 1, 10.

[30] Testimony of Bernard S. Deutsch before Chart. Rev. Comm., May 12, 1935; *Proportional Representation for New York City* (New York: Merchants' Association of N. Y., March, 1937), 5; Letter of John Kirkland Clark to the *N. Y. Sun*, November 3, 1947 (Mr. Clark was State Counsel in the Seabury probe of the District Attorney's office in New York County in 1931). A conspicuous exception was the President of the Board, who was selected by the county leaders.

additional aid from Albany when successful in State politics. Relations with Democratic politicians were most cordial. "When Tammany's on top I do good turns for the Republicans. When they're on top they don't forget me," declared District Leader Plunkitt. "Me and the Republicans are enemies just one day in the year—election day." Some Democrats sneered at Republican "nabobs" for "haughtily ignoring the common man between elections," but in practice there was an exchange of favors between political rivals. Republican district leaders fulfilled contracts involving the municipal government by invoking the aid of their Democratic colleagues, and when their party was in power in the national government the Democrats turned to them for aid in solving their constituents' federal problems. Partly as a result of this friendly collaboration, Republican district leaders secured a small share of commissionerships in municipal offices.[31]

The organization and methods of the Republicans paralleled those of the Democrats. "They are as truly machines as their Democratic counterparts in every respect save that of success in politics," gibed Boss Flynn. Like their opponents, the Republican county leaders easily controlled their county committees. Safely packed with federal jobholders, they appeared to one who had participated in their proceedings as "little more than a joke."[32] Although less numerous than Democratic associations, Republican district clubs also offered "jobs for the faithful and favors for everybody." Republican district leaders, like their Democratic rivals, were responsible for the selection of candidates for the Board of Aldermen from the ranks of party workers. They, too, were disinclined to run for the office themselves. Membership in the board could be a lower rung on the

[31] In 1932 four Republican leaders served as city and county commissioners at an average salary of $9,250. Thomas and Blanshard, *op. cit.*, 33-34; Peel, "Pol. Mach. of N. Y. C.," *Am. Pol. Sci. Rev.*, XXVII, 612, 617; Riordan, *op. cit.*, p. 51; Flynn, *You're the Boss*, p. 8; Pendleton Herring, *The Politics of Democracy* (New York, 1940), p. 143; La Guardia, *op. cit.*, p. 24.

[32] There was a slight difference in the election of the county leaders, for party rules rather than state law guided intra-party election procedures. Conventions elected Republican county leaders, in contrast to the closed meetings of the Democratic Executive Committee.

ladder of political success for a Republican career politician. Henry H. Curran, who was chosen by a Washington Square district leader as alderman, pursued a long and honorable subsequent career as Magistrate, Borough President, Chief Magistrate, and Justice of the Court of Special Sessions. Thomas J. Curran, who had begun his political career as an Assistant District Attorney, was swept into the Board by the Fusion wave of 1933. The following year he succeeded Joseph Clark Baldwin as Minority Leader, a position he held until the last meeting of the Board in 1937. Curran went on to become district leader, Republican Leader of New York County, and political advisor to Governor Thomas E. Dewey, who appointed him Secretary of State in 1941. But no Republican, no matter how he truckled to his leader's wishes, could hold a safe berth in the Board of Aldermen. None could equal the twenty-eight year record held by Cunningham and Molen. In a city that had become overwhelmingly Democratic after World War I, only the "silk stocking" Fifteenth voted consistently Republican.[33]

The major parties devoted their energies to jobs and favors; the minor parties were preoccupied with ideologies. "Only a fool would ask a Socialist to 'fix up' a traffic ticket," reflected one authority. Excepting party office, they had little patronage to offer. Their specialty was open forums for discussion, their aims modification of the social structure. The Socialists reached the height of their influence in the 1918-19 term, but as a "minor minority" they exerted little more than a negative influence. After 1921 no candidate was ever elected without the sponsorship of either of the major parties.[34]

From time to time the aldermen were accused of indolence in the discharge of their duties. The Citizens Union described them as "lazy" and "superficial." It was estimated by an anti-Tammany publicist that their compensation for official duties was

[33] Edward J. Flynn, "Bosses and Machines," *Atlantic Monthly*, CLXXIX (1947), 39; Wirt Howe, *New York at the Turn of the Century* (Toronto, 1946), p. 68; Curran, *Pillar to Post*, *passim*; *New York Times*, December 20, 1942, October 23, 1947.

[34] *Proc. of Council of City of N. Y.*, 1940, I, 20; Peel, *Pol. Clubs of N. Y. C.*, pp. 294-98; *The Searchlight*, VIII, No. 2, 15-16.

$100 an hour. "It would be hard anywhere in the United States to find 64 elected officers who have done so little for their pay as the Tammany aldermen have done," he asserted. In the same vein, a reduction in salaries from $5,000 to $500 a year was suggested by the Executive Director of the City Affairs Committee. "Ten dollars a week is adequate payment for his services for any alderman," he insisted.[35]

Bristling with indignation, the aldermen countered by asserting they were overworked and underpaid. "As an alderman I had plenty work to do," stated Borough President Harvey. "It is a terrific job." A grueling routine it most certainly was. Aldermen were sought out in their homes, at their offices, in the district clubs, and in the streets, at all hours of day and night. To be roused by a worried constituent in the early hours of the morning, to receive an urgent summons from a district worker late in the evening, to be awakened in the small hours of the night by an insistent telephone was all part of the grind. "It was work, work, work," reminisced Henry H. Curran, "morning, noon, and night." [36]

If the alderman's official functions were the sole criteria, the accusations of the reformers were substantially justified. Performing legislative duties, however, was a part-time job; courting the public was a day-and-night affair. "The function of the present aldermen is to work seven days a week for Tammany Hall and twenty minutes a week for the City of New York for $4,640 a year," declared one citizen. The aldermen conceded this quite openly and sought vindication in their incessant efforts to serve their constituents. Aldermanic salaries were regarded as appropriate to the support of extra-official duties.[37]

Henry H. Curran has recalled that as a neophyte among the aldermen he naively expected to qualify for legislative work by

[35] *The Searchlight*, IX, No. 1, 10; Finegan, *Tammany at Bay*, p. 96; Press Release of City Affairs Committee, November 21, 1932.

[36] *New York World-Telegram*, December 4, 1937; Testimony of Borough President George U. Harvey before Charter Revision Commission, April 15, 1935; Curran, *Pillar to Post*, p. 139; Curran, *John Citizen's Job*, p. 200; Interview with the Hon. Walter R. Hart, September 25, 1947; Interview with the Hon. Joseph Clark Baldwin, March 4, 1947.

[37] Press Release of City Affairs Committee, July 12, 1933; Testimony of Kenneth Dayton before Chart. Rev. Comm., March 5, 1935.

studying the city charter and mastering the details of the work of the administrative departments.[38] He was quickly disillusioned. At the first meeting he attended he mentioned the charter to a neighbor, who admonished him:

"Never mind the charter. Did you ever see people reading the charter in the subways?"

"No," I confessed ruefully.

"Well, lay off that highbrow stuff. That's for the reformers, and the mayor—when he feels like it. Do you think you'll get elected by reading the charter?"

"No, but—"

"Say, look here. I heard you're a regular feller, and I'm telling you. The duty of the alderman is to look out for the poor people of his district. That's all. Look out for 'em all the time—jobs, favors, rent, food, outings—anything they want, give it to 'em. Then in November you get the votes and get elected. What good is the charter if you don't get elected?"

I had no answer.[39]

Night after night the alderman made his way to the political clubhouse, the hub of his activities. "Hey alderman—I got a 'contract' for you," was a familiar greeting as district workers beset him with requests for favors. Among the legislators spawned in the club there was a natural division of labor for fulfilling contracts. In federal matters the congressman did the work, in state matters the assemblyman, and in municipal affairs the alderman. But the lightness of his official duties logically made the alderman the district leader's principal flunky.[40]

Relations with constituents varied from neighborhood to neighborhood. Probably no area of comparable size on this planet contained as great a concentration of wealth as Manhattan's "Silk Stocking" district, on the eastern and southern fringes of Central Park. Many residents expended more in rent alone than the yearly income of the average ward politician. Preoccupied with national and international affairs, the Social Registerites usually took local politics as a matter of course. In

[38] Curran, *John Citizen's Job*, pp. 195-96.

[39] Curran, *Pillar to Post*, pp. 128-29.

[40] Former Gov. Alfred E. Smith before Chart. Rev. Comm., June 7, 1935; Curran, *John Citizen's Job*, pp. 195-96, 199; Sherman, *Inside the Machine*, p. 71.

municipal affairs their chief interest lay in the reduction of taxes, and their alderman was pressed by delegations of business men to effect reductions in the annual budget. During the years of Tammany dominance the representatives of the Fifteenth District consistently denounced Democratic finances as wasteful and extravagant. No alderman from the "Silk Stocking" district ever voted for a Tammany-sponsored budget. Blessed with ample leisure time, the blue-blooded ladies of Park Avenue and Fifth Avenue plied their alderman with resolutions to introduce legislation on behalf of their civic-minded projects—Curb Your Dog Committees and Less Smoke Associations.[41]

It was in the tenement neighborhoods that the political machine made its greatest appeal, for there the struggle against poverty was closest. In the slums the political worker became "Big Brother, little sister, and general fixer" to his constituents. The poor looked to him for jobs as watchmen, laborers, and chauffeurs, for permits to sell newspapers, black boots, roast peanuts or keep chickens, for assistance in gaining admission to hospitals, for intercession with the landlord when the rent was overdue, for passing the hat to save the destitute from Potter's Field, or for intervention in the courts when a youth had run afoul of the law. The poorer the district, the greater the number of recent immigrants, the more compelling were its needs.[42]

The manifold services rendered by the alderman—a "helter skelter" lot—defy classification. At one level he interpreted the municipal government to its citizens. A constituent unable to interpret a notice from the Water Department, a delegation of business men desiring to present a petition for a local improvement, a parent anxious to enter a child in school, a would-be driver seeking an automobile license—all were likely to turn to their alderman. One legislator reported his advice had been sought on problems of ejecting a drunk from a saloon, disposing

[41] *Speech of Alderman Ruth Pratt on the Budget for 1928* (Files of Mun. Ref. Library); *New York Herald-Tribune*, July 9, 1934; *Proc. of Bd. of Ald., 1922*, IV, 545; *ibid.*, 1923, IV, 691; *Proc. of Bd. of Ald. and Mun. Ass. Ald. Br., 1924-1933, passim*; Interview with the Hon. Joseph Clark Baldwin, March 4, 1947.

[42] John B. Kennedy, "A Tammany Tour," *Collier's*, XCI (1933), 11; Curran, *John Citizen's Job*, pp. 197-98; Interview with Justice Henry H. Curran, January 24, 1947.

of an automobile in which a dead man had been found, and taking care of a mother in child-birth. Regarding this extraofficial function as the chief duty of the alderman, former Governor Alfred E. Smith, who headed the Charter Revision Commission of 1934, voted in favor of a proposal to merge the two houses of the city's legislature only on condition that a bureau of information be created to continue the work.[43]

In every district the political party met appeals for intervention in the city's courts—requests for release from jury duty, "fixing" traffic tickets, intercession in cases of misdemeanors or petty violations of the law, or aid for suspected felons. An investigation of the magistrates' courts disclosed that magistrates and clerks, who were usually appointed for political considerations, responded to political pressure in the disposition of court business. Aldermen with reputations for probity were disinclined to handle court favors, but not all were squeamish. When the alderman was a district leader himself, the case was readily managed—especially if the magistrate had obtained his position through the leader's recommendation. Most aldermen did not wield such power themselves, but practical politicians were not without resources. Assistant clerks with sharp weather eyes for graft were amenable to the suggestions of their clubhouse henchmen; arresting officers might "throw" cases by testifying lightly enough to gain acquittal; and magistrates themselves could be approached with sly arguments.[44] It was universally believed that the intervention of an alderman in the magistrates' court was more potent than the services of the best lawyer, and the popular conviction was largely true. Aside from the intriguing

[43] During the sessions of the Charter Revision Commission of 1935-36 a central bureau of inquiry was again suggested to fill the gap that presumably would occur if the Board were abolished. *Minutes of the Ninth Meeting of the New York City Charter Revision Commission,* May 28, 1935; Testimony of Kenneth Dayton, March 5, 1935; Curran, *John Citizen's Job*, p. 198; Interview with the Hon. Jos. Clark Baldwin, March 4, 1947.

[44] Two days after he had become an alderman, Henry H. Curran was lectured by a magistrate whom he had interviewed in his chambers about a pending case: "Don't tell him you've known the defendant for ten years, don't ask him to 'turn out' the case or go easy, don't tell him it means a lot to you politically, don't whisper that 'the big feller' is interested—in other words, don't do what an alderman usually does."

possibilities for personal profit, court favors won loyal and grateful friends.[45]

The ceaseless quest for favors ranged far beyond the courts. An enterprising alderman overlooked no possibilities. Denizens of the clubhouses, confederates in the city's bureaucracy, colleagues in the Board of Aldermen itself were exploited. In hearings before city agencies, such as the Department of Licenses, citizens who procured the services of an alderman held a trump card, for his presence implied a threat of reprisal against the presiding official. "What chance has a department head when an alderman appears before him professionally?" demanded Mayor La Guardia.[46]

Their happy hunting grounds were the administrative branches of the city's government. Constituents looked to aldermen for jobs, promotions, transfers, and reinstatements. A convenient handle for enforcing requests was provided by the charter provisions requiring aldermanic approval for fixing the title and salary of every position in every bureau, board, and commission in the city,[47] for granting petty cash for unforeseen departmental expenses, and for contracts in excess of $1,000 without public letting. If the commissioner were concerned about the speedy passage of his proposals by the board, he might well hesitate before denying a request—however irregular—particularly when it emanated from the chairman of an important committee.[48]

When a Fusion administration took office in 1934, Mayor La Guardia resolved to prevent his commissioners from yielding to aldermanic demands. He went to extraordinary lengths to

45 Seabury, *Magistrates' Courts Investigation*, pp. 14-16, 24-26, 44-48, 56-70; Curran, *John Citizen's Job*, pp. 199-210; Curran, *Pillar to Post*, pp. 158-61; *Rep. of Comm. on Bd. of Ald. of Cit. Un. for 1912-13 Term*, p. 10; Finegan, *Tammany at Bay*, pp. 98, 108-11.

46 Remarks of Mayor La Guardia at public hearing of Chart. Rev. Comm., May 7, 1936.

47 For a time county offices in the city were excepted. Local laws regulating the compensation of county officers were declared invalid in *Schieffelin v. Berry* (1926). After the passage of the Smith Amendment to the State Constitution in 1935, local legislatures were granted jurisdiction over county offices.

48 McGoldrick, "Eclipse of the Ald.," *Nat. Mun. Rev.*, XIV, 365-66; Charter, Sec. 56, as amended by Local Law No. 1, 1925; Sec. 187, as amended by L. 1910, C. 683; Sec. 419, as amended by L. 1922, C. 661.

keep legislators and department heads at arm's length. When aldermanic dalliance threatened to obstruct the functioning of city government, little deals were made with Democratic legislative leaders; but the transactions were effected over the mayor's desk rather than in the commissioners' offices.[49]

The aldermen insisted that their wirepulling redounded to the benefit of their constituencies, enabling them to look after their physical needs. Officially the charter designated twenty-four local boards to consider applications of residents for local improvements to be performed by the city government, and each alderman was an ex-officio member of a board embracing his own and adjacent districts.[50] But these bodies proved rather ineffectual, partly because of the limited powers of the local boards, partly because of lack of popular interest.[51] There were some aldermen, particularly the representatives of problem neighborhoods, who took immense pride in the material improvements they won for their districts—parks, playgrounds, play-streets in default of playgrounds, modern street lighting, better policing, adjustments in traffic rules, child welfare stations, and libraries. Peter J. McGuinness became a tireless one-man lobby for Greenpoint, which he glorified as the "garden spot of the universe." It is said that in his farewell speech in the Board of Aldermen he declaimed: "I got Greenpoint three playgrounds,

[49] E.g., in 1936 a Democratic alderman held up an issue of special revenue bonds for two months because the Civil Service Commission had refused to recognize an allegedly illegal reinstatement. The Mayor yielded. William A. Allen, *Why Tammanies Revive* (New York, 1937), p. 120. (Mr. Allen was Secretary to the Civil Service Commission at one time.) Interview with Commissioner Rufus E. McGahen, Budget Director in the La Guardia Administration, October 28, 1947.

[50] Eighteen local boards included three aldermanic districts, five contained two districts, and one was composed of a single aldermanic district. *Manual of Bd. of Ald., 1936-1937*, pp. 33-34.

[51] During the 1916-1917 sessions only nine aldermen attended meetings of their Local Improvement Boards as frequently as once a month, while ten members met with their local boards twice or less during the entire two-year term. *Rep. of Comm. on Bd. of Ald. of Cit. Un. for 1916-1917 Term*, pp. 21-55. The boards in the oldest sections of the city, particularly in Manhattan and Brooklyn, were least needed and functioned least often. Those in the more outlying sections, such as the upper Bronx, Queens, and southern Brooklyn, met more frequently.

the subway, the $1,500,000 bridge on Greenpoint Avenue, and $2,000,000 worth of paving. I done good."[52]

District political workers delighted in representing themselves as public benefactors, sometimes likening themselves to pastors ministering to their flocks. Henry H. Curran described his labors as alderman in lyrical terms:

> I went to every outing and chowder and clambake, every wedding and christening and funeral. I met countless constituents and helped them in countless ways. I never talked politics with them . . . but discussed only their troubles and their jobs. . . . Every minute of it was happiness. For I was the alderman and that opened to me all the little doors to human hearts that are closed to the world in general. "Hello, All'mun!" That was their greeting a hundred times a day. They told me their difficulties and their hopes, there on the street, just as they had always told them to the alderman, whoever he was. Benefactor and friend, translator of city government complications into terms of the individual in trouble, the alderman served as a safety valve to those who mistrusted government as such. To the unfortunate he was a ladder to lighter days. To everybody he was an institution, a wise Santa Claus of all the days of the year, whether or not he bore gifts. If he could not get what was wanted, at least he would try—they all knew that—he would "go to the front" for them.[53]

Curran's rhapsodic portrait contrasted vividly with the low esteem in which aldermen were held. Curran himself once related how his appointment to the board first brought elation, then disillusionment. When he announced the news, friends were prone to commiserate rather than congratulate. That he was a crook was taken for granted. Pitted against him in a political struggle, Mayor Gaynor set his Department of Accounts probing into Curran's life. To the mayor, the Commissioner's report that he was honest was incredible. "Tut, tut," replied the Mayor. "He's an alderman. He can't be honest."[54]

The aldermen were long noted for petty jobbery. At one time the consent of the local alderman was required before a license

[52] Charter, Sec. 432, as amended by L. 1919, C. 323; Sec. 433 as amended by L. 1922, C. 565; Sec. 434; Sec. 435 as amended by Local Law 16, 1927; I. Herschell Philips, "Does the Board of Aldermen Earn Its Sizeable Pay Check?" *Real Estate Magazine*, XXI (1934), 22, 43; Curran, *John Citizen's Job*, pp. 34-35, 122, 140-42, 247-51; Mackaye, *Tin Box Parade*, p. 216; Interview with Justice Henry H. Curran, January 24, 1947.

[53] Curran, *Pillar to Post*, pp. 139-40.

[54] *Ibid.*, p. 155; Henry H. Curran, "Fifty Years of Public Service," *New York Times Magazine*, December 7, 1947.

could be issued for a little newsstand or bootblack stand. Mayor Gaynor accused district leaders of mulcting license applicants of sums ranging from \$5 to \$500. Both Democratic and Republican aldermen, he charged, withheld approval of licenses until the prescribed amounts had been paid over to the local district clubs. Eventually the power to approve licenses was transferred to the city's administrative departments, but the source of scandal did not disappear. Two decades later an investigation revealed that holders of licenses for newsstands were still being mulcted of \$1,500,000 annually, and it was charged that much of the tribute continued to find its way into the aldermen's pockets. A state probe in 1921 disclosed widespread corruption in the issuing and transfer of licenses in the public markets, and aldermen were accused of levying a toll on pushcart peddlers. It was widely believed that court favors yielded substantial returns to aldermen "on the make and on the take." Even honest aldermen were dismayed to find their constituents pressing on them the customary bribes.[55]

During the twentieth century there were no sensational scandals on the grand scale of the "Boodle Board." "More and more its members laid aside the cutlass of the freebooter to assume the dunce cap of the clown," wrote a publicist, "and the air above City Hall, once gay with the tinkle of pieces of eight or sulphuric with arguments over loot carried increasingly the gentle roar of the engaging buffoon." The reason lay partly in successive charter revisions, which had eliminated the lush opportunities for peculation once available to the "Forty Thieves." There were some questionable transactions, however, in connection with the Board's power to vote special revenue bonds in excess of the annual budget. In 1921 it was revealed that an enterprising little band, conspiring to gain lucrative contracts for installing oil heating plants in institutions under the jurisdiction of the Department of Public Welfare, had obtained the assistance of one

[55] *Proc. of Bd. of Ald., 1910*, III, 104-5; *Rep. of Comm. on Bd. of Ald. for 1914-15 Term*, pp. 3-5; *Reports of the New York State Joint Legislative Committee to Investigate the Affairs of the City of New York* (Albany, 1922), pp. 255 ff.; Curran, *Pillar to Post*, pp. 134-35; Blanshard, *Investigating City Govt.*, pp. 35-41; Finegan, *op. cit.*, pp. 97-98, 175-76, 214; *New York World-Telegram*, Dec. 26, 1933, Dec. 2, 1937.

J. J. McManus, a district leader in "Hell's Kitchen," and his brother, Alderman Charles A. McManus. It was Alderman McManus who introduced into the Board a resolution to issue special revenue bonds to cover a contract for $62,500—a proposal that passed unanimously. The contractors had estimated the cost of the project at $26,500, excluding graft, and the alleged price paid to the McManus brothers was $10,000. Alderman McManus was not repudiated by his party for this dubious exploit—he was made majority leader.[56]

The Seabury investigations in the thirties revealed that some local politicians had banked hundreds of thousands of dollars in excess of their official salaries; but among the aldermen opportunities for pelf were limited to small gratuities. One legislator was dubbed "Two-Bit," because his favors were available at cut-rate prices. Petty venality among aldermen was understandable, if not justifiable, for the demands on them for financial contributions were not inconsiderable. As long as the Board of Aldermen remained in existence municipal employees were not required to pay federal income taxes,[57] but from many the party organization exacted its tithe. In the twentieth century party leaders were not ordinarily as candid as the politico who defended the high salaries of aldermen in 1886 by citing the assessments made on them by the political machine; yet Plunkitt correctly expressed their sentiments when he declared, "Office-holders would be ingrates if they didn't contribute to the organization that put them in office." Many aldermen found their district activities a great drain on their finances, for they were expected to contribute heavily to local charities. When largesse had been bestowed upon the deserving poor, little, if anything, of the alderman's salary remained. What could be more appro-

[56] *New York World-Telegram*, December 2, 1937; *The Searchlight*, XI, No. 5, 18; *Proc. of Bd. of Ald., 1921*, III, 2-3; *Facts Versus Flourishes and Ruffles*, pp. 5-6; *Report and Summary of the Evidence of the Joint Leglislative Committee to Investigate the Affairs of the City of New York* (Albany, March 14, 1922), pp. 102-6.

[57] This exemption was wiped out after the case of *Graves v. New York ex rel. O'Keefe*, 306 U. S. 466 (1939). When the Public Salary Act of 1939 was passed municipal employees were subjected to the Federal income tax for the first time.

priate than to balance accounts by pocketing the bounty of those who could afford to pay for their favors?[58]

Few measures were drawn up by the members themselves, and many originated in interviews with constituents at local political clubs. From these unofficial conferences ultimately emerged ordinances and resolutions dealing with local problems —traffic signals, play streets, parks, and playgrounds—or local laws seeking to reduce neighborhood assessments or to reinstate an individual in the municipal civil service. One authority estimated that eighty percent of the business introduced into the board dealt with local district affairs. By a usage known as "privilege," virtually all matters regarding an individual district gained automatic approval in the board if endorsed by its representative. Members of the minority gained a share of local improvements for their neighborhoods by consenting to important measures sponsored by the majority.[59]

Some aldermen considered the introduction of legislation drafted by outsiders as merely another genre of favor for the gratification of the public. The practice occasionally created embarrassment, for the members did not always read the proffered resolutions. At one time an unsuspecting alderman was induced to nominate Noah Webster for Commissioner of Deeds. During the sessions of the board, not long after the consolidation of the city, a reporter mischievously persuaded an Irish alderman to sponsor a resolution providing that City Hall and other public buildings should be decorated on Queen Victoria's birthday. The measure was promptly tabled, but to carry out the joke City Hall reporters notified their papers that it had passed. From all parts of the world communications immediately poured in, denouncing the unhappy legislator, and the next meeting of the board was devoted entirely to vindicating him. Before galleries overflowing with representatives from Irish societies from

[58] Flynn, *You're the Boss*, pp. 114-17; Bryce, *The American Commonwealth*, II, 123; Riordan, *Plunkitt of Tammany Hall*, p. 99; Pratt, "Men Are Bad Housekeepers," *Harp. Mag.*, CLIV, 687; Curran, *John Citizen's Job*, p. 198; *New York Herald-Tribune*, December 26, 1937; J. T. Salter, *The American Politician* (Chapel Hill, 1938), p. 17.

[59] Testimony of Kenneth Dayton and Bernard S. Deutsch before Chart. Rev. Comm.; Peel, *Pol. Clubs of N. Y. C.*, p. 125; Sherman, *Inside the Machine*, p. 24.

every state east of the Mississippi, he pleaded: "Does anyone here think I would have introduced such a resolution if I knew what was in it?"[60]

Utterly subservient to the regnant political machine, the members of the Board of Aldermen introduced an infinitesimal amount of vital legislation on their own initiative. Part of the explanation lay in the character of the membership, for party loyalty rather than a grasp of public affairs was the prime qualification for the post. Essentially the alderman was the district leader's factotum—"something more than an errand boy but less than a hero."[61] Party service was regarded as a full-time job, legislative duty as a sideline. Through the alderman the district organization performed much of its work at the city's expense. "The whole effort is bent toward the goal of offices, jobs and votes for the party with a cheerful unconcern as to what may follow in the way of government," wrote an ex-alderman.[62] Measures introduced into the city legislature revolved about patronage and favors, for in the board as well as extra-legislative work the paramount aim of each alderman was making a showing in his own bailiwick.

[60] Sherman, *op. cit.*, pp. 28-29.
[61] *New York Herald-Tribune*, December 26, 1937.
[62] Curran, *John Citizen's Job*, p. 224.

6. THE GENESIS OF REFORM

The Cincinnati experiment has demonstrated the place of faith in politics. . . . There is faith in this movement . . . the type of religious conviction which is not fanatical; which is not even ecstatic; which is hard headed, and yet idealistic; a conviction, a faith that local good government is a possibility.—CHARLES P. TAFT, *President of the Federal Council of the Churches of Christ in America* [1]

How COULD the moribund Board of Aldermen be resurrected? One school of reformers, the advocates of proportional representation, proposed to reconstruct it by making it more representative. Eventually they persuaded a Charter Revision Commission to offer this system of representation to the voters. When both charter and proportional representation won out at the polls, a campaign extending over many decades bore fruit.

The roots of the movement in the United States go back to the decade after the Civil War; the inspiration came from England. Many years later, the Hare system of representation, which was ultimately adopted for New York's municipal legislature, was to be stigmatized as a device "straight from the Kremlin"—an assertion that would have astonished and amused Thomas Hare, its inventor, and John Stuart Mill, its popularizer. A warm friend of both men, Simon Sterne, published an American adaptation of Hare's volume on the subject in 1871.[2]

Organizer, publicist, and promoter for the cause, Sterne helped found a Personal Representation Society, which aroused con-

[1] *City Management: The Cincinnati Experiment* (New York, 1933), p. 237.

[2] Hoag and Hallett, *Prop. Rep.*, pp. 175-76, 183-85; John Foord, *The Life and Public Services of Simon Sterne* (New York, 1903), pp. 5-7; Simon Sterne, *On Representative Government and Personal Representation* (Philadelphia, 1871), pp. 9-12.

siderable interest in liberal circles in New York, and pleaded for proportional representation before the Constitutional Convention of 1867. In 1872 he was honored by membership in a commission which wrote a plan for minority representation in the Board of Aldermen into a charter drafted to replace "Boss" Tweed's; but it was vetoed by Governor Hoffman, Tweed's creature.[3]

The following year, however, there was enacted a city charter under which aldermen were elected by a system of proportional representation called limited voting. Every district sent three delegates to the Board of Aldermen, voters being permitted two choices each; every elector was allowed four additional votes to help elect six aldermen at large. For almost a decade Republicans and members of all the warring Democratic factions—Tammany Hall, Irving Hall, and the County Democracy—were elected in generous numbers to the board. While the plan operated no outstanding scandals occurred among the lawmakers. A political scientist later noted that the "Boodle Board," one of the most notorious of all boards, was elected the year after the plan was abandoned.[4]

Limited voting was far from perfect in a strict mathematical sense, for minorities were not represented in proportion to their strength among the electorate. Part of the difficulty stemmed from collusion among the various parties and factions. When rival organizations agreed on an apportionment of offices they could guarantee the results in advance. It was said that the plan was sacrificed in 1882 to promote harmony among the several Democratic machines.[5]

[3] Foord, *Simon Sterne*, pp. 96-99, 122-25; *Report to the Constitutional Convention of the State of New York, on Personal Representation* (New York, 1867), *passim*.

[4] Howard Lee MacBain, "Proportional Representation in American Cities," *Political Science Quarterly*, XXXVII (December, 1922), pp. 284-85; John A. Fairlie, "American Municipal Councils," *Political Science Quarterly*, XIX (June, 1904), 240.

[5] Ivins, *Machine Politics and Money in Elections in N. Y. C.*, pp. 79-80; Fairlie, "Am. Mun. Councils," *Pol. Sci. Quart.*, XIX, 240. Some authorities state that the system lasted until 1887, a date accepted by the New York Court of Appeals. See Hoag and Hallett, *Prop. Rep.*, p. 45; *Johnson v. the City of New York, Matter of Bowe v. Cohen*, 274 N. Y. 411, 422. The discrepancy in dates arose from the

Even while this crude plan of minority representation was in operation, P. R. gained official recognition and encouragement. A commission appointed by Governor Samuel J. Tilden to devise a plan of government for New York cities hesitated to impose a newfangled scheme upon localities whose citizens were unacquainted with its merits, but suggested an amendment to the state constitution to permit municipal experiments with P. R.[6]

Reports of state commissions, however, do not ordinarily command a wide audience; rarely do they exert a significant influence on public opinion. Convincing a substantial segment of the electorate of the merits of P. R. required generations of effort by reformers. But after the immediate need for halting the abuses of the Tweed Era had passed, the local movement languished, and for some years it functioned only sporadically.[7]

A new phase began in 1893 at a convention at the Chicago World's Fair. Here scattered groups of proportionalists created a national organization, the American Proportional Representation League, and established a periodical, the *Proportional Representation Review*. While enthusiasm was still running high, a local committee made an unsuccessful attempt to interest the New York Constitutional Convention of 1894. But in 1896 P. R. gained strong endorsement from the commission which drafted the Greater New York Charter. The commission shied away from including it in its draft, however, for fear of violating

---

following situation: The state commission which codified the laws relating to New York City in the Consolidated Laws of 1882 (L. 1882, C. 410) incorporated the existing law on the Board of Aldermen (L. 1878, C. 400). Unfortunately the Legislature reintroduced single member districts that same session (L. 1882, C. 403). The published proceedings of the Board of Aldermen, which then reported the election returns, demonstrate that cumulative voting ended that year. Sixteeen aldermen from plural districts and six aldermen at large were annually elected through 1881. From 1882 onwards 24 aldermen were annually elected from single member districts. *Proc. of Bd. of Ald.*, vols. 149-185, *passim* (The results of the 1881 elections, which were not reported by the Board of Aldermen, appeared in the *N. Y. Times*, November 10, 1881). The terminal date of 1887 is derived from a statute (L. 1887, C. 292) that merely split one district in two.

[6] *Report of a Commission to Devise a Plan for the Government of Cities in the State of New York*, Assembly Document No. 68 (1877), p. 47; Foord, *op. cit.*, pp. 287-92; Simon Sterne, "The Administration of American Cities," *International Review*, IV (1877), 638.

[7] Hoag and Hallett, *op. cit.*, pp. 186-87; *P. R. Review*, II (1895), 114.

"P. R." and the Charter

(With illustrations reprinted by courtesy of American City)

NO matter what the fate of the proposed new City Charter drafted by the Charter Revision Commission, created by the Legislature of 1921, it has at least had the effect of drawing wide public attention in this City to the subject of proportional representation, "P R.," as one means of improving the character of the local legislative body and making it more truly representative The first draft of the Charter contained provisions for the choice of aldermen by "P. R." It was left out of the later draft because of the opinion of Mr F W. M Cutcheon, Counsel to the Commission, that it was doubtful whether the courts would hold it constitutional under existing provisions. The final report of the Commission recommends a constitutional amendment to make its adoption possible without question

The Citizens Union is deeply interested in the subject, and strongly recommended the adoption of "P. R" for aldermanic elections, submitting at the same time reasons for believing in its constitutionality On one point, however, there can be no doubt "P R" would mean the establishment of a really representative legislative body. It would also go far to eliminate the ever-present gerrymander There are presented on this page some rather extraordinary pictures drawn by Mary Spencer Lee of what the gerrymander means in our present aldermanic districting.

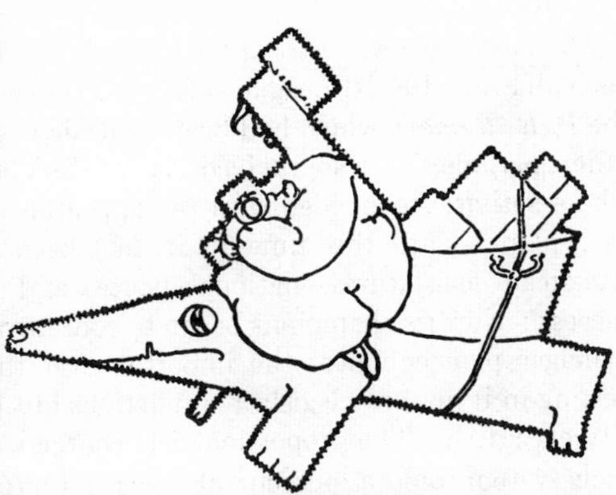

Brooklyn Rapid Gerrymander
(45th Aldermanic District)

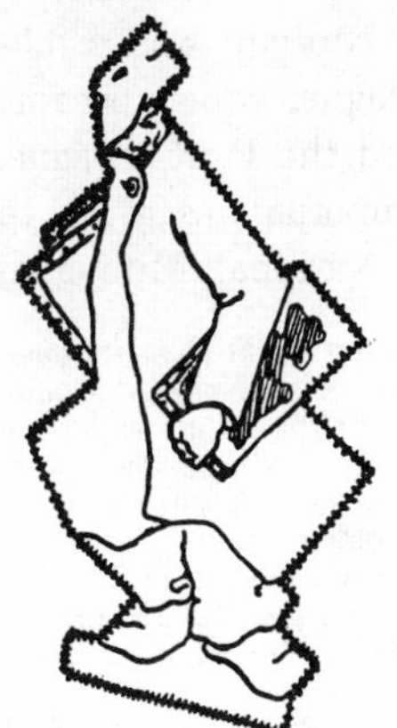

An Unrepresentative Representative
(2nd Aldermanic District)

A Brooklyn Gerry-gander
(34th Aldermanic District)

IN FAVOR OF PROPORTIONAL REPRESENTATION
AND AGAINST GERRYMANDERING

From *The Searchlight,* Vol. XIII, March, 1923

the state constitution. By that time the national movement was declining, and the *P. R. Review* suspended publication as a separate organ.[8]

The next cycle was part and parcel of the Progressive era. In 1909 a national P. R. League Office was set up. Five years later the *P. R. Review,* which had been kept alive as a department of other periodicals, was revived as an independent quarterly. These activities coincided with the appearance of the city manager plan. Until this time P. R. had been advocated for all American legislatures—national, state, and local—with little success. Now its champions began to concentrate on cities. The manager plan enhances the importance of the city council by vesting in it not only legislative functions but also control of the city executive. The proportionalists contended that only under their system could a municipality elect a thoroughly representative city council, capable of exercising its immensely enlarged powers.[9]

From this time on, P. R. in the United States was indissolubly linked with the city manager movement. Indeed, until New York adopted it, every city employing P. R. was governed under the council-manager system. An *entente cordiale* was established between the National Municipal League, which became the chief exponent of the manager plan, and the P. R. League. Eventually the two bodies merged. An impetus was given to P. R. when it was incorporated into the National Municipal

[8] *P. R. Review*, I (1893), 2-5; *An Address to the Members of the Constitutional Convention of the State of New York* (New York, 1894), *passim*; *National Municipal Review*, XXIII (1934), 488; Matthias N. Forney, *Political Reform by the Representation of Minorities* (New York, 1894), p. 2. Forney's book was used as a basic reference by the author of a legal opinion on the constitutionality of P. R., drafted for the Greater New York Charter Commission in 1896. See *Letter to George L. Rives, Esq., Chairman and Member of the Charter Revision Commission Appointed by Governor Roosevelt for the Drafting of Such Amendments to the Charter As May Be Expedient for the Future Government of the City of New York* (New York, 1900), pp. 20-24.

[9] Richard S. Childs, "The League's Second Stretch," *Nat. Mun. Rev.*, XXXIII (1944), 514-17; Hermens, *Democracy or Anarchy?*, pp. 359-64; Chester C. Maxey, "The City Manager Plan and Proportional Representation," *Western Reserve University Bulletin*, XXVII (1924), 9-10; Harold A. Stone, Don K. Price, and Kathryn H. Stone, *City Manager Government in the United States* (Chicago, 1940), p. 12.

League's *Model City Charters,* documents which exercised great influence upon American municipal government. Hundreds of charter revision commissions have been guided by them; in some cases portions of the text were reproduced verbatim in the charters. Sacramento, California, accepted both the manager plan and P. R. in its 1920 charter, adhering closely to the *Model City Charter.* The program of the National Municipal League never gained blanket endorsement from any official body in New York City, but the Thacher Commission, which revised New York's charter, gave both P. R. and the manager plan a full and fair hearing.[10]

Soon after its *Review* resumed publication, the P. R. League plunged into municipal charter campaigns. Its first success was due partly to chance and partly to the eloquence of Prof. C. G. Hoag, secretary and treasurer of the P. R. League. Finding himself in the Ohio lakeport city of Ashtabula one day, Prof. Hoag set in motion a movement which culminated in the first use of P. R. by any American city. Missions were later sent by the League to Kalamazoo, Cincinnati, and Cleveland for municipal P. R. battles. In 1922 officers of the League spent several months in New York, staffing the offices of a local committee and preparing a memorandum for submission to a charter commission.[11]

The heaviest demands on the P. R. League from New Yorkers came at a time when it was losing its separate identity. While the Seabury investigations were revealing "some of the greatest grafting enterprises that ever disgraced an American city," Gothamites were increasingly disposed to heed reformers. The staff of the P. R. League, veterans of many a charter struggle, became invaluable allies of the local reformers, answering inquiries, furnishing information, and distributing literature. Walter J. Millard, Field Secretary of the P. R. League, volunteered

[10] Richard S. Childs, *Best Practices under the Manager Plan* (New York, 1939); Lawrence A. Tanzer, "The Proposed New York City Charter," *Nat. Mun. Rev.*, XXV (1936), 536; Harold W. Dodds, "Model Laws as Aid to Progress," *Nat. Mun. Rev.*, XXXIII (1944), 532, 544.

[11] *P. R. Rev.*, No. 35 (1915), 62; *ibid.*, No. 64 (1922), 63; *ibid.*, No. 65 (1923), 14; Letter of Dr. George H. Hallett to Henry de Forest Baldwin, June 29, 1939 (in the Citizens Union Collection, Columbia University).

his services for the Committee of One Thousand (predecessor of the City Fusion Party, which helped elect Mayor La Guardia), and Dr. Hallett performed anonymous editorial work for them.[12] Not the least of Dr. Hallett's behind-the-scenes accomplishments was to persuade W. Kingsland Macy, state chairman of the Republican Party, of the merits of P. R. for New York. No man worked with greater devotion to promote P. R. in New York than Dr. Hallett, a leading authority on the subject. After he had accepted a position with the Citizens Union, which spearheaded the drive for P. R., he became orator and debater, fund-raiser and campaign organizer, pamphleteer and letter-writer for the cause. When the Thacher Commission wrote its charter, Dr. Hallett was called in to help draft the chapter on P. R. elections.[13]

Conversely, their ventures into New York politics created grist for the mills of the proportionalists. In 1926, when Hoag and Hallett wrote *Proportional Representation,* the standard American treatise on the subject, they drew on the latter's research for New York civic groups in 1922. For years afterwards the *P. R. Review* and *National Municipal Review* made continuous use of current elections in New York to demonstrate the inequities of the single-member district system. To indict the plurality system of elections in the popular pamphlet, *Proportional Representation: The Key to Democracy,* Dr. Hallett employed more illustrations from the New York Board of Aldermen than any other legislative body. There is little doubt that his source was a memorial, prepared in the offices of the Citizens Union, for submission to the Thacher Charter Commission.

After 1932 the educational functions of the P. R. League devolved upon the National Municipal League, with which it was happily united. In both philosophy and functions it qualified as a worthy successor. Like the proportionalists, its leaders as-

[12] Letters of Walter T. Arndt to George H. Hallett, September 4, October 2, 1931; G. H. H. to W. T. A., September 3, 1931 (these letters and those that follow in this chapter are from the files of the National Municipal League).

[13] *New York World-Telegram*, June 19, 1934, October 24, 1936; Letter of Joseph Clark Baldwin to W. Kingsland Macy, September 25, 1931; Dr. Hallett to J. C. B., November 17, 1931, December 2, 1931. Testimony of Dr. Hallet before Charter Commission, November 12, 1935; *Minutes of Executive Meeting of Charter Commission*, November 12, 1935.

sumed that the difficulties of city government are often mechanistic and susceptible to correction by mechanistic alterations. But where the P. R. League had sent shock troops into the fray, the National Municipal League maintained an arsenal of "fact-ammunition," and front-line fighters for P. R. repaired to it to furbish their weapons. Before Judge Seabury made public his epochal report, in which he recommended a legislature for New York City elected by P. R., he secured information and advice from Dr. Hallett.[14] The files of the League bulge with inquiries made after the publication of the Seabury Report. Newspapers, civic organizations, churches, educators, city officials, and private individuals turned to the League as a natural source of enlightenment. The striking similarities in the literature of proponents of P. R. for New York are due partly to a pooling of efforts and partly to the common origin of their arguments.[15]

Gratifying success rewarded the efforts of reformers promoting the city manager plan. By 1936 there were 455 council-manager cities in the United States. But P. R. made slower progress. Proportionalists could boast of an eighth of the world's population governed under P. R., but the P. R. League worked for twenty-three years before a single American municipality was persuaded to adopt it. Up to 1936 only ten cities had accepted P. R., and half of them no longer used it.[16] Endeavoring to embarrass the proportionalists during the New York campaign for P. R. in 1936, its opponents pointed up this seemingly unimpressive record. Friends of P. R. replied that where it had been tried it had produced "miracles of sustained good government," that

[14] Samuel Seabury to George H. Hallett, Dec. 28, 1932. The Hofstadter Committee, for which Judge Seabury served as counsel, also obtained information from the League. William J. Lamont to Elsie Parker, December 10, December 15, 1932.

[15] Childs, "The League's Second Stretch," *Nat. Mun. Rev.*, XXXIII, 519, 530. Leaflets and individual guidance for understanding P. R. were furnished to James Marshall while he was a member of the Charter Revision Commission of 1934. J. M. to Elsie Parker, June 28, 1934.

[16] The courts had declared P. R. unconstitutional in Kalamazoo, Michigan, and Sacramento, California. Use of P. R. in West Hartford had been ended by action of the Connecticut legislature. In Cleveland and Ashtabula the plan was abandoned after popular referenda.

Toledo, Hamilton, Boulder, Wheeling, and Cincinnati were "five of the best governed cities in the United States."[17]

The most conspicuous success was gained in Cincinnati, Mecca of municipal reformers. Afflicted for decades with a government of the "most depraved and rapacious character," it was magically transformed from a "rundown, shabby, despairing, boss-ridden city" to a "forward-looking, confident, clean, and well-conducted" municipality. The metamorphosis was due principally to an independent citizens' movement, a David which slew the Goliath of the local Republican machine. Credit must also be given to the manager plan, the fine record of two city managers, and the personality of Mayor Seasongood. Whatever the essential ingredients, leaders of Cincinnati's Charter Committee insisted that P. R. was requisite for the success of the experiment. "Proportional representation is the shield and essence of the charter," declared the distinguished Murray Seasongood.[18]

With this record Cincinnati was hailed as a beacon light for all municipal reformers. While Judge Seabury was disclosing an apalling record of corruption and dishonesty in New York politics, local enthusiasts began to view Cincinnati's experience as an inspiration and model. There P. R. had enabled independent Republicans to break the stranglehold of the Republican machine in the city council; would it not permit independent Democrats, acting with minority groups, to check Tammany Hall and its allies in New York? If P. R. could regenerate a Cincinnati legislature "as supine and dominated by politics" as New York's

[17] *Municipal Year Book* (Chicago, 1936), p. 236; *P. R. Rev.*, No. 67 (July, 1923), 62-63; *Model City Charter with Home Rule Provisions Recommended for State Constitutions* (New York, 1933), p. 16 n.; Letters to *New York Times*, September 18, September 23, 1936.

[18] Murray Seasongood, *Local Government in the United States* (Harvard, 1933), pp. 30, 69, 106-110; editorial by Alfred E. Smith in the *New Outlook*, CLXI, No. 5 (1933), 11; Geneva Seybold, "Dykstra of Cincinnati," in *Fifteen Outstanding Articles Published by Survey Associates*, 1937 (New York, 1937), pp. 45-47; Hallett, *P. R.: Key to Democ.*, p. iv; Taft, *City Management*, p. 94 ff. A former campaign manager of the Cincinnati Charter Committee felt that the principal importance of P. R. lay in keeping the citizens' movement alive during its lean years. Under the district system it would have fallen apart after it received only 32 per cent of the vote. But under P. R. it always elected three or four vocal and influential members to the Council. Interview with Arthur L. Thexton, July 27, 1949.

Board of Aldermen, was it not reasonable to suppose it would effect an immediate improvement in New York?[19]

Fired by faith in the political miracles they had wrought, a few of the leaders of Cincinnati's citizens' movement prepared to carry their gospel to all corners of the land. Gladly did they extend encouragement and active assistance to their brothers in arms in New York. Henry Bentley, President of the Cincinnati Charter Committee, made a trip to testify in behalf of P. R. and the manager plan at the Seabury hearings. Then the Committee of a Thousand brought him to New York with Murray Seasongood and Charles P. Taft to extol their reforms at Town Hall. When Al Smith singled out P. R. for editorial attack, Bentley and Taft published rejoinders. The Cincinnati crusaders followed developments in New York with keen interest, and the victory of P. R. in the metropolis was a source of deep satisfaction to them.[20]

It was a distinct advantage for local reformers to have at their disposal a thoughtfully deliberated program, tested on a national scale. When the Chairman of the Citizens Union praised the "years of patient and constructive work" of the P. R. League and National Municipal League, his tribute was heartfelt. It is not altogether possible, however, to distinguish between personnel and policies of national organizations and local civic groups. The National Municipal League, in fact, was created by the joint efforts of municipal associations similar to the City Club of New York, and from the very beginning its history was closely

19 *The Searchlight*, XXIV, No. 1, 4; George H. Hallett, "New York City Looks Toward Representative Government," *Nat. Mun. Rev.*, XXIII (1934), 222; "A Citizen's Primer on Charter Reform," *City Affairs Committee Bulletin*, May, 1934.

20 Letter of Henry Bentley to Dr. William Jay Schieffelin, April 14, 1932; "Seabury Minutes," p. 9936 ff.; George H. Hallett, *Proportional Representation: The Key to Democracy* (Washington, 1937), p. 156; Henry Bentley, "A Reply to Alfred E. Smith," *Nat. Mun. Rev.*, XXII (1933), 245-47; Taft, *City Management*, p. 94 ff. Immediately after the adoption of P. R. in New York Henry Bentley sent the following telegram to Dr. Hallett (Nov. 5, 1936): CONGRATULATIONS. NEW YORK CHARTER ELECTION NOT MERELY LOCAL BUT A NATIONAL VICTORY. NEW YORK UNDER P. R. WILL PROVE THE LARGEST CITY IN AMERICA CAN BECOME THE BEST GOVERNED CITY IN AMERICA. THIS VICTORY IS A CHALLENGE TO NEW YORKERS TO ORGANIZE ITS CITIZENSHIP FOR INTELLIGENT POLITICAL ACTIVITY. IT IS POSSIBLE TO DO IN NEW YORK WHAT HAS BEEN DONE IN CINCINNATI . . .

intertwined with that of local organizations. James C. Carter, its first president, was also one of the founders of the City Club and the Citizens Union. At various times in his career the public-spirited Richard S. Childs headed the P. R. League, the National Municipal League, the City Club, and the Citizens Union. Dr. Hallett served simultaneously as Secretary of the Citizens Union and Associate Secretary of the National Municipal League. Generally subscribing to the aims of the National Municipal League, the members of New York civic associations regarded each other as invaluable allies. United fronts and interlocking directorates among municipal organizations were quite common.[21]

As we have said, it required years of persistent work before the proportionalists achieved success in New York. Ephemeral committees were formed to plead the cause before local or state bodies on specific occasions, but they met with little success.[22] It remained for civic organizations with broader interests and deeper roots to kindle public interest and consummate the reform. Until the nineteen twenties they concerned themselves with P. R. only intermittently. Conscious of the merits of P. R., local associations were preoccupied until 1924 with the campaign for home rule, then regarded as the city's most urgent need.[23]

During the twenties the steady proselyting of the P. R. League and National Municipal League began to produce results. Among enlightened public officials and in academic circles there was a growing conviction that the reforms they espoused made for good municipal government. These views transcended national political beliefs, being shared in those days by staunchly

[21] Hallett, *P. R.: Key to Democ.* (1937 ed.) p. 156; *Annual Report of the Secretary of the City Club of New York* (April 2, 1894), pp. 11-12; *The Searchlight*, XII, No. 4, 4-6; Frank M. Stewart, *A Half Century of Municipal Reform* (Los Angeles, 1950), pp. 11-19.

[22] E.g., the Charter Commission of 1900 recommended an amendment to the state constitution to authorize P. R. for municipal elections and former Mayor Seth Low introduced a similar proposal in the State Constitutional Convention of 1915. But nothing came of these gestures. *Report of Chart. Comm. of 1900*, pp. 10-11; *Journal of the Constitutional Convention of the State of New York, 1915*, p. 64.

[23] Walter T. Arndt, *The Emancipation of the American City* (New York, 1917), p. 3 ff.

Republican Ruth Pratt and, at the other end of the political spectrum, Norman Thomas. Visible proof of the need for reform was demonstrated by the Board of Aldermen. A lopsidedly Democratic body after 1918, it became little more than an adjunct of Tammany Hall; for twenty years the local legislators behaved as "mere automatons, answering the bidding of their political bosses without protest or discussion." [24]

In this climate of opinion local organizations began to include P. R. in their programs of reform. A golden opportunity arose in 1921, when the legislature authorized Governor Miller to appoint a Charter Commission for New York City. Its chairman, Henry de Forest Baldwin, a vice chairman of the Citizens Union, publicly proclaimed his faith in P. R. With great confidence, the City Club, the Citizens Union, and a hastily mobilized P. R. Committee memorialized the commission to alter the method of electing aldermen. An impressive list of civic leaders expressed their approbation. Suddenly their hopes faded. In the election of 1922 the Miller administration was swept out of office and the city officials appointed to the commission resigned. Fully aware that its recommendations would never be ratified, the commission completed its task in an atmosphere of futility. "Nothing could have dropped more soundlessly into the ultimate depths than that report," reflected a staff member years later.[25]

Barren as the commission's work then seemed, it occupies an important niche in New York charter history. Deliberating the inclusion of P. R. in its report, the commission responded to its counsel's warnings that it would probably be invalidated by the courts and eliminated it from its still-born charter. Yet its searching analysis of the issues made it an essential tool in the kit of future charter commissions. Again, many citizens in the metropolis gained their first inkling of the reform when over a dozen newspapers carried items on P. R. during the commission's sessions. Most significant of all, after home rule was won, the Citizens Union thoroughly committed itself to P. R. William

24 *New York Times*, April 20, 1931.

25 L. 1921, C. 343; *P. R. Rev.*, No. 64, 63-64; No. 65, 10-14; Interview with Prof. Arthur W. Macmahon, Feb. 25, 1949.

Jay Schieffelin, its chairman for many years, considered the commission's work a landmark in the history of political reform in New York.[26]

For almost a decade thereafter the Citizens Union kept the flame alive in an apparently fruitless campaign to advance P. R. Aldermanic candidates were confronted with questionnaires, testing their views on the subject. Pursuing the Baldwin Commission's recommendation for removing all doubts about the constitutionality of P. R. by amending the state's basic law, request resolutions were introduced at Albany. None ever emerged from committee.[27]

Like many political reforms, P. R. had gone through a long period of gestation. Since Simon Sterne had planted the seed in New York idealists and reformers had pondered and agitated, municipal leagues and national associations had convened and deliberated, political scientists and authors had published and propagandized. Yet scarcely a ripple had been stirred in the public mind. As late as 1932 interest in P. R. was confined to esoteric circles—a few civic organizations and a small body of public officials and intellectuals. Not one in a thousand voters in New York, observed Richard S. Childs that year, thoroughly understood it.[28] The man in the street could no more identify P. R. then than locate Eniwetok or Palau before American troops landed on the isles. Public apathy was not broken until the Seabury investigations set off a chain reaction whose effects were felt for many years. Then the long years of dogged effort by the proportionalists bore fruit. Before turning to the immediate causes of charter reform, however, we may well consider the arguments of the proportionalists and their adversaries.

[26] *P. R. Rev.* No. 65, 9-12; No. 66, 40-43; *Rep. of Chart. Comm., 1923*, pp. 12-15, 319 ff.; William Jay Schieffelin, "P. R. and New Yorkers," *Survey Graphic*, XXVI (July, 1937), 384.

[27] *P. R. Rev.*, No. 70 (April, 1924), 86; No. 91 (July, 1929), 53; No. 94 (April, 1930), 38; *The Searchlight*, XV, No. IV (Oct., 1925), 6-7; XIX, No. 1 (Feb., 1929), 4-6; XX, No. 1 (Feb., 1930), 7; "Seabury Minutes," p. 10013.

[28] Richard S. Childs to George H. Hallett, February 4, 1932.

7. THE IDEOLOGY OF P. R.

A representative body that doesn't represent.[1]

FOR MORE than a decade in the nineteen thirties and forties the method of representation in the city legislature was a subject of controversy in New York politics.[2] The debate stemmed from a long campaign for electoral reform. Critics charged that the single-member district system of representation in the Board of Aldermen, as elsewhere, often made a mockery of democracy. Under the prevailing method the city was sectioned off into aldermanic districts, and the candidate who won a majority or plurality in each territorial subdivision carried the election. After subjecting the entire process of nomination and election to painstaking analysis, the reformers concluded that serious defects and abuses were inherent in the system.

It was argued that the primary elections lent themselves to control of nomination by the local political machines, while the general elections disfranchised minorities and discouraged independent voting. For two decades the single-member system tended to produce legislative majorities for parties lacking popular majorities; then, as the dominance of a single party was established, it invariably overweighted that party's representation. The annihilation of minorities was undemocratic and created monolithic city government. In the city legislature the minuscular opposition was easily brushed aside, and complaisant majorities failed to check administrative debauchery. A system which permitted a few votes in close districts to turn the scales

[1] *The Searchlight*, XX, No. 1 (1933), 7.

[2] In the municipal election of 1947 it emerged as the dominant issue, overshadowing all contests for public office.

in elections created unstable equilibrium and invited corruption. Voters were grouped into artificial districts, an arrangement that made possible gerrymandering and rotten boroughs.

The reformers were under no illusion that primary elections had fulfilled their original purpose of promoting popular control of nominations.[3] Where the preliminary elections were uncontested and the opposition of rival parties in the general elections was perfunctory, obscure and pliable men were named. In such districts the office was actually appointive, for the real choice lay in the hands of the party leaders. Where primary contests did occur, the small, organized group who put up the ticket were supported by armies of political officeholders and their families. Many voters, it was asserted, recognized that scattered and disorganized opposition was virtually helpless before well-disciplined bands of officeholders marshalled by organization leaders. Since most citizens could not make a full-time business of politics, they generally abstained from voting, leaving the elections in the hands of the wardheelers. Consequently, independent candidates were virtually excluded from nominations and the party machine became master of the situation.[4]

In the final elections, it was contended, large segments of the electorate failed to exert any influence on the results. No matter how large the minority in a district, it was disfranchised and the majority over-represented. When a candidate was elected by a plurality the injustice was even more glaring. The accompanying egregious examples are offered in evidence:[5]

[3] Letter of George H. Hallett to *New York Times*, September 23, 1936.

[4] "Seabury Minutes," pp. 9917, 9920; *A Proposal to Change the Method of Electing the New York City Board of Aldermen* (New York, 1922), pp. 10-11 (Henceforth cited as "P. R. Proposal"); *An Analysis of New York Aldermanic Elections Since the Consolidation of the City (1899-1933) Submitted to the New York Charter Commission by the Citizens Union of the City of New York*, January 29, 1935 (Hereafter cited as "Citizens Union Analysis"); *Proportional Representation Review*, No. 64 (1922), 71.

[5] *The Searchlight*, XXIV, No. 1 (1934), 6; *Ann. Rep. of Bd. of Elects., 1919*, p. 36; *1933*, p. 137; "P. R. Proposal," p. 4; "Citizens Union Analysis"; *Proportional Representation Review*, No. 64, p. 64.

Thirty-second Aldermanic District	
(Bronx, 1919)	
Democrat	13,482
Republican	10,154
Socialist	15,660
Scattering	10
Total	39,306

Fifty-third Aldermanic District	
(Brooklyn, 1933)	
Democrat	5,233
Republican and City Fusion	5,190
Socialist	448
Communist	224
Recovery	3,278
Total	14,373

It was emphasized that such elections were hardly isolated incidents; in 1913 more than 40 per cent of the aldermen were elected by a minority of their respective constituencies. There were eighteen aldermanic elections following the adoption of the 1901 charter, and 21.5% of the aldermen elected in them represented a minority of their voters.[6]

The reformers regarded the votes for losing candidates as wasted, for the citizens who cast them were shut out from representation. They calculated that more than 40 percent of all votes cast in the biennial aldermanic elections fell into the "wasted" category.[7]

This immense wastage of votes, it was asserted, discouraged participation in elections, gave disproportionate influence to the party machines, and created public disaffection. In the typical district the voter had a choice only between tweedledum and tweedledee, both organization nominees. "The most I can do is to decide which of two rascals I like the least," a New Yorker observed. Some selected a candidate they did not really prefer merely to defeat his less desirable opponent. Those who voted for independents came to feel they were throwing their votes away. As the incentive to vote faded, many intelligent citizens lost interest in municipal elections, and in disgust refrained entirely from balloting. Public apathy, in turn, weakened the chance of independent and minority candidates and left the professional politicians in undisputed possession of the elections. More and more the people's vote tended to become a nominal operation.[8]

6 *The Searchlight,* XIX, No. 1 (1929), 5; *Citizens Union Analysis; Ann. Rep. of Bd. of Elects., 1935.*

7 *National Municipal Review,* XXII (1933), 143; Hallett, *P. R.: Key to Democracy* (2nd ed.), pp. 16-18. Henceforth all references to the latter volume will cite the revised (1940) edition.

8 *Report of Chart. Comm., 1923,* p. 15; "Seabury Minutes," pp. 10008-10, 10425-26.

Under the system of "winner take all," the electoral reformers pointed out, the errors of the primaries and general elections had a snowballing effect. The size of the majority was accidental, and in eight out of the first ten elections for aldermen under the Charter of 1901 the party in control of the board was elected by an actual minority of voters.[9]

During the nineteen twenties and thirties the prevailing electoral system produced another type of distortion—majorities of the dominant party were magnified out of all proportion. The Democrats consistently seated more aldermen than the number to which their party votes entitled them, while the Republican and minor parties gained but a fraction of their quota in proportion to their vote. The most flagrant instance was the landslide of 1931, in which 64 Democrats were elected by 65% of the vote. Candidates of the remaining parties polled 450,000 votes; yet only one was elected. Table 7 demonstrates this over-representation.[10]

As the proportionalists saw it, the organization Democrats exerted an influence far beyond their actual numbers because the opposition was divided three ways. They vanquished dissident Democrats in the primaries and disposed of Republicans and Socialists separately in the general elections. As a result there were vast discrepancies in voting power. The classic example was the election of 1931, in which the average Democratic vote was worth more than twenty-five times as much as the average Republican vote. Table 8 indicates the votes per party member elected to the Board of Aldermen.[11]

If the Republicans were deprived of an equitable share of representation, other large minorities were entirely excluded from the government. In the last eight elections for the board the Socialists consistently polled enough votes to elect four to ten members had they been concentrated in a few districts; but the single-member system prevented them from gaining a fair share

[9] "P. R. Proposal," pp. 5-6; *P. R. Review*, No. 64, 66-67; *The Survey*, XLIX (1922), 236.

[10] *Citizens Union Analysis*; *P. R. Review*, No. 94 (1930), 38-39; Testimony of Dr. Hallett before Charter Revision Commission, November 12, 1935.

[11] Walter T. Arndt, *Proportional Representation* (New York, 1933), unpaged; *P. R. Review*, No. 64, 67-68; "Citizens Union Analysis."

Table 7. DISPROPORTIONATE PARTY REPRESENTATION ON THE BOARD OF ALDERMEN

Party	*Election Year*	*Votes Cast*	*Seats in Proportion to Votes Cast*	*Seats Won*	*Percentage of Votes Cast*	*Percentage of Seats Won*
Democratic	1921	614,559	35.1	52	54	80
Republican		397,505	22.7	12	35	18
Fusion [a]		6,880	.7	1	1	2
Socialist		113,451	6.5	0	10	0
Others		4,747	.0	0	0	0
Total		1,137,142	65.0	65	100	100
Democratic	1923	562,804	37.4	56	57.6	86.2
Republican		332,316	22.1	8	34.0	12.3
Fusion [a]		6,048	0.4	0	0.6	1.5
Socialist		74,300	4.9	1	7.6	0
Others		1,569	.1	0	.2	0
Total		977,037	65.0	65	100.0	100.0
Democratic	1925	688,447	40.0	61	61.6	93.8
Republican		372,859	21.7	3	33.4	4.6
Fusion [a]		6,921	0.4	1	0.6	1.5
Socialist		47,095	2.7	0	4.2	0
Others		1,706	.1	0	.2	0
Total		1,117,028	65.0	65	100.0	100.0
Democratic	1927	684,137	40.7	58	62.6	89.2
Republican		352,080	20.9	7	32.2	10.8
Socialist		51,629	3.1	0	4.7	0
Others		4,690	.3	0	.4	0
Total		1,092,536	65.0	65	100.0	100.0
Democratic	1929	842,686	40.5	61	62.2	93.8
Republican		428,650	20.6	4	31.7	6.2
Socialist		77,962	3.7	0	5.8	0
Others		4,422	.2	0	.3	0
Total		1,353,720	65.0	65	100.0	100.0

Table 7 (Continued)

Party	*Election Year*	*Votes Cast*	*Seats in Proportion to Votes Cast*	*Seats Won*	*Percentage of Votes Cast*	*Percentage of Seats Won*
Democratic	1931	851,216	42.3	64	65.0	98.5
Republican		339,050	16.8	1	25.9	1.5
Socialist		110,254	5.5	0	8.4	0
Others		8,774	.4	0	.7	0
Total		1,309,294	65.0	65	100.0	100.0
Democratic [b]	1933	969,445	33.3	49	51.2	75.4
Republican [c]		772,463	26.5	16	40.8	24.6
Recovery		28,156	1.0	0	1.5	0
City Fusion		9,807	.3	0	0.5	0
Socialist		75,827	2.6	0	4.0	0
Others		39,112	1.3	0	2.0	0
Total		1,894,810	65.0	65	100.0	100.0
Democratic	1935	1,137,609	43.2	62	66.4	95.4
Republican [d]		447,405	17.0	3	26.1	4.6
Socialist		65,839	2.5	0	3.9	0
Others		61,218	2.3	0	3.6	0
Total		1,712,071	65.0	65	100.0	100.0

Source: See n. 10.

[a] Candidate endorsed by both Democratic and Republican parties.

[b] Includes Democrats running jointly on Recovery and Jeffersonian tickets.

[c] Includes Republicans running jointly on City Fusion, Law Preservation, Taxpayers, and New Deal Party tickets.

[d] Includes Republicans running jointly on City Fusion Party ticket.

Table 8. VOTES PER MEMBER ELECTED TO THE BOARD OF ALDERMEN

Year	*Democratic*	*Republican*	*Socialist*	*Other Parties*
1901	7,539	7,522	15,889 [c]	
1903	6,085	10,905	17,829 [c]	
1905	9,195	6,208	12,532 [c]	12,583 Municipal Ownership [a, c]
1907	5,277	8,804	16,974 [c]	40,088 Independence League [a, c]
1909	6,841	7,584	12,565 [c]	
1911	7,590	6,931	33,155 [c]	
1913	7,490	6,904	33,619 [c]	53,804 National Progressive [a, c]
1915	5,630	11,489	40,685 [c]	
1917	6,661	12,736	16,613	7,365 Fusion [b]
1919	11,002	14,979	36,840	8,459 Fusion [b]
1921	11,818	33,125	113,451 [c]	6,880 Fusion [b]
1923	10,052	41,359	74,300 [c]	6,048 Fusion [b]
1925	11,286	124,286	47,095 [c]	6,921 Fusion [b]
1927	11,795	50,277	51,629 [c]	
1929	13,814	107,162	77,962 [c]	
1931	13,300	339,050	110,254 [c]	
1933	20,359	48,892	75,827 [c]	77,075 Recovery, City Fusion, Emancipation [a, c]
1935	18,459	146,160	66,985 [c]	61,218 City Fusion, Square Deal, Communist [a, c]

Source: See n. 11.

[a] Does not include candidates endorsed by major parties.
[b] Candidates endorsed by both Democratic and Republican Parties.
[c] Elected no one.

of seats. Recognizing the hopelessness of electing their candidates, independent voters refrained from exercising their franchise, thereby surrendering control of the personnel of the board to the dominant party machine.[12]

The prevailing mode of election was said to produce an "invisible" type of error. Citizens who despaired of electing their real favorites suported the most tolerable of the candidates likely to win. Taking into account this deviation from the voters' actual preferences, together with the distortions of the primaries and general elections, some critics asserted that the elections to the Board of Aldermen "violated every tenet of American democracy" by misrepresenting the real preferences of the electorate. Like the French national legislature, the board was a "broken mirror" which distorted the city's political image.[13]

By distorting the will of the majority, the critics declared, the electoral system created a "virtual despotism by the best organized political minority." As a legal creature of the State, the city government was not a self-contained political unit; but within limited confines its authority tended to become absolute. From the outset of Mayor Hylan's regime in 1918 until its displacement by a Fusion administration in 1934, the regnant political party dominated every branch of municipal government. As in European totalitarian states, the legislature degenerated into a "mere collection of yes-men with no more influence on the administration of the city's affairs than had it never been elected."[14]

When a probe of city affairs in the thirties uncovered shocking evidence of corruption, waste, and inefficiency, the State investigating committee attributed the evils partly to the absence of effective opposition in the city legislature. The election of 1931 had left just "one wee little voice and vote" for the entire

[12] *Recommendations from the New York City League of Women's Voters to the Committee on Proportional Representation, New York City Charter Commission* (July 3, 1934); *The Searchlight,* XXIV, No. 1 (1934), 5-6.

[13] "Seabury Minutes," pp. 9996, 10426; *The Searchlight,* XXIV, No. 1, 5-6.

[14] George H. Hallett, "Giving the Charter Back to the People" (Radio address broadcast from Station WNYC, May 26, 1936); Seabury, *Final Report,* p. 20; Statement of William J. Schieffelin at public hearing of Chart. Rev. Comm., May 19, 1936.

minority. Where the opposition was overwhelmingly outnumbered there could be little genuine discussion of majority measures, and dubious proposals were not compelled to run the gamut of critical appraisal. Checks upon the party in power virtually disappeared, for a rubber stamp legislature could hardly restrain an administration that chose to ignore the public interest. The reformers could agree with Alfred E. Smith's dictum, stated when he was President of the Board of Aldermen: "The people rule negatively as well as affirmatively, and a good, healthy, vigorous minority is the necessary check on great power."[15]

Tremendous instability was said to exist under the single-member system, for a relatively slight shift in votes could change the entire complexion of the public assembly. In the election of 1921, in which some 1,137,000 votes were cast for aldermanic candidates, the Democrats obtained 52 out of 65 seats. Yet a hypothetical transfer of 27,662 votes, about two and one-half per cent of the total, in properly selected districts, would have given the Republicans a safe majority of 37 seats. Even the Socialists—*mirabile dictu*—could have increased their representation from no aldermen at all to an actual majority without doubling their vote![16]

The immense interests at stake in the turn of a few votes in strategic districts in the city gave small pressure groups capable of swinging the balance a disproportionate bargaining power and offered a great incentive to corruption. It was common knowledge that right through the last election for aldermen political leaders paid and protected professional gangsters for coercing voters and acting as repeaters. Socialist voters were intimidated, and even Republican watchers were manhandled. In crucial districts Tammany colonized lodging houses and transient establishments with thousands of floaters for illegal voting. A federal judge who tried several cases of election frauds in 1932 strongly condemned the use of "repeaters, strong-arm men, terrorism of

15 "Hofstadter Committee Report," pp. 10-11; Seabury, *Final Report*, pp. 8-10; Philips, "Does Bd. of Ald. Earn Its Sizeable Pay Check?" *Real Est. Mag.*, XXI, No. 5, 19; Norman Hapgood and Henry Moscowitz, *Up from the City Streets* (New York, 1927), p. 149.

16 "P. R. Proposal," pp. 9-10; *Prop. Rep. Review*, No. 62 (1922), 44.

voters, and false returns of a canvass," which had been disclosed during the trials. Where small shifts in votes could turn the scales there was a temptation to employ underhand methods in pivotal districts.[17]

It was unnecessary for party machines to resort openly to dishonest methods, however, when legal means could assure victory in advance. In 1917 the Socialists won seven seats in the board. Then came a redistricting. Almost the same number of ballots were cast for Socialists in 1921; yet their representation had entirely disappeared! The possibilities of gerrymandering could hardly be overlooked. Party managers were understandably reluctant to disclose the maneuvres preceding reapportionment in the state legislature, but it was quite possible to draw district lines that would give the majority party more than an equitable share of representation.[18] A glance at the grotesque contours on a map of the city's election areas, contended the critics of the electoral system, would demonstrate that in New York gerrymandering had been developed into a fine art.[19]

In due course population shifts altered the character of the electorate and negated plans to rig the elections, but failure to redistrict created a "silent gerrymander." As subways were built there was an exodus from the tenements of Manhattan to the other boroughs, as indicated in Table 9.[20]

[17] Lavine, *"Gimme,"* pp. 67, 69; "Seabury Minutes," pp. 10423, 10438; "Hofstadter Committee Report," p. 119; Blanshard, *Investigating City Govt.*, pp. 109-10; *P. R. Review*, No. 62, 44.

[18] How district lines might be drawn as a matter of political expediency is demonstrated by the following story: In the first decade of the century a Republican State Senator from Manhattan was approached by a Democratic leader in his district who feared that a forthcoming state reapportionment would place his clubhouse outside the assembly district, thereby putting him out of business. He offered his support in subsequent elections if the line were extended to contain his clubhouse. The Senator contrived to achieve the desired end and was rewarded in the next election by grateful Democratic support from this assembly district. Interview with confidential source, September 15, 1948.

[19] McGoldrick, "Eclipse of the Ald.," *Nat. Mun. Rev.*, XIV, 367; George H. Hallett, "'P. R.' versus the Gerrymander," *The American City*, XXVIII, No. 1 (1923), 23; "P. R. Proposal"; *The Searchlight*, XIII, No. 1, 6; *P. R. Review*, No. 66 (1923), 56; "Seabury Minutes," p. 9998.

[20] *The World Almanac and Encyclopedia for 1922* (New York, 1921), 563; *Fifteenth Census of the United States* (Washington, 1931), I, 751, 756, 758, 761; *City of N. Y.: Off. Direct., 1935*, p. 7 (The 1921 and 1935 figures are local Board of Health estimates).

Table 9. POPULATION SHIFTS IN NEW YORK CITY

Year	*Manhattan*	*Brooklyn*	*Bronx*	*Queens*	*Richmond*
1921	2,276,778	2,077,674	778,528	497,629	121,252
1930	1,876,312	2,560,401	1,265,258	1,079,129	158,346
1935	1,653,844	2,838,017	1,538,359	1,391,588	179,767

The last reapportionment of aldermen in 1921 had given four boroughs representation roughly proportionate to their population (Richmond had been intentionally overrepresented since its incorporation into Greater New York to provide its fifty-seven square miles with three Boards of Local Improvement). But the rapid growth of the outlying sections of the city was not accompanied by any redistricting. How badly underrepresented the newly developed boroughs came to be at the time of the last election of aldermen is indicated in Table 10.[21]

Table 10. AVERAGE NUMBER OF PERSONS REPRESENTED BY ONE ALDERMAN

Year	*Manhattan*	*Brooklyn*	*Bronx*	*Queens*	*Richmond*
1921	94,866	86,570	97,316	82,938	40,417
1930	77,605	106,633	158,157	179,855	52,782
1935	68,910	118,251	192,295	231,931	59,923

Within individual constituencies the differences were even more pronounced. In 1935 one alderman was elected in Manhattan with 6,140 votes; in Queens 31,066 ballots were cast for a defeated candidate. The latter polled more votes than 55 out of the 65 aldermen elected that day. These inequalities of representation were validated by the courts,[22] but even opponents of proportional representation recognized that the situation was indefensible.[23] It was hardly surprising that the United Civic Organizations of Queens County demanded proportional representation, for the district system was most prejudicial to the interests of that growing borough. Even its leaders who opposed proportional representation were conscious of a pressing need for periodic reapportionment. During this period, however, the

21 Based on representation in the Board of Aldermen as follows: Manhattan, 24 aldermen; Brooklyn 24; Bronx, 8; Queens, 6; Richmond, 3.

22 *People on Relation of Boyle v. Cruise,* 189 N. Y. Supp. 288 (1921).

23 Ferdinand A. Hermens, *Democracy or Anarchy?* (Notre Dame, 1941), p. 395.

elimination of "rotten boroughs" was not even seriously considered, for that would have increased the power of rival city machines at the expense of Tammany Hall.[24]

Finally, it was argued that the district system which herded voters into artificial geographical divisions produced representation "based upon sleep," rather than natural combinations of interest. A given area sent to the Board of Aldermen the delegate who obtained a plurality of votes; but he could not possibly represent all the interests and all classes among his "fellow sleepers" whose residences happened to fall in the district.[25]

To correct these defects in the municipal electoral system, emancipate the voters from political manipulators, and loosen the grip of the party machine, it was proposed to eliminate the evil at its roots and introduce P. R. (as we shall henceforth call proportional representation). The following advantages were claimed for each step in the proposed reform.[26]

The direct primary had failed to transfer power from political boss to the electorate; it was hoped that P. R. would effect this result. Under P. R. it would be impossible to sweep aside the unorganized "better elements" in the primaries, for anyone who could muster 2,000 signatures would have his name on the final ballot. Incidentally, eliminating primary contests would save campaign expenses for independent candidates. In the final elections the voter would have the combined choices of primary and general elections in a single trip to the polls. "Freed from the paralyzing effect of hopeless odds," the independent voters would have an opportunity to wrest control of the machinery of nomination and election from the party organizations.[27]

[24] *The American City*, XXVII, No. 1 (1922), 79; Letter of William D. Bossler, Chairman of Board of Directors of United Civic Organizations of Queens County to Commissioner Thomas I. Parkinson, of the Charter Revision Commission, Jan. 29, 1935; Remarks of Alderman James A. Burke at open hearing of Charter Revision Commission, Mary 21, 1936.

[25] George H. McCaffrey, *An explanation of Proportional Representation for New York City* (New York, 1934), unpaged.

[26] The system outlined in the following pages is the version of the Hare System actually adopted in New York City.

[27] *Proportional Representation for New York City* (New York, 1937), p. 7, *The Searchlight*, XXV, No. 1, 3; "Seabury Minutes," pp. 9919, 9956-57; Walter

Borough-wide districts and a quota of 75,000 ballots to determine the number of legislators to which each borough was entitled would eliminate all possibility of gerrymandering and provide a self-regulating mechanism for periodic reapportionment. Constituencies of more than a million voters would be represented by men of broad vision, capable of looking beyond narrow district boundaries, and the municipal legislature would begin to deliberate on city-wide affairs, rather than concentrate on the problems of sixty-five individual constituencies.[28]

No party emblems—those "magic stars or eagles"—would appear on the ballot.[29] Nonpartisanship was believed desirable to divorce municipal elections from national politics and to induce voters to elect candidates on their own merits.[30]

Multimember districts, with a larger field from which to select candidates, together with the preferential ballot, permitting an unlimited number of choices, would assure citizens they would not be restricted to a "futile selection between the puppets of rival bosses." The conviction that their votes could count towards electing a candidate they really preferred would offer an incentive for independent voters to turn out on election day and provide a fillip for the candidacies of distinguished men. With independent candidates of higher calibre on the same ballot as their nominees, the dominant party would also find it expedient to select more creditable men. Hence the election of able and public-spirited legislators would be ensured. "The P. R. election would remove many of the present type," asserted the chairman of the Citizens Union, "and substitute others so radically different in outlook, philosophy, and capacity as even to make blasé New York sit up."[31]

M. Hinkle, "Proportional Representation—The Keystone of Charter Reform," Radio Address, Station WNYC, July 1, 1934.

28 *Prop. Rep. For N. Y. C.*, pp. 6, 17; *The Searchlight*, XXV, No. 5, 6; *Rep. of N. Y. Chart. Comm., 1923*, p. 14.

29 The endorsement of its county committee, however, permitted the use of a party designation after a candidate's name.

30 "Seabury Minutes," pp. 9925-26; Seabury, *Final Report*, pp. 25-26.

31 *Rep. of N. Y. Chart. Comm., 1923*, p. 15; "Seabury Minutes," p. 9971; Hinkle, "Prop. Rep.—Keystone of Chart. Reform."; Statement of William J. Schieffelin for Citizens Union at Public Hearing of Chart. Rev. Comm., May 19, 1936; William J. Schieffelin, "The City Manager Plan is Suitable for New York," *Nat. Mun. Rev.*, XXI (1932), 294.

The chief advantage claimed for P. R. was its ability to seat a fair share of members of each party or independent group. When the ballots were sorted the candidates receiving 75,000 votes on the first count were to be declared elected. Then, in successive counts, the nominees with the least votes would be eliminated, alternate choices on their ballots going to the remaining candidates. Ultimately the field would shrink to the quota of councilmen assigned to the borough. This system was held to guarantee justice to all parties, affording representation to every shade of public opinion in aproximately the proportion in which it existed among the electorate. No longer could a single party dominate the Board; the city legislature would now represent all the people.[32]

Strengthened by revived public interest in its deliberations, by the election of more capable legislators, and by the presence of spokesmen for every substantial group in the city, the representative assembly would become a forum for public discussion of city problems. Regardless of the prevailing type of electoral system, an overwhelmingly Democratic city like New York would normally seat a majority of Democrats. A P. R. legislature, however, would install Democratic insurgents capable of combining with members of political minorities to curb one-party dictatorship. The majority would find a critical minority acting as a gadfly and counterweight. Genuine opposition would test out administration policies and prevent a relapse to the "depths of misrule" exposed by the Seabury inquiries. "Majorities will be vastly more careful," declared an anti-Tammany writer, "if there is a constant and broadcasting minority on the alert to discover and disclose in advance where the public is about to be robbed." In such a legislature it would be infinitely more difficult for majorities to "sell the city's birthright for a mess of pottage" or to "acquiesce in administrative debauchery."[33]

Depriving the party bosses of the power to control all nominations and compelling their nominees to meet open competi-

[32] *Prop. Rep. For N. Y. C.*, pp. 7-14; "Seabury Minutes," pp. 9945-46.

[33] *Chart. Rev. For City of N. Y.* (N. Y. U. Plan), pp. 7-8; George H. Hallett, *Real Majority Rule* (Brooklyn, 1935), pp. 6-7; William J. Schieffelin, "P. R. and New Yorkers," *The Survey*, XXVI (1937), 386; Finegan, *Tammany at Bay*, p. 39; Hinkle, "Prop. Rep.—Keystone of Charter Reform."

tion at the polls involved a shift in the balance of power. "The government (of the city) is almost wholly in the hands of a single dominant political party," wrote Judge Samuel Seabury. "P. R. cannot fail to shatter the completeness of this domination." The reformers planned not only to alter the structure of municipal government, but also to curb the power of the machine. P. R. was advanced as a device to weaken boss rule, to "cut the tiger's claws close to the quick."[34]

Some advocates of P. R. maintained it would purify politics, acting as a deterrent to fraud. Corrupt methods could not be used to turn the scale in a few close districts; in the greatly enlarged constituencies they would be reflected only proportionally in the results. Unfortunately this was a delicate issue, for P. R. implied a reversion to paper ballots with attendant possibilities of manipulation. It was a tremendous relief to the reformers when a voting machine capable of handling preferential ballots was invented and exhibited towards the end of the campaign.

P. R. was vigorously opposed by such groups as the five regular Democratic organizations, the Brooklyn Bar Association, and the Home Rule League. But its opponents did not argue their case as effectively or as copiously as their adversaries. Perhaps they scorned to emulate the "library politicians," those devotees of good government whose "highly worded resolutions" were regularly discarded as rubbish when received in the Board of Aldermen. The dominant political organization, chief foe of P. R. in the 1936 campaign, relied on methods other than intellectual persuasion. Denizens of the clubhouses, described by the chairman of the Charter Revision Commission as "The Light Brigade—they never reason why," were simply ordered to vote against the charter. The Democratic machine never seriously believed P. R. would come to a vote, and when a Court of Appeals decision was handed down less than a month before the election sanctioning the appearance of P. R. on the ballot it was caught unprepared. It had required years of intensive research

[34] Seabury, *Final Report*, p. 20; Schieffelin, "City Manager Plan is Suitable for N. Y.," *Nat. Mun. Rev.*, XXI, 294.

to hammer out the P. R. argument; to whip up a reply in a few weeks was no simple matter.[35]

In the scant literature issued by the opponents of P. R. before its adoption they insisted that it was thoroughly impractical—too complicated to work smoothly and too involved for the average voter to understand. P. R. was denounced as an "erratic fad," so confoundingly complex that its authors had "wandered into a wordy morass out of which not even the ingenuity of Edgar Wallace could extricate them." Operating this "implausible eccentricity" would wreak havoc. Open nominations would encourage "every seeker of notoriety and crackpot" to stand for office; perhaps 500 names would be placed on a single ballot. An "elaborate system of ballot marking and juggling" and a colossal number of votes under the system of unlimited preferential voting (perhaps 500,000,000 in a borough the size of Brooklyn) would create bedlam in the canvass. The element of luck in the transfer of ballots would turn elections into lotteries, with freakish results. Completing the count would take weeks. Endless litigation would ensue, with the winners of disputed elections unable to take office on the statutory date. So complicated a gadget might work in smaller towns, but for a city the size of New York it was thoroughly impractical.[36]

Mastering the gymnastics of P. R. voting was like "solving a jig-saw puzzle in the dark." Nine tenths of the electorate would find the system beyond their understanding, and introducing it would be feasible only after years of instruction. Bewildered by the intricacies of voting, many good citizens would spoil their ballots. Hence P. R. would replace majority rule with the dominion of an intellectual élite—a blow at universal suffrage. The fate of their ballots after voters left the booth would be another mystery. For that matter, the actual processing was unscientific. Was it logical to equate the second and lower choices with

[35] Curran, *John Citizen's Job*, pp. 155-56; *New York Times*, October 26, 1936; *New York World-Telegram*, November 3, 1936; *Matter of Mooney v. Cohen*, 272 N. Y. 33 (1936).

[36] Editorial signed by Alfred E. Smith in the *New Outlook*, CLXI (Feb., 1933), 10-11; Statement of Tammany Executive Committee, *New York Herald-Tribune*, Oct. 30, 1936; Letters to *New York Sun*, March 3, 1933, Oct. 28, 1936; *New York Sun* editorial, Nov. 2, 1936; Letter of Alexander U. Mayer, Counsel, Taxpayers Alliance of the Bronx, to Chart. Rev. Comm., July 17, 1935.

the voter's first preference? "Would the horses in a race on the track be rated as equally of the same value in the betting ring?" [37]

P. R., it was contended, could easily deprive majorities of proper representation. The obliteration of district lines made it possible for every legislator in a borough to live in the same apartment house. Hence the majority of districts would lose their spokesmen and neighborhood viewpoints could not be presented in the municipal assembly.[38]

In the local legislature, it was asserted, the representation of "every political bloc and clique and ism" would destroy party responsibility and disrupt city government. Effacing party designations from the ballot and permitting innumerable "crackpots" [39] and "wild-eyed ginks" to run on "all sorts of crazy platforms and impossible promises" would make for irresponsible management of municipal affairs, and put an end to party rule. Governments like the French, which relied on uneasy coalitions, had proven notoriously unstable. Did not the fate of the German Republic prove the danger of installing a score of clashing factions in the legislature? By promoting disunity and chaos in the Reichstag P. R. had paved the way for the Nazi dictatorship. Strong majorities were required for the successful conduct of public affairs and experience had demonstrated that replacing them with the European bloc system would inevitably lead to obstruction and disintegration. "A City Council selected in this way," declared Alfred E. Smith, "would be the most unworkable, disorderly, irresponsible spectacle we have ever seen in our government." [40]

P. R., it was argued, was a radical experiment, of foreign origin and alien to American life. It would introduce subversive elements into the city legislature, invite destruction of the two-party system, and divide the electorate into racial and religious

[37] *New York Sun*, March 3, 1933, October 28, 1936; *Tammany Statement*; Testimony of George McAneny before Chart. Rev. Comm., June 13, 1935, 2; *Taxpayers Alliance Letter.*

[38] *New Outlook*, CLXI, No. 5, 11; *New York Sun*, November 2, 1936.

[39] In political parlance a "crackpot" is an independent or insurgent.

[40] *New Outlook*, CLXI, No. 5, 11; *New York Times*, July 2, 1934, October 31, 1936; *New York Enquirer* editorial, February 5, 1933; Testimony of Alfred E. Smith before Charter Revision Commission, May 28, 1935.

voting blocs. Few American cities had seen fit to adopt P. R., and most of those had abandoned it. It was unconstitutional and un-American.[41]

Years of effort had gone into the movement to introduce voting machines. Under P. R. they would be scrapped at considerable financial loss. Ballots would be transferred to an armory where the tedious count would cost a half million dollars, and, in close elections, tempt mobs to tear the buildings down. In place of "impartial and imperturbable" machines, producing prompt and accurate results, it was proposed to return to the iniquities of paper ballots—clearly an invitation to fraud.[42]

Historic reforms are not consummated by argument alone; they await the logic of events. For years an interest in P. R. had been confined to limited circles. Its approbation by almost a million citizens was one of the consequences of a political tidal wave that swept in a reform administration and left lasting effects on the city government. In the next chapter we shall turn to the historic background preceding P. R.'s adoption.

[41] *Tammany Statement; New York Times*, Sept. 28, 1936; *New York Sun*, Oct. 28, 1936; Testimony of Borough President George U. Harvey, April 15, 1935.

[42] *New York Sun*, March 3, 1933; *Taxpayers Alliance Letter; Tammany Statement*; Testimony of Harvey.

8. TAMMANY COLLAPSES

When Murphy died, "the brains of Tammany were laid away in the cemetary."—EX-MAYOR JAMES J. WALKER [1]

TAMMANY HALL reached the zenith of its power in the 1920's. Under Charles F. Murphy's leadership (1902-24), the longest and most successful in Tammany history, the Hall dominated the city democracy, controlled governors and state legislatures, and influenced national conventions. For years after his death positions of power were filled by Murphy protégés—Al Smith, Governor and Presidential nominee, Robert F. Wagner, legislative pilot of the New Deal, Edward J. Flynn, campaign manager for President Roosevelt, Surrogate James A. Foley, and the brilliant but irresponsible Mayor Walker.[2]

Following the principle that "clean politics was judicious politics," Murphy made Tammany comparatively respectable. Conspicuous city offices were filled with honest and capable men; the thieving impulses of party functionaries were curbed with iron discipline. After the Triangle Shirtwaist fire of 1911, a horrible factory disaster, the organization sponsored the most progressive factory laws in the country, and an impressive body of social legislation was passed at Albany. Decent government and the promotion of social welfare raised Tammany's popularity to new levels. For some time after Murphy's death, the "New Tammany" was in good repute with political scientists, who

1 Salter, *The American Politician*, p. 19.

2 Hapgood and Moscowitz, *Up from the City Streets*, p. 81; Isabel Patterson, "Murphy," *American Mercury*, XIV (1928), 352; Julius Henry Cohen, *They Builded Better Than They Knew* (New York, 1946), p. 76; Arthur Krock, "The Brown Derby and the Bee: Profile of Alfred E. Smith," *The New Yorker*, II (May 29, 1926), 16.

compared its rule favorably with Chicago under "Big Bill" Thompson and Philadelphia under Boss Vare.[3]

None of Murphy's successors achieved his mastery of party politics. George W. Olvany (1924-29) paid lip-service to the "New Tammany," but followed Croker's policy of "working for his pocket all the time." His own law firm accepted fabulous fees from clients doing business with the city. Governor Smith and Mayor Walker never yielded him the deference accorded Murphy, while leaders of the city's other county machines asserted their independence. Relegated to the level of patronage dispenser, Olvany was unable to discipline his cohorts, and under the complaisant Mayor Walker "the boys stole and stole and forgot to give the city much in the way of government in return."[4] A contemporary reporter described the corruption which permeated the city:

> Nothing was too big and nothing too small for the district leaders and wardheelers who made the city pay dividends during this era. The system was organized for profit from the top to the bottom, and no bets were overlooked. Politicians in the upper stratum of power took their cut on such ambitious projects as the leasing of piers, the purchase of real estate for public improvements, the sale of building materials, the granting of franchises. . . . The lesser fry collected the small change. Building inspectors accepted a ten-spot here and a ten-spot there to overlook illegal kitchenettes and violations of fire laws. . . . The unromantic brownies who picked up garbage took their weekly cash collections from cafés and business places. Nothing came free in New York.[5]

Signs of deterioration appeared during Mayor Walker's first term (1926-29). Important city offices were placed on the auction block and inferior administrative and judicial appoint-

[3] Gustavus Myers, "The New Tammany," *Century Magazine*, CXII (1926), 391; Jacob Knickerbocker, *Then and Now* (Boston, 1939), pp. 232-33; Lowell M. Limpus, *History of the New York Fire Department* (New York, 1940), pp. 305-6; Frances Perkins, *The Roosevelt I Knew* (New York, 1946), pp. 24-25; *New York Times*, August 17, 1927.

[4] Myers, "The New Tammany," *Cent. Mag.*, CXII, 385, 391-93; William B. Northrop and John B. Northrop, *The Insolence of Office* (New York, 1932), p. 168 ff., 193 ff.; Johnston, "No More Lawyers," *The New Yorker*, VII, No. 7, 24-25; McGoldrick, "The New Tammany," *American Mercury*, XV, 2; Moscow, *Politics in the Empire State*, p. 95.

[5] Mackaye, *The Tin Box Parade*, pp. 26-27.

ments followed. Scandals broke out almost continuously; one rocked the Queens Democratic organization. In 1928 the Republicans professed to find the entire city administration "honeycombed with graft." It was said that Tammany insiders jocularly boasted of outclassing Tweed himself.[6]

Still, no political upheaval was imminent. Little real opposition came from New York's moribund Republican machine in the twenties. Even the Citizens Union, a leading reform group, designated no preference in the mayoralty election of 1929 between Tammany's Jimmy Walker and the Republican La Guardia. Civic consciousness, rarely strong in the metropolis, flickered feebly in the era of the great Wall Street boom. During the "intoxicating orgy of private and public gambling and spending" reckless expenditures by local politicians were easily condoned. "Preoccupied with picking up greater and greater profits from speculation, few citizens were concerned with the honesty of public officials."[7]

Few suspected that the Great Depression would destroy the "bull market in graft" and revolutionize New York politics. The city's principle source of revenue was real estate taxes: booming realty values permitted extravagant expenditures and a doubling of the annual budget in a single decade with little change in the tax rate.[8] Judge Seabury's historic report described the fattening of the machine at public expense:

> The affairs of the City of New York are conducted, not with a view to the benefits which can be conferred upon the residents of our city, but for the profit which the dominant political organization . . . and its satellites can make out of the running of it. . . . Widespread inefficiency and sloth are tolerated in politically appointed and protected city

[6] McGoldrick, "The New Tammany," *Am. Merc.*, XV, 7, 12; Flynn, *You're the Boss*, p. 139; Raymond Moley, *Tribunes of the People* (New Haven, 1932), pp. 37-38; Allen, *Al Smith's Tammany Hall*, p. 297 ff.; 320-21; *The New Tammany* (New York: Republican State Committee, 1928), 24.

[7] McGoldrick, "The New Tammany," *Am. Merc.*, XV, 10, 12; *The Searchlight*, XIX (October, 1929), 4; Cleveland Rodgers, *New York Plans for the Future* (New York, 1943), pp. 102-3; Harold Seidman, *Investigating Municipal Administration* (New York, 1941), p. 92.

[8] Nevins and Krout, *The Greater City*, pp. 169-72; Alva Johnston, "The Scandals of New York," *Harper's Magazine*, CLXII (1931), 412; Joseph D. McGoldrick, "Storm Warnings in New York City's Finances," *National Municipal Review*, XXI (1932), 171-72.

employees, and every subterfuge is availed of to furnish excuses for the spending of money, not because the spending thereof is necessary, or even desirable . . . but because [of] the opportunities for graft incident thereto. . . . The costs of our public improvements are vastly in excess of their reasonable value, the difference representing the "rake-off" of the politicians and the allowances made for grafting officials.[9]

The economic downswing in the thirties cut city revenues and ended riotous spending. Signs of financial strain appeared after 1931. American cities were facing their greatest crisis, and New York's credit deteriorated more seriously than most. With defaults on payrolls and maturing bonds imminent, the city government capitulated to banking pressure and agreed to curtail expenditures and seek new sources of revenue.[10]

But no Tammany administration could solve the dire budget problem. Realty values were dropping, tax delinquencies increasing, and unemployment relief needs mounting. The administration deferred public improvements, applied to the state legislature to authorize additional taxes, and desperately juggled the city's books. To no avail—the budget for 1934 contained a deficit estimated at $30,000,000. What was needed was a thorough housecleaning to rid the city payrolls of a "horde of superfluous, incompetent chairwarmers." But that would have meant suicide for the dominant political organization.[11]

The depression also loosened a flood of exposure which swept that organization out of office. Auditing of the books of bankrupt firms uncovered evidence that implicated city judges in dubious financial ventures and indicated the purchase of judgeships. The sentencing of a justice to prison for mail fraud and the removal of a magistrate who had been consorting with crimi-

[9] Seabury, *Final Report*, pp. 2-3.

[10] F. L. Bird, "American Cities Face 1933," *Nat. Mun. Rev.*, XXII (1933), 53; Paul V. Betters, "Bolstering Municipal Credit," *Nat. Mun. Rev.*, XXII (1933), 268-70; T. D. Zuckerman, "The Story of New York City in Interest Rates," *Nat. Mun. Rev.*, XXIII (1934), 673-78.

[11] *Fiscal Facts Concerning the City of New York* (New York, 1940), p. 18; McGee, *Finances of the City of New York*, p. 7; Harry H. Freeman, "How American Cities are Retrenching in Times of Depression," *Nat. Mun. Rev.*, XXI (1932), 267; *Thirtieth Annual Report of the Committee on Legislation of the Citizens Union of the City of New York for the Regular Session of 1934 and the Special Sessions of 1933 and 1934*, pp. 4-5, 9; John Palmer Gavit, "New York—The Second Biggest Job," *Survey Graphic*, XXII (1933), 155.

nals prompted Governor Franklin D. Roosevelt to request an investigation of the Magistrates' Courts of Manhattan and the Bronx.[12]

Under Referee Samuel Seabury, the inquiry revealed a "hideous caricature that paraded as justice" in those courts. There emerged a sordid picture of police brutality, stealthy "fixing," frameups of innocent women, extortion, and inefficiency. Justice was dispensed in a "fetid atmosphere of political self-interest." The heart of the evil lay in the system of appointment and promotion. Nominally chosen by the mayor, but actually designated by district leaders, grateful magistrates could hardly bar their benefactors from their chambers or disregard their counsel on pending cases. An official trial calendar was discovered with the names of politicians penned in opposite the printed names of defendants. During the investigation two magistrates were removed and three resigned under fire.[13]

The magistrates' probe was only the beginning. New York County had seen such fighting District Attorneys as William Travers Jerome and Charles S. Whitman; Governor Thomas E. Dewey and Frank S. Hogan were later to make outstanding records in the same office. By no stretch of the imagination could Thomas C. T. Crain be included in their number. Responding to serious charges, Governor Roosevelt appointed Judge Seabury to investigate Crain's conduct in office. It was demonstrated that precisely when serious crimes were increasing, the city's law-enforcing authorities had made a "complete and abject surrender" to racketeers. In the absence of wilful dishonesty, however, the charges were dismissed.[14]

[12] Johnston, "Scandals of N. Y.," *Harp. Mag.*, CLXII, 413-15; Allen, *Since Yesterday*, p. 66; Northrop and Northrop, *The Insolence of Office*, p. 3 ff.

[13] Seabury, *Magistrates' Courts Investigation*, *passim*; Moley, *Tribunes of the People*, *passim*; Arthur Train, *From the District Attorney's Office* (New York, 1939), pp. 47-48; Raymond Moley, "When Politics Seasons Justice," *Yale Review*, XXI (1932), 449-53; Thomas and Blanshard, *What's the Matter with New York*, p. 92 ff.

[14] Northrop and Northrop, *op. cit.*, p. 115 ff.; Edward A. Williams, "The Crain Removal and the Statistical Charts," *Nat. Mun. Rev.*, XXI (1932), p. 232 ff.; *Report and Opinion of Samuel Seabury, Commissioner, in the Matter of the Investigation, under Commission Issued by the Governor of the State of New*

The trail of "honest graft" led to the staff of the President of the Board of Aldermen, where a ring of profiteers had planted a listening post. Here Chief Examiner McEneny had collaborated with a confederate in the Board of Education to obtain advance knowledge of school building sites. Acting through dummies, favored politicians and real estate speculators converted this information into a highly lucrative means of milking the city treasury. After the leader of the Brooklyn machine had been implicated, many suspected that other key political figures were involved.[15]

The time was ripe for a full-dress investigation of the city's politics. It could hardly originate in the Board of Aldermen, where top-heavy Tammany majorities shielded rather than exposed the administration to embarrassing inquiry. Republican-dominated state legislatures, however, had frequently undertaken such probes. Touched by recent scandals themselves, Republican managers saw an opportunity to disclose a "saturnalia of graft" in the Tammany stronghold. It seemed good strategy to divert attention from their own transgressions, to loosen the Democratic grip on the metropolis, and to endanger the presidential aspirations of Governor Roosevelt. Yet some Republicans hesitated, possibly fearing retaliatory investigations of upstate cities. State Chairman Macy drove the resolution through the legislature by the narrowest of margins, and then only after a personal phone call by Herbert Hoover from the White House.[16]

Judge Seabury's courage in attacking an entrenched machine, his distinguished conduct of the magistrates' inquiry, and his eminent reputation in the legal profession made him the logical

---

York, of Charges Made Against Honorable Thomas C. T. Crain, District Attorney of New York County (New York, 1931), *passim*; Interview with Justice Jacob Gould Schurman, August 1, 1949.

[15] Finegan, *Tammany at Bay*, pp. 125 ff., 264; Julius Isaacs, *Oath of Devotion* (New York, 1949), pp. 129-32; Thomas and Blanshard, *op. cit.*, pp. 234-38; Lavine, "Gimme," pp. 238-40; Leonard M. Wallstein, *Report on Law and Procedure in Condemnation Applicable to Proceedings Brought by the City of New York* (January 28, 1932), p. 44 ff.

[16] Lavine, "Gimme," pp. 30-33; Moscow, *Pol. in the Emp. State*, pp. 70-74, 138; *New York Times*, July 4, 1930; James A. Farley, *Behind the Ballots* (New York, 1938), pp. 167-69; *Nat. Mun. Rev.*, XX (1931), 183-84; Alva Johnston, "The King: Profile of W. Kingsland Macy," *The New Yorker*, VII (Sept. 12, 1931), 25-27.

choice as counsel for the Joint Committee. Technically it was a legislative investigation; actually the brilliant young Seabury staff bore the brunt of the gigantic operation. Seabury's purpose was not to catch petty miscreants, but to demonstrate that the city's machinery of government was infested with "sickening corruption," from top to bottom. Consequently he trained his guns on ranking figures in the dominant political party.[17] His ultimate aims were to drive that party from office by arousing the public's conscience and to limit future wrongdoing by revising the city charter.[18]

The fateful probe revealed a "metropolis ravaged by corruption and public betrayal." District leaders had effected a lucrative alliance with the underworld, giving professional gamblers sanctuary in political clubs. The law firm of a Tammany leader had sold "political influence under the guise of legal fees" and banked $5,000,000 in seven years. What made this the most devastating scrutiny of New York politics ever undertaken by the legislature was the effective use of the subpoena. The city's highest public officials and party potentates were haled to the witness stand to be discredited by their own testimony. Some sought refuge in fantasy. Sheriff Tom Farley explained that his swollen bank accounts had originated in a magic tin box. Thereafter "tin boxes" became "folk-symbols of graft without tell-tale bookkeeping." [19]

Revelation followed revelation, as a "shameless history of laxity, graft, and special privilege" was unfolded. Overshadowing all else was the prosecution of Mayor Walker for participa-

[17] He was willing to embarrass Republicans, too, as demonstrated by his exposé of Col. Edward E. Carrington, Republican candidate for Borough President of Manhattan. But their control of the city government gave the Democrats greater opportunities for peculation. Hence the investigation dealt principally with Democratic malfeasance.

[18] Richard O. Boyer, "Inquisitor: Profile of Samuel Seabury," *The New Yorker*, VII (June 17, 1931), 23; Samuel Seabury, *The Power of an Ideal* (New York, 1931), pp. 5, 7; Seabury, *Intermediate Report, passim*; Walter Chambers, *Samuel Seabury* (New York, 1932), pp. 344-47, 354-55.

[19] Salter, *op. cit.*, p. 4; Seabury, *Intermediate Report, passim*; Lowell M. Limpus, *Honest Cop: Lewis J. Valentine* (New York, 1939), p. 144 ff.; Nevins and Krout, *The Greater City*, p. 98; Interview with Justice Irving Ben Cooper, August 28, 1949.

tion in a notorious bus conspiracy and acceptance of "beneficences," his abrupt resignation, and his eclipse in city politics. An era in New York history was closing.[20]

Informed citizens had long been aware of the misgovernment revealed by Judge Seabury. Five years before "Tin Box" Farley's sins were publicly exposed, his assemblyman became so disgusted with the bunco game of politics in the district that he severed all connections with the machine. At that time, however, the electorate was "almost mockingly indifferent." When La Guardia's disclosure of shocking civic abuses sounded the tocsin in 1929, the "Little Flower" was overwhelmingly defeated. But as the new decade opened the public began to stir out of its complacency. As city officials and party leaders writhed under Judge Seabury's relentless grilling, newspapers gave the examinations floods of publicity. Many who usually took no interest in municipal problems followed hearings avidly, particularly after the tabloids spiced their coverage of the police "Vice Squad" inquiry with a sensational combination of crime, corruption, and sex.[21]

Public indignation against Tammany was fed not only by adverse publicity, but also by the desperate economic situation. Apart from the usual resentment against the party in power in hard times, important economic groups discovered how heavily they were paying for a profligate government. Landlords were in no mood for rises in assessments or tax rates in the midst of a bitter depression. Numerically more important were the civil service employees, threatened with pay slashes while time servers still infested the city pay rolls. As haphazard handouts failed

[20] Robert S. Allen (ed.), *Our Fair City* (New York, 1947), p. 47; Seabury, *Second Intermediate Report*, p. 76; Welling, *As the Twig Is Bent*, pp. 84-85; Gene Fowler, *Beau James: The Life and Times of Jimmy Walker* (New York, 1949), p. 293 ff.; John Dewey (ed.), *New York and the Seabury Investigation* (New York, 1933), p. 24 ff.

[21] Ernest S. Griffith, *Current Municipal Problems* (New York, 1933), p. 138; Frederick L. Hackenberg, *A Solitary Parade* (New York, 1929), pp. 289-95; McGoldrick, "The New Tammany," p. 11; Howard P. Jones, "The Seabury Revue of 1932," *Nat. Mun. Rev.*, XXI, 147; Oren C. Hervitz and William G. Mulligan, "The Legislative Investigating Committee," *Columbia Law Review*, XXXIII (1933), 5 n. A series of lurid articles, based on the revelations of "stool pigeon" Chile Acuna, ran in the *Daily News*, November 24 through December 1, 1930.

to meet relief needs, armies of unemployed found they had been "humbugged, swindled and betrayed." [22]

Tammany had its own troubles. The deepening depression had created a problem of mass unemployment too complex for the machine's customary methods of relief. Yet organization revenues from big business were falling off. Following the rift between Al Smith and Governor Roosevelt, Tammany leaders opposed the nomination of Roosevelt for President and Lehman for Governor—decisions fraught with unpleasant consequences. Inside Manhattan, the Hall was rent by factional feuds; in the outlying boroughs revolt was brewing against its domination of city politics. After Mayor Walker's sudden resignation the five county leaders momentarily staved off disaster, uniting behind the dull, respectable Surrogate O'Brien in the mayoralty race. Their unanimous backing and the Roosevelt landslide of 1932 ensured O'Brien's election. Impressed with Mayor McKee's efforts at administrative efficiency, however, 234,000 voters pencilled in his name on the ballots, and possibly 200,000 others unsuccessfully attempted to follow suit—a remarkable display of independent voting.[23]

During the ensuing year, the administration of bumbling Mayor O'Brien, "sterile intellectually in the face of economic disaster and bankrupt morally," made token gestures towards reform and economy. Shaken by exposure and internal dissension, a discredited Tammany faced the 1933 elections with trepidation. Since the consolidation of the city the pattern for defeating the regnant organization has been investigation of a corrupt administration, public reaction in favor of reform, and synthesis of anti-Tammany forces into a Fusion movement. These conditions were successfully fulfilled in 1933. When Bronx Leader Flynn was encouraged by the national administration to support a third candidate, Aldermanic President McKee,

[22] Joseph D. McGoldrick, "Again the Tiger is Challenged," *New York Times Magazine,* June 19, 1932; Gavit, "N. Y.—The Second Biggest Job," *Surv. Graph.,* XXII, 152-55; Johnston, "The Scandals of N. Y.," *Harp. Mag.,* CLXII, 412-13, 418; Finegan, *op. cit.,* p. 139 ff.; Seabury, *Final Report,* p. 104.

[23] Peel, *Pol. Clubs of N. Y. C.,* p. 330; Flynn, *op. cit.,* pp. 127-30; Joseph D. McGoldrick, "Tammany Totters But Triumphs," *Nat. Mun. Rev.,* XXI (1932), 640; *ibid.,* 700; *Ann. Rep. of Bd. of Elects. for Year 1932,* p. 82.

Tammany's defeat was assured. Flynn saved his county ticket, but in the municipal race the unhappy O'Brien ran third.[24]

Only a Fusion victory could produce a thoroughgoing revision of the city charter. Tammany leaders understandably did not relish fundamental changes, particularly the reform of a body so admirably suited to their purposes as the Board of Aldermen. As long as the Tiger remained in power no new charter could originate in the city, for changes in the city's framework of government under the Home Rule Act could only be initiated by the municipal legislature. No one seriously believed that a majority of aldermen would support an important measure without the consent of their party.[25]

La Guardia's election elated the reformers. In 1922 both he and Samuel Seabury, his sponsor in the Fusion movement, had signed a manifesto advocating P. R. for the city legislature. Seven years later he had called for the elimination of the Board of Aldermen as a "worthless body." In 1934 he denounced the existing document as a "Horse Car Charter in an Airplane Age" and pledged his administration to charter revision.[26]

The La Guardia regime left a deep imprint on New York politics. Few reform mayors in any American city have succeeded themselves; La Guardia was elected for three four-year terms. (Not since Peter Stuyvesant's day has a chief executive in the city held office longer than twelve years.) Finding "demoralized departments, shaken confidence, impaired credit, disorganized institutions," he resolved to clean out the city's Augean stables—a herculean task of exposure, reform, and reconstruction. In his first administration (1934-37) the New Broom swept out old abuses, restored fiscal solvency, and established a tradition of good government. From these efforts emerged a new charter.[27]

[24] Salter, *op. cit.*, pp. 18-22; Flynn, *op. cit.*, p. 132 ff.; Lowell M. Limpus and Burr W. Leyson, *This Man La Guardia* (New York, 1938), pp. 361 ff.

[25] Lawrence A. Tanzer, "Political Strategy Nullifies Home Rule in New York," *Nat. Mun. Rev.*, XXII (1933), 16; Walter Davenport, "Tammany's Own," *Collier's*, XCI (March 4, 1933), 17; City Home Rule Law (L. 1924, C. 363), Sec. 20, as amended by L. 1927, C. 501.

[26] *Nat. Mun. Rev.*, XXII (1933), 613; John Franklin Carter, *La Guardia* (New York, 1937), p. 113; *New York Times*, October 17, 1929, January 15, February 11, February 12, 1934.

[27] Carter, *La Guardia*, p. 115; John Palmer Gavit, "La Guardia—Portrait of a Mayor," *Survey Graphic*, XXV (1936), 58.

9. WRITING THE NEW CHARTER

New York is at the parting of the ways. We have been a Greater City for thirty-five years. We can either sit still and do the usual, lazy, thoughtless, unimaginative thing and tinker with our situation, or we can stir ourselves and . . . provide a constructive, a forward-facing and an imaginative solution of our problem.—NICHOLAS MURRAY BUTLER, in 1932 [1]

THERE WAS A TIME when reformers believed that evils in municipal government could be eradicated by "turning the rascals out." Repeated experience taught them that palace revolutions brought fleeting results, that permanent changes were effected only by reconstruction of local institutions. Consequently the revolt against Tammany in the nineteen thirties became a two-pronged drive—to blast the Walker administration out of office and to obtain sweeping changes in the city charter.

After the work of the Baldwin Commission (1921-23) leading civic associations evinced sporadic interest in P. R. for elections to the Board of Aldermen. But discussion of the subject was academic and lacked popular appeal. As late as 1931 the Citizens Union did not seriously contemplate charter changes. It sought merely to pave the way for future action, sponsoring an amendment to the state constitution authorizing P. R. elections for municipal legislatures.[2]

The year 1931 marked a turning-point in charter history. When the fateful Seabury investigations revealed a panorama of municipal corruption, reformers began to demand constructive change. "The objective of the investigation," asserted the

[1] Seabury, *Final Report*, p. 105.

[2] George H. McCaffrey, "Proportional Representation in New York City," *American Political Science Review*, XXXIII (1939), 841; *New York Times*, January 5, 1931.

Citizens Union organ, "must be both the discovery of wrongdoing and the proposal of specific measures for improving the machinery of government." In that year Dr. William J. Schieffelin, long-time Chairman of the Citizens Union, organized the Committee of a Thousand to drive Tammany from power, to install the manager plan, and to obtain P. R. By 1936 a score of civic bodies were participating in the campaign for charter revision.[3]

Tammany's political opponents soon sensed the possibilities of reform. They were obvious to the Socialists, who had consistently polled enough votes, on a proportionate basis, for a modest delegation to the Board of Aldermen, but failed to elect a single candidate since 1919. The American Labor Party, born during the campaign for P. R., anticipated the same benefits. Dedicated from the beginning to charter revision, the City Fusion Party supported P. R. "to a man." Republicans were more chary. The best answer to municipal misrule, they frankly declared, was to replace the Tammany administration with men of integrity—themselves. Charter revision was regarded as a secondary remedy. From time to time, however, Republicans spoke up for city manager government, for P. R., or for a unicameral legislature.[4]

Public attention began to focus on charter revision in the Fall of 1932. During the city-wide investigation Democratic leaders had rebuked the legislative committee for confining itself to a "manhunting job" instead of preparing constructive legislation. Actually Judge Seabury intended to perform both tasks—to disclose the "low and sordid estate" to which the city had sunk and to offer positive remedies. With the resignation of Mayor

[3] *The Searchlight*, XXI, No. 1 (1931), 2; *Reminiscences of William Jay Schieffelin* (Oral History Project, Bancroft Fund Collection, Columbia University), p. 35.

[4] *Nat. Mun. Rev.*, XXI (July, 1932), 442-43; *New York Times*, February 20, 1930, April 20, 1931, March 20, 1933; *New York Sun*, November 4, 1936; Chambers, *Samuel Seabury*, p. 344. "There is no question but that P. R. would help us Republicans here in town—which is why I am interested. On the other hand the wider aspects of the matter may not be so alluring," wrote Joseph Clark Baldwin, Minority leader of the Board of Aldermen, to Republican State Chairman W. Kingsland Macy, November 17, 1931.

Walker the first mission was triumphantly completed. Capitalizing on the front-page publicity gained by his spectacular revelations, he called to the witness stand public officials, university scholars, and leaders of civic societies—a cross-section of informed public opinion—to present their views on charter improvement.[5]

There followed a spate of plans. Ex-Governor Smith advocated a bicameral city legislature, patterned after the state government. George McAneny and Acting Mayor McKee suggested reducing the number of aldermen and electing them by P. R. Even Mayor-elect O'Brien appointed a committee to prepare charter changes acceptable to Tammany. (This was the first of a series of maneuvres to forestall fundamental charter revision.) The Seabury Report itself borrowed liberally from the municipal reform program, recommending a single-chambered legislature, elected under the Hare system of P. R., with nonpartisan ballots. The city manager plan, however, was discarded. In New York any system of elections was likely to yield the dominant party a majority; under the manager scheme this majority would select the Mayor and city manager. Appointed agents of Tammany, both would be out of reach of the electorate. Substantially the same recommendations for a city council were made by the Hofstadter Committee, which Judge Seabury had served as counsel.[6]

All signs seemed to point to concrete legislative action in 1933. Throughout 1931 and 1932 the strategy of the Republican high command had been to mark time pending completion of the Seabury inquiry. Almost the last of Governor Franklin D. Roosevelt's messages to the Legislature in 1932 pleaded for a revamping of local government; one of Governor Lehman's first, the following year, called attention to the very same issue. En-

[5] Joint Legislative Committee to Investigate the Departments of the City of New York, *Minutes of Executive Sessions*, pp. 102-4; Seabury, *Intermed. Report*, pp. 174-75; "Seabury Minutes," pp. 9, 636 ff.

[6] The Hofstadter Committee suggested a council consisting of Mayor, Comptroller, and 15 Councilmen, elected from two districts (Manhattan-Bronx and Brooklyn-Queens-Richmond), as well as small borough councils elected by P. R. *Mun. Ref. Lib. Notes*, XIX (Feb. 1, 1933), 17-19; *Nat. Mun. Rev.*, XXII (Feb., 1933), 71-72, 79; Joseph D. McGoldrick, "Proposals for the Reorganization of the Government of the City of New York," *Am. Pol. Sci. Rev.*, XXVII (1933), 337; Seabury, *Final Report*, p. 18 ff.; *Hofstadter Committee*, pp. 8-18, 29-33.

couraged by these developments, the reformers launched a vigorous charter campaign. The City Affairs Committee appealed to the general public through mass meetings, "flying squadrons" of orators, and addresses from the pulpit. The City Party, an outgrowth of the Committee of One Thousand, proselyted the civic organizations.[7]

But all hopes for charter reform were dashed by the Legislature. The Hofstadter Committee's plans were introduced by the principal author of its report, Assemblyman Moffat, the Seabury proposals by Senator Desmond. Neither passed. As a last resort a group of civic societies drafted an amendment to the Home Rule Law, permitting the voters themselves to create a local charter commission by petition. Somehow opposition from up-state Republicans and the city's Democratic contingent was surmounted in the Assembly. In the Democratic-controlled Senate, however, even a special message of endorsement from Governor Lehman was ineffective. The message was never read and the measure died in the closing hours of the session.[8]

Having thwarted charter changes which threatened its stranglehold on the Board of Aldermen, Tammany proposed a counter-reformation. A local law was pushed through the Municipal Assembly placing on the ballot a referendum to authorize the Mayor to appoint a charter commission. It was charged that this measure, giving the voters the alternative of a Tammany charter or no revision at all, was designed to frustrate rather than promote real reform.[9] Earlier in the year a commission

[7] W. Kingsland Macy to George H. Hallett, February 19, 1932; *New York Legislative Documents, 1932: Extraordinary Session,* XX, Document No. 1 (Dec. 9, 1932), 5-6; *Public Papers of Herbert H. Lehman, 1933* (Albany, 1934), pp. 14-15; City Affairs Committee, *Press Releases on Matters Related to the Administration and Finances of the City of New York,* January 1, 4, February 13, March 25, 1933; *Reports Adopted by Second Session of Civic Conference on Charter Revision* (N. Y.: City Party, 1933), *passim.*

[8] *New York Times,* March 22, April 7, 1933; *Twenty-Ninth Annual Report of the Committee on Legislation of the Citizens Union* (New York, 1933), pp. 15-17; *New York Legislative Documents, 1933,* XX, Document No. 1; *Nat. Mun. Rev.,* XXII, 48, 186-87, 244-45, 256.

[9] It was common knowledge that Mayor O'Brien never displayed independence in his appointments. Asked whom he would name Police Commissioner, he blurted out: "I don't know. I haven't got the word yet." Allen, *Our Fair City,* p. 49.

chosen by Mayor O'Brien had given the existing charter sweeping endorsement—their only suggestion for the Board of Aldermen had been transfer of authority to inspect electric signs. When the voters rejected both Mayor O'Brien and his charter proposition in the 1933 elections, the whole scheme collapsed.[10]

For almost a year charter reform had been stalemated. The O'Brien administration had effected scattered changes, none drastic.[11] In the 1933 elections, however, the Fusion slate pledged itself to general charter revision, including a new city council that would give minorities fair representation. The Fusion victory that fall gave the reform movement a flllip. When the Board of Aldermen convened in 1934 its new presiding officer informed the assemblage it was an "outworn institution."[12]

Once again advocates of charter revision converged upon the state legislature. After prolonged negotiations, the city administration and legislative leaders agreed on a Commission to draft a charter and refer its work to the people. The Democrats, however, were anxious to balk charter revision without outraging public opinion. As the 1934 session was ending they thrashed about in the Assembly in a series of frantic maneuvres that almost killed the bill. Only the last-minute intervention of Governor Lehman saved the Commission.[13]

Two unusual features of the law were provision for separate submission to the voters of any proposals for P. R. and the nam-

10 *Mun. Ass. Rec.*, IX, No. 10, 3; *Preliminary Report of Charter Revision Committee Appointed by Hon. John P. O'Brien, Mayor* (New York, 1933), pp. 3, 18; *City Aff. Comm. Press Releases*, November 28, 1932, April 24, Nov. 4, 1933; *New York Times*, May 22, 1933; *Mun. Ref. Lib. Notes*, XIX (November 15, 1933), 83.

11 Of these, only the executive budget, giving the Mayor responsibility for budget preparation, and a capital outlay budget for public improvement projects, impinged on the work of the Board of Aldermen. At that, the latter was suspended until November 30, 1935.

12 *Has Tammany Reformed?*, *passim*; *Proc. of Bd. of Ald. and Mun. Ass., Ald. Br., 1933*, I, 1441-47; *ibid.*, 1934, I, 9; *New York Times*, November 5, 1933; Tanzer, *New York City Charter,* p. 82; *Address by Samuel Seabury before the Proportional Representation League, November 25, 1935*, p. 5.

13 *Thirtieth Ann. Rep. of Comm. on Leg. of Cit. Un.*, pp. 11-14; Russell McInnes, "New York Legislature Again Impedes a Progressive Governor," *Nat. Mun. Rev.*, XXIII (1934), 386-87; Geo. H. Hallett, *The Legislature and Charter Revision* (Radio Address over Station WOR, April 28, 1934).

ing of the commissioners in the act itself. Opponents of charter reform reasoned that even if a new charter were adopted, P. R. could be beaten if referred separately; reformers also welcomed the clause on the theory that some who favored revision but opposed P. R. would be induced to vote for a new charter. But Mayor and charter revisionists alike had grave misgivings about the Tammany-selected majority on the Commission. Two months after it had started work, its Chairman, ex-Governor Smith, confirmed their worst fears. Resigning in a huff, he condemned that majority as "stowaways who were put on board with monkey wrenches to throw into the machinery to scuttle the ship."[14] Vice Chairman Samuel Seabury was more explicit. He charged that—

> The very pen which drew the legislation took pains to insert into it the names of commissioners who would prevent any real benefit accruing to the people of this city from it. The politicians contrived to load the commission with sufficient machine men to make sure that the balance of power was in their hands and that any serious attempt at improvement could be checkmated by them.[15]

Meetings of the Commission were stormy; arguments turned into fights. "There was thundering and yelling and out-yelling," declared Richard S. Childs, "so that at times our proceedings must have been audible out in Foley Square." It is hard to see how a document satisfactory to all parties could have been drafted. Neither Governor Smith nor the Tammany faction exhibited genuine openmindedness. In the end, worn out by endless bickering, advocates of substantial revision quit in despair (Alfred E. Smith, Samuel Seabury, Mrs. George E. Wyeth, George Brockaw Compton, James Marshall, and Charles H. Tuttle). Judge Seabury bitterly reproached the majority:

> This group from the very commencement engaged in a series of . . . filibustering tactics. Every expedient for delay was availed of. . . . It was obvious that they were not amenable to reason, that they were not interested in the merits of the questions presented, and that they had a single desire, to wit: to perpetuate a governmental structure under

[14] McCaffrey, "Prop. Rep. in N. Y. C.," *Am. Pol. Sci. Rev.*, XXXIII, 842; *Nat. Mun. Rev.*, XXIII, 268-69; *New York Times*, August 7, 1934.

[15] *New York Times*, August 9, 1934.

which every existing opportunity for graft, patronage, and misgovernment would be retained.[16]

The Commission reorganized and offered to carry on, but Mayor La Guardia vetoed their plans. Judge Seabury, for whom he had the highest regard, advised that the rump body was "merely the mask behind which the safe Tammany majority would see to it that nothing worth while was accomplished." The Mayor observed to Richard S. Childs, the new chairman, that the Commission resembled a small-town girl with a tarnished reputation. No matter how stainless her actual conduct, her usefulness in that community was ended.[17]

The commission wrote no charter, but its deliberations produced one tangible result—an opportunity to cut superfluous jobs from municipal payrolls. As Governor, Alfred E. Smith had promoted a more efficient state government; as Chairman of the charter commission the elder statesman sincerely desired a charter that would bear his name. He proposed an amendment to the State Constitution to authorize consolidation of county offices, saw it through the commission, and persuaded Governor Lehman to call a special session of the Legislature to save a year. (Constitutional amendments in New York require legislative approval for two successive years, then acceptance by the voters.) Endorsed overwhelmingly at the polls, the amendment offered partial relief for the city's financial problems. But political machines rest on patronage, and elimination of placeholders threatened their power. Hence bills to implement the measure were bottled up in committee, first in the Board of Aldermen, later in the City Council. Eventually civic associations carried out the

[16] *New York Times*, August 9, 1934. Norman Thomas acknowledged that "it was apparent from the beginning that some members of the commission wanted no revision or very little revision of the charter. In some cases their motive was doubtless loyalty to a particular organization." Yet he believed the resignations had taken place "without exhausting every possibility . . . of reaching some agreement." *New York Times*, August 10, 1934.

[17] *Minutes of Meetings of New York City Charter Commission*, August 7, August 9, 1934; *New York Times*, August 9, 1934; *Nat. Mun. Rev.*, XXIII, 477; Interview with Richard S. Childs, March 9, 1949.

reform by initiative and referendum, charter innovations introduced by a later commission.[18]

Viewed in retrospect, the Commission's work did influence the later course of charter revision. Almost unanimously, civic societies had advocated the city manager plan under a one-house legislature, elected by P. R. The manager plan was rejected without discussion, despite the presence of its intellectual father, Richard S. Childs, on the Commission. ("A snap decision," complained Mr. Childs). In considering the city legislature the Commission ran against a snag; indeed, that was one of the questions on which it foundered. After a month's debate it voted in favor of a Board of Estimate and Council. But the commissioners could not agree on the duties of the Board of Estimate, for they had become embroiled in a dispute over borough autonomy. As for the Council, Judge Seabury regarded it as the same old Board of Aldermen, dressed up with a new name and reduced personnel, but "lacking any powers worthy of a legislative body." The one ray of hope was the determination to honor the Legislature's mandate and submit P. R. separately. Most Commissioners opposed P. R., however, and their decision could hardly be construed as a positive recommendation. Discouraged by this experience, the reformers were disposed to settle for something less than the full program of the National Municipal League's Model City Charter.[19]

During the Commission's deliberations these civic associations discovered they could perform a vital role in mobilizing public interest. Apart from their own spokesmen, attendance at public hearings, even on the most controversial subjects, was meager. Both major parties disregarded the original public sessions of the subcommittee on P. R.; there was great difficulty in gaining expressions of opinion from representative groups. Clearly

18 *Minutes of Meetings of N. Y. C. Chart. Comm.*, May 25-July 17, 1934; *Nat. Mun. Rev.*, XXIII, 389, 411-12, 443-44, 457-58; *The Cost of the Administration of County Government in the City of New York* (New York, 1934), p. 251 ff.; *The Searchlight*, XXV, No. 3, 7; Smith, *Citizen and His Govt.*, p. 247.

19 *Nat. Mun. Rev.*, XXIII, 330-31, 389-90, 398, 444-45, 485; *Minutes of Charter Comm.*, June 26-August 2, 1934.

an educational campaign was needed to overcome public inertia.[20]

The successors of the Smith Commission did accept one of its basic decisions—to draw up a "skeleton" outline of government and relegate details governing the municipal departments to an administrative code. A compound of prior revisions, piecemeal amendments, and the "incrustation of a generation of interpretations by the courts and corporation counsels," the existing charter was an oversize document, big as a telephone book. Even trained lawyers were perplexed by this confused mass of law. Well might the Thacher Commission take pride in reducing the city's fundamental law to a brief and simple grant of power which any intelligent citizen could understand. Under Reuben A. Lazarus, who had served as Associate Counsel to the Smith Commission, the Board of Statutory Consolidation performed the heroic task of analyzing the accumulated disorder of thousands of pages of detailed regulations and preparing a simple, up-to-date administrative code to supplement the structural framework of the new charter and guide the work of the administrative departments.[21]

An invaluable legacy to its successor was the Smith Commission's counsel. Furnishing the Commission with authoritative data for their deliberations and incorporating their decisions into a charter harmonious with the laws of the State called for a scholar thoroughly grounded in political institutions, a skillful billdrafter, and an expert on constitutional law. Governor Smith and Judge Seabury persuaded Professor Joseph P. Chamberlain, Director of the Legislative Drafting Fund at Columbia University, to serve. When the Thacher Commission commenced its

[20] *Minutes of Chart. Comm.*, July 17, July 19, 1934; *New York Times*, July 10, 1934; Roy V. Peel and Paul Studenski, *A New Charter for New York City* (New York, 1934), p. 4.

[21] *Min. of Chart. Comm.*, June 12, 1934; Rankin, *N. Y. Advancing: 1934-35*, p. 356; Tanzer, *N. Y. C. Charter*, pp. 17-21, 486, 523-25; *Report of Special Committee on Reorganization of City Government to the Board of Directors of the Merchants' Association of New York*, February 2, 1933; *Statement of the Hon. Thomas D. Thacher, New York Times*, November 1, 1936; Reuben A. Lazarus, "A New Administrative Code for New York City," *Nat. Mun. Rev.*, XXVII (1938), 92-95.

work the following year a capable staff and the fruits of their research had already been assembled. At that time Lawrence A. Tanzer, a leading authority on home rule, became Associate Counsel, and Mrs. Norman S. Goetz, a volunteer worker of unusual industry and ability, assistant secretary.[22]

The Smith Commission had dissolved during a special session of the Legislature. Then a "political miracle" occurred. At the Governor's urging, the Legislature unanimously authorized the appointment of a new Charter Commission. The reformers could hardly ask for more—a wieldy body appointed by a Fusion Mayor and recognition of the principle of Home Rule. Why did the Democrats shift their strategy? With an election impending, they were hardly disposed to buck public opinion, which favored charter revision. On the other hand they believed Mayor La Guardia could not fulfill his promise to draft a new charter and that he would be discredited in the attempt. Later they realized how seriously they had miscalculated. At this period Tammany leadership was at a low ebb.[23]

During his first administration Mayor La Guardia made a number of distinguished appointments. The new Commission was no exception. Governor Lehman had suggested a "truly representative" body of commissioners of "character and attainments that would command the respect of all residents of the city." His recommendation was scrupulously fulfilled. The commission was comprised of Republicans, Democrats, and a Socialist, culled from all five boroughs. It balanced the President of the Chamber of Commerce and a real estate operator, Thomas I. Parkinson and Charles G. Meyer, with a Socialist lawyer and a past champion of labor, S. John Block and Justice

[22] *Min. of Chart. Comm.*, June 19, 1934; Lucille J. Buchanan, "The New York City Charter Commission" (New York, 1934), 3-4; Tanzer, *N. Y. C. Charter,* pp. 475-76; Genevieve B. Earle, *Reminiscences* (Oral History Project, Columbia University, 1950), p. 24. The Institute of Public Administration also helped with a comparative study of European municipal governments. Luther Gulick to Thomas I. Parkinson, January 18, 1936; Sarah Greer and Lawrence Chamberlain, *Outline of Governmental Organization within the Cities of London, Paris, and Berlin* (New York, 1935).

[23] *Nat. Mun. Rev.*, XXIII, 477; *30th Ann. Rep. of Comm. on Leg.*, p. 37; Rankin, *N. Y. Advancing*, p. 355; *Address by S. Seabury*, p. 4; Tanzer, *N. Y. C. Charter*, pp. 519-22.

Frederick L. Hackenberg. An impressive array of legal talent was prepared to grapple with thorny constitutional questions—Judge Thomas D. Thacher, President of the city's Association of the Bar, Charles E. Hughes, Jr., son of the Chief Justice of the United States, and Justice Joseph M. Proskauer, a former member of Governor Smith's Kitchen Cabinet. One of the most valuable members was Professor Joseph D. McGoldrick, whose incumbency as City Comptroller had transformed him from a keen student of municipal affairs to a seasoned expert. He was given the responsibility of drafting the financial aspects of the new charter, and most of the fiscal reforms embodied his ideas. The civic associations were ably represented by Mrs. Genevieve B. Earle, Executive Secretary of the Women's City Club, who later spent a dozen years in the legislature she had helped devise.[24]

Taking up its tasks in May, the Smith Commission had worked at breakneck speed in order to submit a charter in the fall elections. The Thacher Commission proceeded more deliberately. At the outset every shade of public opinion was given an opportunity to be heard in public hearings or through written briefs. Then followed a year of intensive but quiet study. Realizing that no intelligent revision was possible without first-hand knowledge of the operation of the city government, they called upon presiding officers and party leaders of past Boards of Aldermen, municipal administrators, and other qualified witnesses. From their executive meetings emerged a preliminary charter draft, which was subjected to public hearings. After revising their tentative charter in the light of public discussion, the Commission saw it submitted at the polls in November, 1936, almost two years after they had been appointed.[25]

The reformation of the Board of Aldermen was almost in-

[24] *Mun. Ref. Lib. Notes*, XXI (March 13, 1935), 17-18; Isaacs, *Oath of Devotion*, p. 120; Earle, *Reminiscences*, p. 24. Adverse criticism of the Commission may be found in the *N. Y. Post*, September 25, 1936 and Allen, *Why Tammanies Revive*, p. 111.

[25] Tanzer, *op. cit.*, pp. 4-5, 474-75; Rankin, *N. Y. Advancing*, pp. 356-58; "Charter Revision" (Dialogue delivered by Mrs. Harry Whitney and Mrs. John Philip Cunningham over Station WHN, Dec. 28, 1935); *Nat. Mun. Rev.*, XXIV (1935), 184.

evitable. "No single feature of the city government has been subject to such severe and unanimous criticism," reported the Charter Commission. It was almost universally agreed that its size was too cumbrous, its constituencies too small. A mere diminution in numbers, however, fell far short of the reformers' objectives. Could a "crying evil and a longstanding disgrace" be eliminated merely by cutting it in half?[26]

Civic societies submitted the self-same recommendations as the previous year: to replace the Board of Aldermen and Board of Estimate with a unicameral body elected by P. R.,[27] and a city manager, chosen by the Council, to act as administrative head of the city. A titular mayor, appointed by the Council, would preside over the city legislature. There was little hope that the manager plan would be adopted, but prospects for a single-chambered legislature and P. R. seemed brighter. Mayor La Guardia leaned toward these changes and Judge Seabury had sponsored them in the Smith Commission. "Proportional representation may mean all the difference between sustained good government year in and year out," declared Seabury, "and a spasm of reform once in a generation." [28]

As anticipated, the commission quickly vetoed the council-manager plan. Three years before Professor McGoldrick had been perturbed by pleas for concentrating legislative and administrative responsibility in a single council. The Commissioners accepted his viewpoint and his arguments. For New York, they wrote, it involved dangers "too grave to risk." Exciting mayoralty campaigns stimulate an interest in municipal politics that a score of councilmanic contests can never match. Then there was the problem of finding a suitable manager for

[26] Tanzer, *N. Y. C. Charter,* p. 487; "The Central Government of the City" (Memorandum prepared for the Charter Commission by Professor Joseph P. Chamberlain and Lawrence A. Tanzer, June 3, 1935) and Communication of the Rev. John Haynes Holmes to Hon. Thomas D. Thacher, December 16, 1935 (*N. Y. C. Charter Commission Documents,* Vol. IV).

[27] Non-partisan ballots, borough-wide districts, and a fixed quota were suggested.

[28] Cf. Buchanan, *N. Y. C. Chart. Comm. of 1934* and *The Searchlight,* XXV No. 1 (1935), 1; *New York Times,* August 17, 1934, February 20, 1935; Richard S. Childs, "New York City Elections as a Problem in Political Science," *National Municipal Review,* XXIV (1935), 25-26; *Address by S. Seabury,* pp. 6, 10.

the nation's biggest city. Perhaps the most powerful objection at the moment was that P. R. would be submitted separately. If the manager plan were adopted and P. R. rejected at the polls, Tammany would be assured an automatic majority in the Council, and the city administration permanently handed over to it.[29]

Whether to retain two deliberative bodies or to merge them into a single chamber presented a more troublesome problem. Critics of the Board of Estimate and Apportionment maintained that the Borough Presidents, who comprised most of its membership, represented mere local areas. Being "borough-minded," they were hardly concerned with the welfare of the entire city. Again, the Borough Presidents who expended the city's funds as local administrators appropriated those very funds in the Board of Estimate. Hence the larger interests of the city were overlooked; log-rolling and back-scratching were the rule.[30]

The Commission based its decision on its concept of a municipality's functions. A legislature may shape policies for the entire state, they held, but the governing house of a city is concerned largely with administrative functions—the authorization of capital expenditures, the granting of franchises, or the location of public buildings. In the daily conduct of the modern municipality's business, policies "too important or too doubtful to be left to the decisions of a single, executive head, and not sufficiently general and fundamental to be suited to the deliberations of a representative assembly" could be handled most effectively by a small group of representative and responsible officials. They saw little fundamental difference between the controlling board of a private corporation and a municipal business directorate, save the enormity and complexity of the latter's problems. In

[29] Joseph D. McGoldrick, "Is the City Manager Plan Suitable for New York?" *Nat. Mun. Rev.*, XXI (1932), 291-92; Chamberlain and Tanzer, "Central Govt. of the City; Memorandum of Conclusions Reached by Commission at Its Meeting Held May 23, 1935"; Tanzer, *op. cit.*, p. 486; Remarks of Commissioners Hughes, Block and McGoldrick during testimony of Richard S. Childs, June 6, 1935; Interview with Richard S. Childs, March 9, 1949.

[30] *Monthly Bulletin of the Chamber of Commerce of the State of New York*, XXVIII (1936), 37; Testimony of Mayor F. H. La Guardia, May 9, 1935; Testimony of Gov. Alfred E. Smith, May 28, 1935.

this capacity the Board of Estimate and Apportionment had served New York exceptionally well.[31]

A compelling reason for preserving two chambers was the realization that the charter would be submitted at the polls. The borough autonomy issue had shipwrecked the Smith Commission and the Thacher Commission could founder on it as well. Retaining the borough presidents on the Board of Estimate forestalled criticism that the outlying boroughs were being deprived of representation in the city government. Again, there was the circumstance that P. R. would be presented separately. Arguments for a unicameral legislature rested on the premise that P. R. would assure the election of a thoroughly representative body. But what if the charter were adopted and P. R. rejected?[32] While the charter was pending Chairman Thacher explained the commission's reasoning:

> We had to propose a charter which would serve the City's interests with or without proportional representation. If proportional representation is voted down next fall, what alternative could we have proposed for the election of such a (unicameral) council? There are only three that can be imagined: either an election of twenty councillors or more on a city-wide ballot so long that no voter at the polls, except a few, would know more than two or three of the men that they were voting for; or a ballot on a borough-wide basis, which would have the same evil, though not to the same extent . . . ; or election by districts . . . , as the Board of Aldermen are now elected. This Commission could not in conscience propose any such consolidation of powers in a council chosen by any of these methods of election. If that had been done and proportional representation rejected, the adoption of the charter would have delivered the City for generations to some body, boots and breeches to the dominant political organization, and the people in the street wouldn't have known how to get rid of that domination.[33]

Having made its decision the commission undertook to remedy existing defects in the Board of Estimate. It sought to pre-

[31] *Bull. of Chamb. of Comm.*, XXVIII, 36; Chamberlain and Tanzer, "Cent. Govt. of the City;" Remarks of Commissioners Thacher, Proskauer and McGoldrick during testimony of Governor Smith, May 28, 1935; Tanzer, *op. cit.*, p. 488; Joseph M. Proskauer, *A Segment of My Times* (New York, 1950), p. 174.

[32] Testimony of Mayor LaGuardia, May 9, 1935; Statement by Judge Proskauer during testimony of Gov. Smith, May 28, 1935; Tanzer, *op. cit.*, p. 492.

[33] *Bull. of Chamb. of Comm.*, XXVIII, 38.

vent log-rolling inspired by local interests by "confronting the (local) representatives with the interests of the public at large." For this purpose a Planning Commission was created to plan and budget the city's permanent improvements. Capital expenditures unauthorized by this independent body could originate in the Board of Estimate only with the approval of twelve votes. Hence two members elected by the city at large, men who saw "the interest of the city as a whole," could check back-scratching among the Borough Presidents.[34] Some of its members regarded the newly created custodian of the city's future as the commission's outstanding achievement. In urging adoption of the charter, Professor McGoldrick reported they were "practically willing to let their case rest on the creation of the City Planning Commission." [35]

If two chambers were to be retained, a clear line of demarcation between the functions of both bodies would have to be drawn. In a haphazard way the Board of Estimate had been gradually taking over administrative duties performed by the aldermen. The result was a crazy quilt pattern of jurisdiction, confusing even to experts in municipal government.[36]

In redistributing authority the commissioners sought to make the Board of Estimate the "heart and soul of business control and management" of the city, vesting it with broad, semi-executive powers. It retained decisive control over the budget, appropriations, and franchises; as board of directors of the municipal corporation it gained exclusive control over borrowings, contracts, and salaries not fixed by law. The new charter divested the Board of Aldermen of the last of its administrative functions. Too often had these been employed to mend the fences of individual aldermen. Aldermanic power to authorize

[34] The three city-wide officials in the Board of Estimate (Mayor, Comptroller, and President of the Council) have three votes each; the five Borough Presidents seven among them.

[35] Tanzer, *op. cit.*, pp. 81-82, 482-84, 492-98; *Bull. of Chamb. of Comm.*, XXVIII, 39; Fritz M. Marx, *Elements of Public Administration* (New York, 1947), pp. 128-29; *New York Times*, October 2, 1936.

[36] Newbold Morris, "Advantages of the New City Council over the Old Board of Aldermen," *Flatbush Magazine*, XVI, No. 9 (1938), 1, 6; *Cent. Govt. of the City.*

contracts over $1,000 without public letting had afforded the Committee on Public Letting a first-rate opportunity to exchange favors with department heads, while authority to fix grades and salaries of public employees had enabled the legislators to apply pressure on the commissioners to fulfill sundry requests for their constituents.[37]

Like the Charter Commission of 1900, which had attempted to make the Board of Aldermen the "real director of local policy," the Thacher Commission sought to cloak the board's successor with full legislative power. Following the principle of divorcing administrative and legislative functions, it established a new City Council as the sole municipal legislative body under the Home Rule Law. The artificial distinction between ordinances enacted by the Board of Aldermen and local laws passed by the Municipal Assembly was eliminated; henceforth all legislation would be by local law. Only the City Council could initiate and pass local laws,[38] with the proviso that charter amendments or laws touching on the administration of municipal affairs or the structure of city departments required approval of the Board of Estimate.[39]

Separation of administrative and legislative functions also dictated exclusion of executive officers from the legislature. The department heads lost their voice and borough presidents their vote in the new City Council. This, in turn, meant a more cosy and less cluttered chamber during legislative sessions.[40]

It was a foregone conclusion that the city legislature would be more compact—almost everyone conceded that the Board of Aldermen was too large and unwieldy. Enlarging the legislative districts, the commissioners believed, would attract men of broad

[37] *Bull. of Chamb. of Comm.*, XXVIII, 37; Reuben A. Lazarus, "The Council: Origin, History, Evolution" (Typewritten copy of address delivered at the College of the City of New York, November 18, 1941), p. 4; Tanzer, *op. cit.*, pp. 46-50, 111-13, 480-81, 488; "Memorandum on Conclusions Reached by New York Charter Commission at Meeting Held June 4, 1935."

[38] Like national laws, local laws were to be subject to the Mayor's veto; but a two-thirds vote of the Council could re-pass them over his veto.

[39] In some cases charter amendments also required a referendum. Tanzer, *op. cit.*, pp. 27, 40-44, 480, 488-91, 514; Lazarus, "The Council," p. 5; "Cent. Govt. of the City."

[40] Tanzer, *op. cit.*, pp. 28, 45, 489.

vision and stature, thereby enhancing the City Council's dignity and usefulness. Early in their deliberations they had agreed that a maximum of thirty councilmen, elected from borough-wide constituencies, would produce a body small enough to operate expeditiously, yet large enough to represent all the chief interest groups in the community. No final decision could be reached, however, because the question of P. R. had to be submitted separately. Eventually two alternatives were presented. If P. R. were approved, the borough would become the constituency, with one councilman for every 75,000 valid ballots.[41] (Had aldermen been elected under these rules in 1935, 23 would have been elected). If P. R. were rejected, the legislators would be elected from State Senate districts. Unfortunately, there had been no state reapportionment since 1917. To provide the boroughs of Brooklyn, Queens, and the Bronx with their equitable share of representatives, each would be granted three councilmen at large, pending reapportionment.[42] This alternative provided for 32 councilmen. In either case, Staten Island would have one representative.[43]

No charter proposal was acclaimed more enthusiastically by reformers than P. R. The Citizens Union regarded it as the "chance of a lifetime to escape from political despotism and establish true representative government." Officially the Commission preserved strict neutrality on the subject; indeed, they never formally canvassed the question among themselves. The state legislature had stipulated that P. R. could be adopted along

[41] A remainder of 50,000 or more valid ballots would entitle a borough to an additional Councilman.

[42] The original charter draft provided for two Councilmen at large for each of these boroughs. At public hearings in the spring of 1936 the Commission was convinced that three apiece would be more appropriate. Cf. Section 22 in *Preliminary Report and Draft of Proposed Charter for the City of New York, Published by the New York City Charter Revision Commission, April 27, 1936*, and *Proposed Charter for the City of New York, Filed with the City Clerk on August 17, 1936 and Report of the New York City Charter Revision Commission.*

[43] Tanzer, *op. cit.*, pp. 27-30, 479, 487-89; Chamberlain and Tanzer, "Cent. Govt. of the City;" Statement of Chairman Thacher in *New York Times*, November 1, 1936; Remarks of Commissioner Block during testimony of Gov. Smith, May 28, 1935; *The Searchlight*, XXVI, No. 1 (1936), 4; "Minutes of Executive Meeting of Charter Commission, November 12, 1935.

with the charter if submitted separately; the commission voted unanimously to respect this mandate. Later it became apparent that a majority, but not a unanimous majority, had favored P. R.[44]

What form of P. R. should be employed? Civic associations were dismayed by reports that Mayor La Guardia was advocating the party list system, a plan widely used on the European continent. This method, under which voters ballot for a list of candidates without expressing a preference for individuals, had long been rejected by proportionalists, who maintained that it failed to eliminate machine control of politics or to promote a discriminating selection of nominees. With the exception of the Communist Party, which favored a version of the list system used by the ill-starred Weimar Republic, all civic parties or groups interested in P. R. approved the Hare Plan, which allowed the elector unrestricted choice of candidates and permitted him to cross party lines freely. Their preference was respected; the Hare Plan, which has been employed almost exclusively in English-speaking countries, was adopted.[45]

Devising a practical system of P. R. posed a difficult problem. Some Commissioners suggested authorizing the first City Council to implement the plan, following general principles they themselves would outline. In the end, a complete system, with all details necessary to hold an actual P. R. election, was threshed out. It was only natural that the commission employ the broad experience of Dr. Hallett, the leading authority on P. R., and this part of the charter was drafted under his guidance. Lawyers of

[44] Judge Proskauer vehemently denounced P. R. while Dr. Hallett was testifying in its behalf, November 12, 1935. During a campaign for repeal of P. R. in 1940, Commissioners Thacher, Earle, McGoldrick, Hughes, and Block publicly defended it. *The Searchlight*, XXVI, No. 1, 3; Holmes to Thacher, December 16, 1935; Tanzer, *op. cit.*, pp. 479, 521; *Bull. of Chamb. of Comm.*, XXVIII, 38; *Prop. Rep.: What It Is and How It Works in N. Y. C.*, pp. 13, 33; "Minutes of Executive Meeting of Chart. Comm.," April 21, 1936.

[45] *P. R. Review*, No. 59 (July 21, 1921), 43-46; George H. Hallett to Thacher, November 12, 1935; Communication of Merchants' Association to Charter Revision Commission, December 17, 1935; Richard S. Childs, President of the City Club, to Chairman Thacher, January 20, 1936.

the Citizens Union and the Merchants' Association also contributed their services.[46]

These and other civic groups realized that the Commission could hardly accept all their recommendations without imperiling the charter at the polls. The Merchants' Association stated the case cogently:

> While we believe that a charter based on the . . . city manager plan, with p.r. used as a method of electing a representative body, would be the best form of government for the city, we recognized that would be almost a revolutionary step and that it is reasonable to take the position that it is better to advance toward the goal of better municipal government by shorter and more certain steps than to risk the continuation of the present cumbersome and antiquated machinery in an attempt to make too much progress at one time.[47]

At the same time they sought to leave the door open for future reforms, such as extending the powers of the City Council, if the experiment with P. R. proved successful. Time and again hostile majorities in the city legislature had proven an insuperable barrier to constructive reform; hence they proposed by-passing the new City Council entirely. Acceding to their demands, the commission introduced the initiative for charter amendments. Proposals for changing the method of election, abolishing offices, or creating new ones could be placed on the ballot for referendum by a petition signed by 50,000 voters. With this innovation the reformers were assured that their full program could be adopted "when the people were ready." Along with P. R. it helped reconcile them to the new charter.[48]

The commission realized that their determinations would set the framework of the city's government for a generation. Whatever the merits of the charter, however, their work would come to naught if it were not ratified by the voters. What was the most auspicious time to present it? The authorizing statute specified either a general election or a special city election. Pro-

[46] "Minutes of Executive Meetings of Chart. Comm.," March 24, 31, June 11, July 15, 22, 1936; Hallett to Thacher, June 11, 1936.

[47] Merchants' Association to Thacher, December 17, 1936.

[48] Hallett to Thacher, December 24, 1935; Tanzer, *N. Y. C. Charter*, pp. 202-3, 486, 514-16; George H. Hallett, "Giving the Charter Back to the People" (Radio Address over Station WNYC, May 26, 1936); *New York Times*, April 29, 1936.

fessor Chamberlain, counsel to the commission, reported that past experience proved that special elections attracted only a small portion of the electorate; on such occasions the machine vote counted heavily. Hence the commission decided to submit the charter at the general elections of 1936, when the electors of the city would turn out *en masse* to vote for a President.[49]

Throughout most of 1935, when the Commission was pursuing its exhaustive study of the city's government, it had dropped out of sight. Disinclined to direct the charter campaign themselves, the Commissioners were intensely concerned, nevertheless, about the need for reawakening interest and educating the public on the merits of the new charter. Fortunately the civic associations had promised "aggressive support." [50]

Seizing their long-awaited opportunity, the charter revisionists plunged into the campaign with remarkable fervor and zeal. For tactical reasons, conservatives who favored the new charter but distrusted P. R. were organized into a Citizens Charter Campaign Committee, headed by Judge Morgan J. O'Brien, a former Tammany sachem. The labor element and borough autonomists who were more enthusiastic about P. R. than the charter formed a Proportional Representation Committee, led by Dr. Henry Moscowitz, a former associate of Governor Smith. In practice the two groups blended efforts for a common victory. Few channels for reaching public opinion were overlooked. A corps of trained speakers delivered scores of radio addresses. Hundreds of public meetings were held. More than 2,000,000 pieces of campaign literature were distributed—even cartoons were created and fed to the press. Enthusiastically assisted by the important city-wide civic organizations and supported almost unanimously by the metropolitan daily newspapers, the reformers overcame the distractions of the state and national campaigns and gained the initiative.[51]

[49] "Minutes of Executive Meeting of Chart. Comm.," January 30, 1936; Address by Chairman Thacher to Lawyers Club, May 28, 1936 (*N. Y. C. Chart. Comm. Docs.*, IV); Tanzer, *N. Y. C. Charter*, p. 521.

[50] Whitney and Cunningham, *Charter Revision; Nat. Mun. Rev.*, XXV (1936), 736; Hallett to Thacher, June 1, 1936.

[51] *Nat. Mun. Rev.*, XXV (1936), 376-77, 627-28, 680, 736-37; William J. Schieffelin, "P. R. Thwarts Machine Politicians," *Readers Digest*, XXXI (1937), 44-45; Schieffelin, "P. R. and New Yorkers," *Survey Graphic*, XXVI, 385.

Powerful aid came from the political parties that had been consistently under-represented in the Board of Aldermen. With the exception of the Communists, the minority parties supported the new charter enthusiastically. Originally cool to charter reform, the Republicans eventually saw the light. Just before election orders were issued by Kenneth Simpson, Republican leader of New York County, that the clubhouse "boys" were to range themselves with the "forces of righteousness" against the "forces of corruption." Naturally Mayor La Guardia's Fusion administration backed a charter which struck at Tammany's interests.[52]

As the campaign opened, Tammany saw no cause for alarm. Charter revision had been balked for years; with proper maneuvring it could be staved off again. Certainly it presented no dangers if it never reached the ballot. Late in August a truck driver who happened to be a member of a Democratic club decided to hire an expensive lawyer to institute action for wiping the charter and P. R. off the voting machines that fall. The Supreme Court barred both questions—some called it a political decision.[53] But when the Court of Appeals reversed the opinion in October, the organization was caught flat-footed. A tardy but vigorous campaign was organized to stem the rising tide in favor of P. R. and mandatory instructions were sent to the clubhouse element to "kill the charter."[54]

They came too late. The new charter carried decisively—959,519 to 603,072, with an affirmative majority in 59 out of the city's 62 assembly districts. P. R. was voted in by an even greater margin—923,186 to 555,127. What made the results

[52] *Nat. Mun. Rev.*, XXV, 680; Limpus and Leyson, *This Man La Guardia*, pp. 399-400, 403-4; *P. R.: What It Is and How It Works in N. Y. C.*, p. 36; Interview with Manhattan Republican district leader, May 21, 1948 (Confidential source).

[53] *New York Post*, September 25, 1936.

[54] *Nat. Mun. Rev.*, XXV, 621-22, 680, 736; Limpus and Leyson, *op. cit.*, p. 400; Tanzer, *op. cit.*, pp. 7-9; *Am. Pol. Sci. Rev.*, XXXIII, 843-45; *Matter of Mooney v. Cohen*, 272 N. Y. 33; Remittitur Amended, 272 N. Y. 597 (1936); *New York World-Telegram*, November 3, 1936; Interview with Dr. George H. McCaffrey, Assistant Campaign Manager of Citizens Charter Campaign Committee, October 30, 1947.

most impressive was the unusual number of preferences recorded. In the years 1931 to 1940 the electorate never expressed itself on public questions in greater numbers than in 1936. Never were more "yes" votes registered. There was a higher ratio of "yesses" for the P. R. option than in 78% of all other referenda during the decade, a higher ratio of affirmative votes for the charter than 83% of all other propositions.[55] Contemporary observers recognized the ratification of the charter as a "significant manifestation of the public will."[56]

In the face of these striking results, opponents of the charter have created the impression that the election was won by default. Notwithstanding the unprecedented campaign waged by reformers, one critic charged that the voters had "little information and less thought" on the subject. Immediately after election day, however, a local newspaper stated editorially: "Explanation, discussion, and support has been wide and thorough —worthy of the charter's high importance. No one can say either was voted blindly or from snap judgment."[57]

The triumph of the charter and P. R. were not altogether unexpected, but the margin of victory came as a distinct surprise. Aside from the enthusiastic campaign carried on by charter advocates, it was due partly to the wisdom of the Charter Commission, which composed internal differences to present a unanimous report. Again, P. R. offered an effective solution to the vexatious reapportionment problem (Brooklyn, which gained first place in number of Councilmen under P. R., voted for it almost 2 to 1. Staten Island, which lost two representatives, was the only borough to reject it).[58] Some of the opposition's most telling arguments had been that paper ballots would delay

[55] The proportions of "yesses" are based on total votes registered on the public counters. Since there was a referendum on a city matter in only one other year during the decade, the above statistics are based on the votes cast on both city and state questions. Tanzer, *op. cit.*, pp. 9-14; *Ann. Reports of Bd. of Elections in the City of N. Y., 1931-40, passim; Nat. Mun. Rev.*, XXV, 745-46.

[56] *New York Times*, November 15, 1936.

[57] Allen, *Why Tammanies Revive*, p. 48; *New York World-Telegram*, November 4, 1936.

[58] Actually Staten Island's representation dropped only from 4.6% of the Board of Aldermen to 3.8% of the first Council.

the count and make fraud possible. The answer was found, late in the campaign, when a P. R. voting machine was invented. Contrary to expectations, a heavier plurality was recorded for P. R. than the charter itself, partly because radical groups instructed their adherents to reject the charter but vote for the new electoral system. One observer accused the voters of going on a "yes-debauch." Curiously enough, this sneer contained an element of truth. On the same voting machine was an amendment giving firemen a three-platoon system. To ensure victory, the firemen, their families, and friends voted "yes" on every proposition.[59]

The proportionalists proclaimed their triumph the "greatest of the victories of P. R. in North America." Further to emphasize it, they pointed out that in 1936 Tammany yielded the Democratic presidential candidate a whopping majority, yet it was trounced on the charter issue. These are surface facts, wrenched out of context. Actually Tammany displayed veiled hostility toward the "Roosevelt brand of Democracy" that year. It was Mayor La Guardia, a supporter of *both* the President *and* the charter who was really close to the New Deal.[60]

It cannot be gainsaid that P. R. has made great strides in the United States during waves of reform. Richard S. Childs has pointed out that the revival of the P. R. League in 1909 was part and parcel of the Progressive movement, which sought to cure democracy's ailments by transforming our political institutions. In Cincinnati, where P. R. achieved its greatest triumph, its adoption in 1924 was blessed by Robert M. La Follette, whose Progressive Party workers gave it their enthusiastic support. After the Seabury investigations P. R. was openly linked to reform in New York. "The badge of liberalism was to favor P. R.; and the badge of conservatism was the other way," declared a member of the Smith Commission. It can hardly be denied that the citizens of New York who voted overwhelmingly for Presi-

[59] *New York Times,* November 4, 1936; *New York World-Telegram,* November 4, 1936; *Nat. Mun. Rev.,* XXV, 432; Schieffelin, "P. R. and New Yorkers," *Survey Graphic,* XXVI, 385; Allen, *Why Tammanies Revive,* p. 48.

[60] Hallett, *P. R.: Key to Democracy,* p. 147; Carter, *La Guardia,* 127; *New York World-Telegram,* November 10, 1936.

dent Roosevelt's program of "bold, persistent experimentation" were disposed to accept a new charter and P. R.[61] One newspaper hailed the public's approval of these innovations as New York's "own New Deal." When New York abandoned P. R. during the sessions of the first anti-New Deal Congress, the circle was completed. A former chairman of the Citizens Union declared it was repealed at the behest of the "reactionaries."[62]

Few lamented the demise of the Board of Aldermen. The very name had long been associated with such episodes in its unsavory history as Tweed's "Forty Thieves" and the "Boodle Board." To remove the stigma it was rebaptized the City Council. As the old board passed quietly out of existence, a reporter voiced popular opinion about it with a paraphrase of a jingle about George II:

Farewell the Board of Aldermen
Whose word no one relied on
Who seldom did an honest thing
And never did a wise one.[63]

[61] After the President's death, Dr. Hallett revealed that Franklin D. Roosevelt himself had cherished an abiding faith in P. R. *Nat. Mun. Rev.*, XXXIV (1945), 304-5.

[62] Childs, "The League's Second Stretch," *Nat. Mun. Rev.*, XXXIII, 514-15; Interview with Athur L. Thexton, former campaign manager of the Cincinnati Charter Committee, July 27, 1949; *Reminiscences of Leonard M. Wallstein*, p. 101; *New York World-Telegram*, November 4, 1936; *Reminiscences of William J. Schieffelin*, p. 55.

[63] *New York World-Telegram*, December 4, 1937.

10. THE NEW COUNCIL

Every city needs local legislation enacted by a local body clothed with ample legislative authority and locally elected by methods which make its members responsible and responsive to the local electorate.—HORACE DEMING[1]

THE NEW GOVERNMENT was not a radical reconstruction of the old. Seeking reforms principally within the existing framework, the Charter Revision Commission had retained the strong-mayor form and two deliberative bodies. In their disappointment, some reformers criticized the commission for merely "replacing the piston rings and getting some new tires for the same old car." Samuel Seabury regarded the new charter as only a "step, although a very short step," in the right direction.[2]

The commission's restraint was due partly to conviction, partly to strategy. "The notion that New York City's charter needs drastic reorganization is much exaggerated. There are one or two major operations that are called for," Commissioner McGoldrick had declared in 1932. "Some of the things that most need doing would, however, occasion bitter controversy."[3] Anticipating an uphill battle, the commission had realized that moderate changes would arouse less opposition than revolutionary proposals.

The new charter seemed to augment the City Council's dignity and importance, lodging in it full legislative authority. With the Board of Estimate and Apportionment no longer a co-

1 *The Government of American Cities*, p. 149.

2 Whitney and Cunningham, *Charter Revision*; Holmes to Thacher, December 16, 1935; *New York Times*, April 27, May 3, 1936.

3 McGoldrick, "Is the City Manager Plan Suitable for N. Y.?" *Nat. Mun. Rev.*, XXI, 292.

ordinate branch of the Municipal Assembly under the Home Rule Law, the City Council gained sole power to initiate local laws. Nevertheless the Board of Estimate (successor to the Board of Estimate and Apportionment) remained the more important house. One observer estimated that it performed 98 per cent of the job. The Charter Revision Commission might have questioned his arithmetic but agreed with his broad conclusions. They themselves had realized that the functions of a city government are preponderantly administrative rather than policy-making. Hence the Board of Estimate, the board of directors of the municipal corporation, rather than the City Council, the regulator of broad policy, was destined to play a decisive role in municipal affairs.[4]

Even in the sphere of policy-making, the most important of the Council's decisions were subject to the approval of the Board of Estimate. All local laws that amended the charter, modified the duties of city officers, or reduced taxes required ratification by the latter. The purpose of this provision was to prevent a City Council "not charged with the responsibility of conducting the city government, perhaps hostile to the administration or unfamiliar with the practical requirements of the situation" from hampering the Board of Estimate in its management of city business.[5] In effect it gave the Board of Estimate a substantial voice in policy determination; but no reciprocal check on administrative decisions was granted the City Council.[6]

The old Board of Aldermen was limited by the Mayor's veto; this curb has been retained.[7] In addition, the new charter trans-

[4] Tanzer, *op. cit.*, pp. 27, 480, 488; Allen, *Why Tammanies Revive*, p. 114; Chamberlain and Tanzer, "Cent. Govt. of the City;" Charter, Sec. 21 (Hereafter all references to the city charter relate to the document in effect Jan. 1, 1938).

[5] The Lyons Residence Law offers an excellent example of an enactment that could hamstring an unfriendly administration. The Borough President of Manhattan during Mayor LaGuardia's second administration wrote: "We suffer today because of that unfortunate 'Lyons Law' which makes it impossible to appoint a non-resident to an important city position without the concurrence of the Board of Estimate and the Council. That was put over because Mayor La Guardia had an unfriendly Board of Aldermen at the time." Letter of the Hon. Stanley M. Isaacs to author, November 23, 1949.

[6] Tanzer, *op. cit.*, pp. 43-44, 489-90; Charter, Sec. 39.

[7] A public hearing must be held before the Mayor signs a local law. If he takes no action within thirty days it is deemed signed. His veto may be over-

ferred several legislative powers to administrative agencies. Aldermanic ordinances governing pedestrian and vehicular traffic have been replaced by Police Department rules and regulations. The Department of Water Supply, Gas and Electricity formerly submitted its rules to the aldermen for approval; now they are presented to the Board of Estimate. Rules and regulations promulgated by administrative agencies may supplement local laws. Since the courts are now required to take judicial notice of these rules, they are actually a species of subordinate legislation.[8]

To a limited degree the people, too, may check the City Council. Under the Home Rule Law referenda for certain types of local laws amending the charter are mandatory. The Charter Commission made substantial additions to the list.[9] What is more, they made it possible to bypass the local legislature entirely, for fundamental charter changes may be accomplished by initiative and referendum. If the City Council proves a bottleneck to a popular reform, the citizens may place the issue directly on the ballot.[10] Incidentally, this provision inspired an extension to the state Home Rule Law in 1937, permitting voters in all New York cities to amend their charters in similar fashion.[11]

In any government the power of the purse is far-reaching; in municipalities the annual budget goes far towards determining legislative and administrative policies a year in advance. But the City Council plays a minor rôle in budget-making. The Charter Commission developed two basic reforms originating in Mayor O'Brien's administration—a separate budget for public

ridden by a vote of two-thirds of all the councilmen. Such measures are not reconsidered by the Board of Estimate, even if its concurrence was originally required.

8 Tanzer, *op. cit.*, pp. 170, 183; Charter, Secs. 38, 435, 734, 885; *Administrative Code*, Sec. 982-80.

9 A summary of types of local laws subject to popular referendum under the Home Rule Law appears in Tanzer, *op. cit.*, pp. 200-1. For additional classes of local laws prescribed by the Charter Commission, see *ibid.*, p. 201. Section 40 of the Charter details amendments in both categories.

10 These relate to the mode of electing city officers and abolishing or creating offices. An initiative petition by not less than 50,000 voters is required.

11 Tanzer, *op. cit.*, pp. 202-3, 486; Charter, Secs. 40-41, 44-45; Winston W. Crouch, "The Initiative and Referendum in Cities," *American Political Science Review*, XXXVII (1943), 504; *Nat. Mun. Rev.*, XXVI (1937), 310.

improvement projects and an executive budget for operating costs. It decided that the capital budget would be prepared by the City Planning Commission and the expense budget, as heretofore, by the Mayor's Bureau of the Budget. Both would be presented to the Board of Estimate and the City Council.

The Council gained a slight advantage over the Board of Aldermen in considering the budget—added time to investigate. The old Board had 20 days to study the estimates; the Council has 50 days for the expense budget and 57 days for the capital budget. Again, under the new charter the fiscal year for the expense budget commences July 1 instead of January 1. Hence the preliminary work occurs in the spring instead of during the legislators' vacation, and the Finance Committee now has an opportunity thoroughly to familiarize itself with the document during the crucial stages of preparation. But its fiscal powers are still slight. It may reduce or delete items not mandated by law in the expense budget or strike out any authorization in the capital budget, but it may not vary the terms or conditions of either. What is more, its decisions on the expense budget are subject to the Mayor's veto.[12]

Some of the financial powers enjoyed by the defunct Board of Aldermen have not devolved upon the City Council. The old charter provided for concurrent action with the Board of Estimate to authorize corporate stock for the city's capital improvements or special revenue notes (now tax notes) for emergencies. The new charter stripped the City Council of these powers. The President and Finance Chairman of the Board of Aldermen had been Commissioners of the Sinking Fund, which disappeared in the new charter. The Council still sets the tax rate, but the actual calculations are made in the Comptroller's office. A ministerial duty, it is still vested in the Council only because the Charter Commission deemed it essential to have a public announcement and recording of the figures.[13]

[12] If the Mayor vetoes its changes, a three-fourths vote of all the Councilmen is required to restore them. *Mun. Ass. Rec.*, IX, No. 10, 3; Tanzer, *op. cit.*, p. 59 ff.; Charter, Secs. 111-26, 211-24.

[13] *Manual of Bd. of Ald., 1936-37*, pp. 17-18; Tanzer, *op. cit.*, pp. 47, 74, 95, 502-3; Charter, Secs. 169, 242, 249; Chamberlain and Tanzer, *The Central Govt. of the City*.

Why are the City Council's fiscal powers so restricted? The Charter Commission never intended to make it responsible for municipal finances. In recent years the trend has been toward careful planning of expenditures by a single authority. The British budget is prepared by the Chancellor of the Exchequer, and Parliament may only reduce or eliminate items. So too, the executive budget has been adopted by our federal government and New York State. The Charter Commission realized that the City Council could not conduct hearings and produce an orderly financial policy as effectively as the executive departments or the City Planning Commission. It decided to have budgets submitted to the city legislature chiefly because it wanted to give citizens who objected to individual items another opportunity to present their views at public hearings. Incidentally, the City Council now reviews the capital outlay budget, a power never exercised by the Board of Aldermen.[14]

In most municipalities the City Council is the dominant body, with full responsibility for the authority exercised by the municipal corporation. In New York the new charter underscored the "virtual disappearance of the legislative branch and the enlargement of the executive."[15] Those who doubted the efficacy of P. R. regarded a weak legislature as insurance against disaster, should the new mode of election operate badly. Its proponents were confident the new City Council would exercise its limited authority with greater vigor and independence than the moribund Board of Aldermen. Galvanized by an aggressive minority, the City Council would become a real law-making body, a prophylactic against epidemics of misgovernment. The Chairman of the Citizens Union explained his organization's views:

> We are satisfied . . . that even under the present draft of the charter the Council would have enough power so that if P. R. is adopted it should be an effective agency for keeping the city permanently out of the depths of misrule revealed by the Seabury investigation.[16]

[14] Local Law 15 of 1933.

[15] Rexford G. Tugwell, "Implementing the General Interest," *Public Administration Review*, I (1940), 2.

[16] Statement of William J. Schieffelin at public hearing of Charter Revision Commission, May 19, 1936.

Nevertheless good government forces hoped the Council's powers would be extended after P. R. demonstrated its merits. At any rate, the provisions in the charter for two-thirds and three-fourths votes would acquire meaning for the first time in decades. No longer would it be possible for the dominant party to railroad a bill through the legislature after perfunctory consideration. A third of the legislators could insist it remain on the members' desks at least eight calendar days. Nor could lopsided majorities blackmail a reform Mayor of another political persuasion by enacting obnoxious local laws or arbitrarily slashing the budget, then threatening to override his veto.[17]

Any municipal legislature, no matter how vigorous or well-intentioned, would have difficulty in surmounting the limitations of the Home Rule Law. Home Rule had not perceptibly augmented the authority of the old board; but then the aldermen had never been really interested in broad municipal problems. In 1936, however, the charter was overhauled by a local body and ratified by the local electorate, instead of being imposed by Albany. This procedure, declared the Chairman of the Charter Commission, "firmly established for the first time the principle of home rule in New York." A number of circumstances gave point to his observation. Although the Thacher Commission had received statutory sanction to amend special legislation pertaining to New York, it had deliberately confined its attention to matters within the ambit of the home rule power and excluded matters beyond that power. As a result, there was not a single item in the new charter that could not be amended or repealed by municipal authorities. With the creation of a City Council that promised to concern itself with city-wide rather than narrow neighborhood problems, there was hope that the state legislature would recognize its competence and cease intruding into the city's affairs. "The year 1938 should prove the turning point in the possibilities for municipal freedom in local

[17] To be passed over the Mayor's objections, local laws require a two-thirds majority, budget changes three-fourths. *Nat. Mun. Rev.*, XXV, 299; Charter, Secs. 37, 38c, 125; Letter of Councilman Stanley M. Isaacs to author, November 23, 1949.

affairs," declared the City Council's President at the opening session.[18]

To clinch it, the city administration pleaded with the State Constitutional Convention of 1938 to extend the powers of cities over their own affairs. In response, city councils obtained a new grant of power. Heretofore special laws affecting any of the state's 62 cities had been considered by the Legislature after a message of necessity from the Governor; now, instead, a request from both mayor and council of the city itself was required.[19] Furthermore, a council could present such requests without the Mayor's concurrence, if adopted by two-thirds of the body. By this measure the City Council acquired authority to determine the necessity for legislative action on the city's affairs at Albany. What is more, local laws initiated by the City Council could supersede the Legislature's special laws passed since 1924.[20]

Examined more closely, these gains proved illusory. The City Council's new power—to amend special laws passed after 1924—was trifling compared with the authority withheld, for the most burdensome legislation was enacted *before* 1924. Moreover the city lost important powers over local legislation. It could no longer regulate the retirement systems of public school employees and serious barriers were placed in the way of reorganizing county offices. Nor did the new restrictions on special laws affecting cities really restrain the Legislature. It could still enact general laws governing all cities, and those limited to cities with a population with a million or more would apply to New York alone. What is more, they were easier to pass than special laws; a bare majority was required, and no special requests were necessary.[21]

18 *N. Y. World-Telegram,* November 4, 1936; Tanzer, *N. Y. C. Charter,* pp. 516-17; Morris, *Mun. Home Rule under the City Council; Proc. of Council, 1938,* I, 2.

19 A two-thirds vote of both houses was still required to enact such special laws.

20 Nathaniel L. Godstein, "March Towards Home Rule," *Nat. Mun. Rev.,* XXXIV, 171; Constitutional Convention of 1938, *The Constitution of the State of New York to Be Submitted to the People at the General Election of 1938* (Document No. 16), Art. 9, Secs. 11-12.

21 Lazarus, "The Council," pp. 10-11.

Under the circumstances, charter-tinkering in Albany continued. Even before the new charter went into operation, the Legislature began amending administrative details within the scope of the Home Rule Law. A group of civil servants who believed the charter militated against their interests persuaded the 1937 Legislature to enact a special law to remedy the situation. Curiously enough, Mayor La Guardia himself endorsed the bill.[22] Yet the Mayor later complained bitterly to the Council that both branches of the municipal government were unable to cope with local problems for lack of adequate authority:

> We are geared for local government . . . , and yet we are responsible for a government that is larger than any state in the Union. I haven't any extra powers because of this added responsibility and you gentlemen haven't the full powers of the Legislature of the State. That makes it extremely difficult. . . . There's a feeling of hopelessness that comes over us . . . on a great many things we'd like to do and want to do but just haven't the power.[23]

As long as responsibility was divided between Albany and City Hall, the Council could not function freely. As President of the City Council, Newbold Morris repeatedly urged the majority and minority to join forces to secure added powers from the State Legislature, but his pleas fell on deaf ears. Indeed, when the minority introduced a resolution asking the Legislature to yield control over salaries in the city's courts, the majority lined up solidly against it.[24]

In one area the new charter did seem to provide an expansion of the Council's powers—in its authority to investigate. Here would appear to lie a new safeguard against malfeasance. Formerly the Commissioner of Accounts acted as the "eyes and ears" of the Mayor; the Commissioner of Investigation, his successor under the new charter, is now at the disposal of the City Council as well.[25] The new charter also amplified the legisla-

22 Lawrence A. Tanzer, "The Home Rule Situation in New York State" (Mimeographed copy of address delivered Jan. 10, 1938, in files of National Municipal League); Tanzer, *N. Y. C. Charter*, p. 402; Charter, Sec. 683; L. 1937, C. 922.

23 *Proc. of Council of City of N. Y., 1939*, I, 7.

24 *Ibid., 1938*, I, 2, *1940*, I, 11; *The Searchlight*, XXIX, No. 1, 11-12.

25 Under the new charter the Commissioner of Investigation is no longer required to report to the city legislature. Hence it has been argued that a

ture's independent authority to investigate, extending it to any matter relating to the property, affairs, or government of the city. The City Council's first President believed the absence of city commissioners from its deliberations would further strengthen this power. "Department heads must stand or fall by their own administration," he declared. With the notable exception of the Curran Committee's probe of the Police Department, aldermanic inquiries had rarely been in the public's interest. In periods of widespread corruption the power had lain dormant; invariably legislative majorities had invoked it against hostile administrations.[26]

The new City Council was to employ this power vigorously, if not wisely. It was twice sanctioned in the courts, however, against the city administration. When a special committee of the City Council summoned the director of the municipal radio station before them, he challenged its authority, asserting that the resolution creating the special committee had never been approved by the Mayor. The highest court in the state held that the appointment of such a committee was not part of the City Council's ordinary law-making power and did not require the Mayor's signature. This opinion, vindicating the City Council's power to pursue independent investigations, was followed some years later by an important precedent-setting case. Mayor La Guardia had sought to withhold from an investigating committee a confidential paper. Once again the Court of Appeals upheld the City Council, ruling that the municipal executive department is not immune from councilmanic investigations. In the same decision it laid down the principle that the separation

---

"potential lever for prying out information which the public needed," was eliminated. This provision in the old charter, however, had long been a dead letter. The new charter merely regularized existing practices. Vid. *Nat. Mun. Rev.*, XXVI, 54; Allen, *Why Tammanies Revive*, p. 116; Seidman, *Investigating Municipal Administration*, pp. 93, 125.

26 Tanzer, *N. Y. C. Charter*, pp. 45, 190; Charter, Secs. 43, 803; Seidman, *Investigating Municipal Administration*, pp. 123-24, 177; Sophia A. Olmstead, "The Municipal Power of Investigation," *Nat. Mun. Rev.*, XXV, 652-53; Morris, *Mun. Home Rule Under the City Council.*

of powers between the executive and legislative branches does not apply to the governments of cities.[27]

It was inevitable the New York's experiment with P. R. would attract widespread attention. Fortunately, the Charter Commission could draw upon twenty years of experience by American cities with P. R. elections. Dr. Hallett, whom they had called in to help draft this part of the charter, was thoroughly conversant with the record of the ten municipalities that had employed P. R. The result was a streamlined version of the Hare System. "The details are simpler than the rules of baseball," declared the Chairman of the Citizens Union.[28] In Appendix E is a summary of the salient features of the system used in New York.

There was one provision that proportionalists regarded as inconsistent with the spirit of P. R. They wanted vacancies filled by a preferential recount of the ballots that had elected the vacating member. The charter, instead, directed the City Council to name a successor from the same borough and party. When a Brooklyn Democrat resigned in 1940 a Democrat was designated to replace him. The state constitution, however, provides that such an appointment last only until the end of the year it is made and that a popular election be held for the remainder of the unexpired term. Since the session extended through 1941 such an election became necessary. How should it be conducted? The charter did not specify. An application for an order to require a P. R. election was rejected by the courts, which directed that it be held under the plurality system. In this instance a Democrat was elected. In 1946, however, two vacancies left by Democratic Councilmen were filled by Republicans in the general elections, paring down the Democratic majority from three to one. Municipal reformers held that such shifts in the balance of power could leave voters unrepresented, particularly if the

[27] *In the Matter of Radio Station WNYC (Morris Novik)*, 169 Misc., N. Y. 502; 255 N. Y. 844; 255 N. Y. 950 (1938); *Matter of La Guardia v. Smith*, 288 N. Y. 1 (1942); *Nat. Mun. Rev.*, XXXI (1942), 223.

[28] Schieffelin, "P. R. and New Yorkers," *Survey Graphic*, XXVI, 386.

minority were reduced. They proposed that alternate councilmen be chosen in the original P. R. elections.[29]

One unfilled City Council vacancy raised an interesting question—what is a legal party? State law defines it as a group that nominates a candidate for Governor and polls 50,000 or more votes for him. When Communist Councilman Peter V. Cacchione died late in 1947, the remaining Communist in the Council presented the recommendation of the Kings County Communist Committee for the interim vacancy. But the Council adopted a committee report stating that it was powerless to follow the charter provision for filling the vacancy with a person of the "same political party" because the Communists had failed to achieve a legal status. The committee originally decided to let the courts decide. After the Communists announced they would not test the issue in the courts, however, the Council specifically rejected the nomination. In the absence of any judicial determination there was no definitive interpretation of what constitutes a legally recognized party.[30]

Aside from the abolition of P. R. itself, only one basic change relating to the City Council passed in the twelve years that P. R. obtained (1938-49). This was the extension of its term of office. Early in 1945 the Fusion administration introduced a charter amendment increasing it from two to four years and making it coextensive with that of the Mayor. The Councilmen were delighted, for it would assure them a longer term of office. P. R. elections in New York provided for a fixed quota, with the result that the number of Councilmen elected at a given time depended on the number of valid ballots cast. Experience had shown that more Councilmen were seated in Mayoralty elections than off-years.[31] Hence the amendment would maintain the same num-

[29] Charter, Section 24; *Ross v. Cohen et al.*, 238 N. Y. 388; 28 N. E. 2nd 883 (1940); *Nat. Mun. Rev.*, XXIX (1940), 629-30, XXXV (1946), 434, XXXVI (1947), 167-68.

[30] Letters of Councilman Benjamin V. Davis, Jr., to *New York Times*, December 15, 1947, to *N. Y. Herald-Tribune*, February 21, 1948; Letters of Councilman Louis P. Goldberg to *P. M.*, February 13, 1948, to *N. Y. Herald-Tribune*, February 24, 1948; *Proc. of Council, 1948*, II, 65.

[31] In the mayoralty elections of 1937 and 1941 twenty-six Councilmen were elected; in the off-year elections of 1939 and 1943 twenty-one and seventeen, respectively.

ber of Councilmen in the second half of a Mayor's administration as the first. When the bill came to a vote Republicans, Democrats, Communists, and American Labor Councilmen eagerly assented. Only one Councilman voted against it.[32]

Civic reformers opposed it on the grounds that freezing Councilmen into office for four years violated the principle of responsibility. They wanted the Council's actions frequently reviewed by the public. P. R. contests would always be subordinated to the more dramatic Mayoralty campaigns, they asserted. As the councilmen saw it, the change would eliminate the rigors of a grueling campaign in off-years. Relieved of half their election headaches, the legislators would be under less temptation to play partisan politics and would have greater opportunity for constructive study of long range municipal problems. Each campaign cost a candidate more than a year's salary, and the measure reduced the city's expenses as well.[33]

From the viewpoint of the reformers, the city legislature had been granted trivial powers. It was excluded from the management of city affairs. Important policies originating in the Council could be annulled by the Board of Estimate, the Mayor, or the electorate. Its influence on the budget was slight. P. R. was their bright and shining hope: P. R. was expected to end one-party dictatorship and to produce an alert and numerous minority, capable of acting as a gadfly and check upon the majority.[34]

Yet a public-spirited legislator could realize some real advantages from serving on a body endowed with moderate powers. Stanley M. Isaacs, who had once served as Borough President of Manhattan, observed that in his executive post he had formulated administrative policy in a limited sphere. In the city

[32] *Proc. of Council, 1945*, I, 205, 935-36; Earle, *Reminiscences*, p. 91; Local Law No. 32 of 1945.

[33] Three Mayoralty elections produced an average of 25 Councilmen, two off-year elections 19. On this basis the six hypothetical additional Councilmen for 1948 and 1949 drew $60,000. Since each P. R. election cost over $200,000, the amendment saved the city $140,000 when the 1947 election was eliminated. *Proc. of Council, 1945*, I, 2-3, 936; *Citizens Union Press Release*, June 5, 1945; *Nat. Mun. Rev.*, XXXIV (1945), 419.

[34] George H. Hallett, "The Case for P. R.," *The American Scholar*, XII (1943), 164, 167.

legislature, however, he was at liberty to advocate broad concepts of social progress. Independent Councilmen could and did make the city legislature a sounding-board for their ideas.[35]

[35] Stanley M. Isaacs, *Reminiscences* (Oral History Project, Columbia University, 1950), p. 141; Adam Clayton Powell, *Marching Blacks* (New York, 1945), p. 156.

11. FIVE P. R. ELECTIONS AND REPEAL

In a representative body actually deliberating, the minority must of course be overruled. . . . But does it follow that the minority should have no representation at all? . . . In a really equal democracy every or any section would be represented, not disproportionately, but proportionately.—JOHN STUART MILL [1]

THE FIRST P. R. election in New York marked the Hare system's greatest victory and its greatest challenge. Never before had it been employed on so large a scale or among so diverse a population. The electorate of Ireland, which had adopted it for national elections, was less than half the size and far more homogeneous than the voters of New York. For these reasons it was inevitable that the city's experiment with P. R. would attract wide attention.

Unfortunately the very officials responsible for putting it into effect were hostile. Although court decisions bearing on the constitutionality of P. R. were rendered too late to enable them to order voting machines in time for the first election, the politically controlled Board of Elections failed to complete plans for counting paper ballots until the last possible moment. Samuel Seabury charged that they deliberately used dilatory tactics to discredit P. R. and pave the way for the return of the district system of voting. The Civil Service Commission accused them of failure to comply with the charter provisions for testing candidates for voting canvasser.[2]

[1] *On Liberty, Representative Government, the Subjugation of Women* (London, 1948), p. 248.

[2] In *Finegan v. Cohen*, 275 N. Y. 432 (1937), the right of the Civil Service Commission to give an examination for employees in the central count was upheld. See also George H. McCaffrey, "New York's 1937 Election and Its Results," *Nat. Mun. Rev.*, XXVII, 42; Samuel Seabury, "Proportional Representation and

Whether impaired by deliberate sabotage, inexperience with P. R., or defects inherent in the system, the election provided an excellent source of ammunition for P. R.'s opponents. There were hordes of candidates, 232 in all. Delayed by litigation, the Civil Service Commission was unable to check the requirements of candidates for canvasser in the central count, with the result that forty were later found to have police records! Little wonder that criminal alterations were found in 580 Bronx ballots. It turned out that four canvassers had been tampering with ballots with bits of graphite hidden under their finger nails. Canvassers as a group had every incentive to soldier on the job, since they were on a *per diem* payroll. Consequently the count proceeded so slowly that the results were not known for 28 days. (Meanwhile the numbers racket paid off on the figures that came up in the Manhattan vote, instead of digits in the stock exchange, or clearing house statements.) The election cost $700,893. Pronouncing the event a "ridiculous and obscene farce," the tabloid *Daily News* censured the Board of Elections and called for their respective scalps. Later the editorial policy shifted, and the "fantastic farce" was attributed not to politicians, but to the system itself.[3]

In later elections many of the "bugs" were eliminated. The Board of Elections completed plans for the 1939 count well in advance instead of the day before election. Paying canvassers a fixed sum not only reduced the count to eleven days, but also cut the cost more than two-thirds.[4] Only 100 candidates appeared, instead of 232, on the five borough ballots that year.[5] Yet opponents of P. R. found it expedient to hark back to the first

the Constitutional Convention," *Nat. Mun. Rev.*, XXVI, 570; *What "P.R." Is: How It Works* (New York, 1937), p. 3.

[3] Howard R. Penniman, *Sait's American Parties and Elections* (N. Y., 1948), pp. 630-31; Hermens, *Democracy or Anarchy?* p. 397; "Report of R. Lawrence Siegal, Special Assistant District Attorney, Relative to the Irregularities Marking the 1937 Election of Councilmen in the Borough of the Bronx to John J. Bennett, Jr., Attorney-General of the State of New York (Aug. 30, 1938), pp. 8, 15-21; *New York Daily News,* November 12, November 30, 1937.

[4] In 1941 the count took 9 days, 9 in 1943, and 12 in 1945. The $700,893 spent in 1937 was reduced to $267,604 in 1939, $242,155 in 1941, and $202,416 in 1943.

[5] The number was further reduced to 88 in 1941, 65 in 1943, and 96 in 1945.

election as if it were typical rather than exceptional. The four-foot Brooklyn ballot, containing 99 names, has become a classic in anti-P. R. literature.[6]

Probably the fairest criterion for judging P. R. would be its success in fulfilling its objectives. One genuine accomplishment was to guarantee each borough equitable representation. There was no state reapportionment between 1917 and 1943, yet the P. R. election in 1937 automatically ensured every borough a fair share of delegates to the City Council. Table 11 contrasts the representation of the five boroughs in the last Board of Aldermen and the first City Council.[7]

Table 11. BOROUGH REPRESENTATION IN THE LAST BOARD OF ALDERMEN AND FIRST CITY COUNCIL

	1935		1937	
	Percentage of Voters	*Percentage of Aldermen*	*Percentage of Voters*	*Percentage of Councilmen*
Manhattan	25	37	25	23
Brooklyn	36	37	35	35
Bronx	18	12	20	19
Queens	18	9	17	19
Richmond	3	5	3	4
Total	100	100	100	100

Since the election district was broadened to include the entire borough, overrepresentation of depopulated districts and underrepresentation of newly built areas was eliminated. Needless to say, gerrymandering also became impossible.

Did P. R. offer independents a better chance? The answer must be a resounding yes. Boss Flynn once observed that among the Democrats in the Bronx no legislative candidate who challenged the machine ever won out, for the county organization could pour overwhelming resources into a single district's primary fight. P. R. bypassed primary elections, with their opportunities for manipulating paper ballots, and placed well-qualified candidates on the final ballot if they could obtain a mere 2,000

[6] McCaffrey, "N. Y.'s 1937 Election and Its Results," *Nat. Mun. Rev.*, XXVII, 44; *Prop. Rep.: What It Is and How It Works in N. Y. C.*, *passim.*

[7] Testimony of Dr. Hallett before Charter Commission, November 12, 1935; *Ann. Rep. of Bd. of Elects., 1937*, pp. 43-46.

signatures. In the election of 1939, three candidates were elected without the designation of any of the three legal parties—Mrs. Genevieve B. Earle in Brooklyn, and Alfred E. Smith, Jr. and Robert K. Straus in Manhattan. Later the Republicans were glad to offer their endorsement to Mrs. Earle and Stanley M. Isaacs, who won a seat in 1941 as an independent. Without P. R. these exceptionally qualified legislators might have disappeared from public life. To see mavericks gain office without organization support was galling to the political bosses.[8]

The most drastic change lay in the caliber of the legislators. "It seems to be the consensus of opinion that the new Council will have the best personnel of any city legislative body since the greater city was formed," enthused a proportionalist after the first election. There is no general agreement on the qualifications of the ideal councilman, but nominees in this election passed all tests with flying colors. Never before had such a galaxy of candidates entered the field—sixty-one earned the accolade of the Citizens Union.[9]

Among those elected, the number with records of distinction was surprisingly high. Not a single member of the last Board of Aldermen had rated mention in the then current *Who's Who in New York*. Ten were returned to the new Council. Among the sixteen new legislators, however, no less than five merited a place among the celebrities. A study of the personnel of the Council revealed that as a group they had attained a distinctly higher level of education and occupational experience than their predecessors. What is more, a process of selection took place among the ex-aldermen. Newbold Morris, a veteran alderman presiding over the Council, observed that the Democrats weeded out their inarticulate hacks and put up their more vigorous and capable representatives for Councilman.[10]

[8] Flynn, *You're the Boss*, p. 227; Charter, Sec. 1004; *Nat. Mun. Rev.*, XXVIII (1939), 882-83.

[9] McCaffrey, "N. Y.'s 1937 Election and Its Results," *Nat. Mun. Rev.*, XXVII, 35; *The Searchlight*, XXVII, No. 2 (1937), 12-18.

[10] *Who's Who in New York* (New York, 1938), *passim*: Helen H. Prince, "The New York City Council" (Master's thesis at Columbia University Library, 1940), pp. 24-25; Rovere, "Good Citizen," *The New Yorker*, XX, No. 38, 32.

One reason for the dead level of mediocrity in the Board of Aldermen had been the quick turnover among men of promise. In the City Council the high caliber of the original body was not merely maintained; it actually rose. Comparative studies of the personnel of the two bodies indicate not only that the most independent and effective legislators in the Council remained; but also that in its latter years the City Council attracted additional men and women of intelligence and repute. Few aldermen could match the distinguished record of public service Mrs. Genevieve B. Earle brought to the city legislature. A former director of the Women's City Club and member of the Charter Revision Commission, she remained for twelve years in the legislature she had helped fashion. Minority leader for a decade, she won universal respect for her courage, her vast fund of information, and for her sponsorship of constructive legislation. Few men who had held important executive posts had ever been elected to the city legislature. Stanley M. Isaacs, a former Borough President of Manhattan, brought to the City Council a record of administrative achievement and practical experience in municipal affairs unsurpassed among novice legislators. Either would do credit to any legislative body. It has been observed that the P. R. Council was dominated by former aldermen. This was largely true, but they were the more valuable aldermen. The rubber stamps had largely disappeared. It was a far cry from the old days when mention of the Board of Aldermen produced derisive snickers.[11]

Did P. R. make the people's vote count? Opponents charged that the new and intricate way of voting so baffled the electorate that thousands were disenfranchised. Certainly the P. R. ballot was more complicated than the voting machine. It was designed to make it more difficult to vote a "straight" ticket—voters could not locate a star or eagle, then automatically flick down a horizontal row of levers. Each name had to be searched out individually. After P. R. was adopted in Cincinnati, large numbers of wardheelers had been unable to vote at all. The Republicans actually set up schools to teach their cohorts how to mark the

[11] Gustaferro, "Personnel of the Board of Aldermen," pp. 17-26, 42, 56; *The Searchlight*, XXVII-XXXVII (1937-1947), *passim; Nat. Mun. Rev.*, XXXIII, 264, XXXV (1946), 46.

ballot. In New York the civic organizations that had put over P. R. waged an intensive campaign to educate the electorate in the mechanics of P. R. voting before the first campaign. Nevertheless, over the course of five elections almost 14% of the ballots were left blank or invalid. Even more were exhausted before the alternate votes could be transferred to a winning candidate. All told, 30% of the total vote was ineffective in electing candidates.[12]

But P. R. did enable larger numbers of voters to elect some nominee than the majority system. Although unmarked or invalid ballots were not a serious problem in aldermanic elections, a greater proportion was wasted in the sense that they elected no one. Since the consolidation of Greater New York 41% of the ballots cast for aldermen had been frustrated votes. Proportionalists estimated that almost half a million more voters helped elect someone in the first councilmanic elections than in the last aldermanic race.[13]

One of the avowed purposes of the new charter had been to shatter Tammany domination of the city legislature, to "cut the Tiger's claws close to the quick." Precisely that was accomplished. As a result of each of the five P. R. elections the city's dominant political organization was confronted with a substantial minority in the City Council. Even in 1945, a year of a Democratic landslide, almost 40 per cent of the seats were won by the minority. The party representation in the Council after each election is given in Table 12.[14]

In their enthusiasm, some proportionalists had even envisaged a "good government" majority of independent Democrats, Republicans, and Socialists. Except for a brief period in 1938, this hope was never fulfilled. Nevertheless the new charter was quickly recognized as a staggering blow to the Democratic machine. "No more signal, far-reaching triumph over bossdom has ever been achieved in this city," crowed one editor. Apart from

[12] *Nat. Mun. Rev.*, XXVI, 380, 512; Seasongood, *Local Govt. in the U. S.*, p. 108; *Prop. Rep.: What It Is and How It Works in N. Y. C.*, pp. 16, 41-42.

[13] *Problems Relating to Legislative Organization and Powers* (Albany, 1938), pp. 257-58; Hallett, *P. R.: Key to Democ.*, pp. 16-17.

[14] Belle Zeller and Hugh A. Bone, "The Repeal of P. R. in New York City—Ten Years in Retrospect," *American Political Science Review*, XLII (1948), 1132.

Table 12. PARTY REPRESENTATION IN THE CITY COUNCIL AFTER FIVE P. R. ELECTIONS

Party	*1937*	*1939*	*1941*	*1943*	*1945*
Democratic	13	14	17	10	14
Republican	3	2	2	3	3
Insurgent Democratic	2	1	..	..	..
American Labor	5	2	3	2	2
City Fusion	3	2	3	..	..
Liberal	..	..	..	..	2
Communist	..	..	1	2	2
Total	26	21	26	17	23

Source: See n. 14.

a relaxation of their grip on the city legislature, the dominant organization lost dozens of $5,000 a year jobs. The first City Council included thirty-nine less Democrats than the Board of Aldermen. Acutely conscious of the threat embodied in P. R. the Democrats spent a decade ridding themselves of this incubus.[15]

One of the proportionalists' most powerful arguments had been that a P. R. legislature would reflect the fine shades of public opinion with mathematical accuracy. Opponents, however, called P. R. the "Great American Sweepstakes," which produced freakish rather than arithmetical results. They found immense discrepancies between the first-choice votes and the final outcome. Table 13 indicates the results of the 1937 election.[16]

Table 13. PERCENTAGE OF FIRST-CHOICE VOTES AND PERCENTAGE OF MEMBERS ELECTED, 1937 ELECTION

Party	*Percentage of First-Choice Votes*	*Percentage of Members Elected*
Democratic	31	50
American Labor	12	19
City Fusion	11	11.5
Republican	9	11.5
Insurgent Democratic	5	8
Communist	4	..
Socialist	1	..
Others	27	..
Total	100	100.0

[15] Testimony of Dr. Hallett before Charter Revision Commission, November 12, 1935; *New York Sun, New York Herald-Tribune, New York Post, New York World-Telegram,* Nov. 4, 1936; *New York Times,* Nov. 5, 1936.

[16] Louis Cohen, *P. R. Unmasked* (New York, 1940), p. 1; Robert Moses, *Theory and Practice in Politics* (Cambridge, 1939), p. 39; Hermens, *Democracy or Anarchy?* pp. 397-98.

But after the wildcat and hopeless candidates had been eliminated (and they would have been even more hopeless under the district system) the final results were roughly proportionate to the first balloting. Table 14 compares the proportion of votes distributed among successful candidates on the first ballot with the final outcome.

Table 14. PERCENTAGE OF VOTES GAINED BY SUCCESSFUL CANDIDATES ON FIRST BALLOT AND PERCENTAGE OF COUNCIL SEATS GAINED, 1937 ELECTION

Party	*Percentage of Votes on First Ballot*	*Percentage of Council Seats Gained*
Democratic	45.8	50.0
American Labor	17.6	19.3
City Fusion	16.6	11.5
Republican	13.2	11.5
Insurgent Democratic	6.8	7.7
Total	100.0	100.0

The avowed purpose of P. R., however, is to give representation to the greatest number of voters. For that reason, when a voter's favorite is defeated, alternate preferences are permitted. These secondary choices are an integral part of the Hare System, and in all fairness, judgment cannot be passed on its functioning without considering them. If the votes cast on the final count are reviewed, there will be found a remarkably close correspondence between the deciding count and the number of Councilmen actually elected. The results of the five P. R. elections are given in Table 15.[17]

Proportionalists presented these statistics to prove that "you couldn't get closer to accuracy without dividing Councilmen up into fractions." The figures were authentic enough, but they gave no inkling of the maneuvering that produced them. No one seriously believed that 9% of the city's electorate were extreme radicals. But how did it happen that two Communists were elected in 1943 and again in 1945? Part of the answer lay in the technique they developed. Realizing they could scarcely seat

[17] Commerce and Industry Association, "Report Concerning Election of the New York City Council by Proportional Representation" (September 24, 1947), 11-12.

Table 15. VOTER STRENGTH AND REPRESENTATION BY PARTIES, 1937–1945

Party	1937 Percentage of Seats	1937 Percentage of Votes	1939 Percentage of Seats	1939 Percentage of Votes	1941 Percentage of Seats	1941 Percentage of Votes
Democratic	50.0	47.0	66.5	65.5	65.5	64.0
Republican	11.5	8.5	9.5	8.0	7.5	6.5
Insurgent Democratic	8.0	7.0	5.0	4.0	...	...
American Labor	19.0	21.0	9.5	11.5	11.5	11.5
City Fusion	11.5	10.5	9.5	11.0	11.5	12.5
Communist	...	2.5	...	...	...	...
Others	...	3.5	...	...	4.0	5.5
Total	100.0	100.0	100.0	100.0	100.0	100.0

Party	1943 Percentage of Seats	1943 Percentage of Votes	1945 Percentage of Seats	1945 Percentage of Votes
Democratic	59.0	53.0	60.0	59.0
Republican	17.0	22.0	13.0	15.0
American Labor	12.0	11.0	9.0	10.0
Communist	12.0	14.0	9.0	7.0
Liberal	...	...	9.0	9.0
Total	100.0	100.0	100.0	100.0

Source: See n. 17.

more than one candidate in any borough, they instructed their adherents to cast a single vote, without secondary preferences. "Bullet" voting, as it was called, assured such candidates of a solid block of votes. But a Communist could not muster the required quota among the party faithful alone. Hence they selected men with a broad appeal. Benjamin V. Davis, Jr., a handsome and intelligent graduate of Amherst College and Harvard Law School, was a Negro who had participated in the legal defense of the Scottsborough boys and Angelo Herndon. An all-out drive in 1943 had enlisted the American Labor Party and leftist trade unions, such as the National Maritime Union, in his behalf. Negro issues were emphasized in Harlem, where he was endorsed by Negro clergymen, writers, musicians, and athletes, including Joe Louis (who had also accommodated the Republicans by supporting Landon in 1936). A variety of appeals and popular front tactics won a City Council seat for Davis in two elections.[18]

Viewing these developments, Democrats contended that P. R. had produced misrepresentation, giving a "lion's roar to irresponsible fleas." Yet as reluctant participants, they played the game for all it was worth. After watching their candidates compete against each other in borough-wide elections in 1937, they evolved their own technique for obtaining maximum representation. Each borough was divided into the same number of zones as the number of councilmen it seemed likely to select. Within each zone the district leaders agreed upon a candidate. Then the entire slate was reviewed by the County Leader and Executive Committee, who ordered the party's adherents to follow an identical pattern of voting—i.e. the number to be placed beside each candidate's name in each zone was determined in advance. Proportionalists and their opponents agree that under this system in the 1939 election the Democrats massed their strength for optimum effectiveness.[19]

Independent organizations often lacked the cohesion and discipline necessary to execute such maneuvres. Although the City Fusion Party's objectives parallelled those of the Citizens Non-Partisan Committee, they did not always work as a team. Sometimes they offered rival candidates who competed for the votes of like-minded citizens. Since their adherents were not instructed on how to transfer votes, their ballots tended to become exhausted before electing anyone. It would appear that even under P. R. political acumen, organization, and party discipline counted. Under P. R., however, there was a limited sphere for manipulation. It could never produce the distortions of the aldermanic race of 1931, where the minority gained 35% of the vote and received 1.5% of the seats. Nor would it be possible for the minority parties to obtain almost 40% of the votes, as

[18] *Danger*, Leaflet of Keep P. R. Committee, 1947; *Nat. Mun. Rev.*, XXXII (1943) p. 619; Adam C. Powell, *Riots and Ruins* (N. Y., 1945), p. 161; Robert Minor, *Tell the People How Ben Davis Was Elected* (N. Y., 1946), *passim.*

[19] Letter of State President of Affiliated Young Democrats to *New York Times,* Aug. 25, 1947; Hermens, *Democracy or Anarchy?* pp. 410-13; *Nat. Mun. Rev.,* XXVIII, 884.

they did in the last five aldermanic elections, but average less than 10% of the representation. P. R. reflected the political viewpoints among the city's electorate with relative accuracy, assuring each party of consequence an equitable share of delegates.[20]

If diversity of membership is the measure of popular government, the first P. R. City Council was the most democratic ever elected in New York. Organization Democrats mingled with Republicans, insurgent Democrats, Fusionites, and Labor Party men. The old Tammany crowd still played a prominent part, but the minority seemed a microcosm of the city. There was Joseph Clark Baldwin III, product of St. Paul's and Harvard, former representative of the Silk Stocking district, noted for his correct evening dress. Directly behind him sat B. Charney Vladeck, a former Socialist alderman, who had been imprisoned in Russia. Mrs. Genevieve B. Earle, an independent Republican, rubbed elbows with Salvatore Ninfo, organizer for the American Federation of Labor, and Robert K. Straus, a brain-truster in Franklin D. Roosevelt's first administration. Newbold Morris repeatedly called it the most representative body in the world.[21]

That was precisely what irked the dominant party. "A political organization has as one of its dearest wishes continuance in office," remarked a Democratic Councilman.[22] P. R. had dealt his party a stunning blow, destroying its near-monopoly in the governing body as it provided articulation for minorities.

Opponents contended that P. R. involved abuses unknown to the majority system of election. In contrast to the quick and orderly procedure where voting machines are used, a member of the Board of Elections found P. R. counts "confusion confounded." Councilman Earle, a member of the Charter Revision Commission, took pains to answer this argument after the first P. R. balloting. "The alleged confusion was more apparent than real," she wrote, "like the ordinary confusion of a football

[20] Hugh A. Bone, "Political Parties in New York City," *American Political Science Review*, XL (1946), 276; *Nat. Mun. Rev.*, XXVII, 54.

[21] *Proc. of Council, 1939*, I, 2; *1942*, I, 4; *1945*, I, 2.

[22] Cohen, *P. R. Unmasked*, p. 13.

team running through plays. The players are apparently running helter-skelter; but actually according to a well-defined plan. To those who understand what was being done there was very little confusion in the 1937 count." That there was more confusion than necessary in the first election she attributed to the "scuttling tactics" of a hostile Board of Elections.[23]

It was argued that P. R. was an overgrown bingo game in which the transfer of votes from one candidate to another was often determined by their accidental positions on the ballot. Glaring examples of alphabetical voting were found: when Keshner was eliminated in the first Brooklyn count Kiernan and Klein gained the major part of his vote; in the same election Sullivan and Surpless inherited the bulk of Stimson's ballots. The Charter Commission had been aware of this problem—it had been demonstrated in other cities that candidates at the bottom of the ballot stood little chance of election. Hence they had provided for alphabetical rotation of names by election districts. The "dumbbell" vote is not confined to P. R., but it shows up more clearly in the transfers of P. R. ballots.[24]

A serious accusation against P. R. elections was that they fanned racial feeling. A thoughtful publicist described the type of balloting revealed by the transfer of votes in the P. R. counts:

> Joe Murphy, an ardent exponent of the principles of the Christian Front, might be eliminated from the race on the fourth transfer of choices, and of his ten thousand assorted votes, probably as many as eight thousand would go to McShane, also an Irishman, but a Communist, or at least a fellow traveler. Simon Schwartz, old-time Socialist, would lose out, and most of his votes would go to Schapiro, a labor-baiting dress manufacturer. Salvatore would get the votes of Santini. There would be no rhyme or reason for these transfers except that furnished by names, coupled with alphabetical proximity on the paper ballot.[25]

Creating self-consciousness among the numerous nationalities of a cosmopolitan city could lead to ugly consequences, particularly in a period of violent agitation by the German American

[23] *New York Sun*, Nov. 5, 1947; Letter of Mrs. Genevieve B. Earle to John A. Heffernan of the *Brooklyn Eagle*, October 24, 1938 (Earle Papers).

[24] *Probs. Rel. to Leg. Org. and Powers*, pp. 268, 270; Charter, Sec. 1005.

[25] Moscow, *Politics in the Empire State*, p. 49.

Bund and the Christian Front. But the fact is that ethnic and religious sentiments have always exerted a powerful influence in American elections—a lesson underscored by Al Smith's defeat in 1928. Boss Flynn once revealed how his Democratic organization deliberately selected candidates of Irish, Jewish and Italian extraction to cater to these groups, representing the bulk of the Bronx population. "Our whole system of government is based on proportional representation," he wrote. "Special interest groups have a perfect right to be represented in the bodies that govern us all." Successful reform coalitions in New York have followed the same principles. The Fusion ticket elected in 1933 was headed by La Guardia (a Protestant who could attract the Italian vote), Cunningham (a Catholic), and Deutsch (prominent in Jewish circles).[26]

To prove that religion was the most vital consideration in the voters' minds, a councilman cited the Bronx P. R. elections of 1939: When Deering was eliminated the bulk of his vote was transferred to Keegan and Kinsley, Irish Democrats, but Cohen, a Jewish Democrat, received only a small fraction of his ballots. Distribution on the ninth count is given in the accompanying table.[27]

Louis Cohen, Dem	2,105	Salvatore Ninfo, ALP	1,175
James A. Deering, Dem	Eliminated	Michael Quill, ALP	990
Charles E. Keegan, Dem	22,892	Ballots exhausted on this count	3,461
Joseph E. Kinsley, Dem	10,581		

Did Keegan gain Deering's votes because he was Irish, Catholic, Democratic, or the next name on the ballot? The fact that Kinsley received less than half the number he did suggests that many Democrats who voted a straight ticket turned to Keegan because his was a prominent name and it came directly after Deering's. Significantly, Cohen, a Democrat, gained more of Deering's votes than Ninfo or Quill, Catholics endorsed by the American Labor Party. The results hardly demonstrate that religious or ethnic factors provided the sole motivation.

[26] Flynn, *You're the Boss*, pp. 222-23; J. H. Wallis, *The Politician: His Habits, Outcries, and Protective Coloring* (New York, 1935), pp. 105-7.

[27] Cohen, *op. cit.*, pp. 4-5; *Ann. Rep. of Bd. of Elects., 1939*, pp. 32-33.

Intensive studies of P. R. vote transfers in New York indicate that it is difficult to isolate religious, national, and racial influences, but that party loyalty is the most important consideration. With almost 44% of the Bronx population in 1937, Jewish voters failed to elect a single Jewish councilman from that borough. Protestants, who comprise 46% of the city's population, elected only 21% of the councilmen in five P. R. elections, while 53% of the Council seats went to Catholics, estimated at 22% of the population. Although the city contains the highest concentration of Negroes in the Western Hemisphere (468,000 in 1940), they were totally unrepresented in the first two Councils. A political scientist who surveyed Cleveland's first P. R. election reached the conclusion that the system neither intensified nor reduced racial and religious prejudices. New York's experience with P. R. yielded similar deductions. P. R. has given us an insight into the psychology of voting; but it can hardly be proved that it accentuated or diminished prejudices and tensions.[28]

Democrats (and sometimes organization Republicans) often argued that P. R. deprived whole communities of representation in the City Council. Al Smith pointed out that the 1939 elections left Manhattan without a single City Councilman living below 59th Street; a legislator observed that all Manhattan Councilmen came from two State Senatorial districts.[29] They dwelt on the countless services the alderman had rendered in his bailiwick. Recalling his career in the old Board of Aldermen brought Henry H. Curran a warm glow:

> When we lost them we lost something of value in New York, something of safety, of help in the manifold joys and sorrows of helter-skelter humanity. These new Councilmen are not the same. . . . There is in the Councilman no responsibility to a local district, no sound knowledge of a neighborhood's needs, no touch with all the modest people in odd corners of a great city who need every day the simple human help that only an alderman can give. All that is gone.[30]

[28] Zeller and Bone, "Repeal of P. R. in N. Y. C.," *Am. Pol. Sci. Rev.*, XLII, 1139-42; *1949 World Almanac and Book of Facts* (New York, 1949), p. 205; Powell, *Marching Blacks*, pp. 152-53; Maxey, "City Manager Plan and P. R.," *Western Reserve University Bulletin*, XXVII, No. 7, 25.

[29] *Proc. of Council, 1940*, I, 20.

[30] Curran, *Pillar to Post*, p. 140.

The professional kindliness displayed by these servitors had been one of the secrets of the ward machine's success. But with Councilmen elected from boroughs rather than neighborhoods, the district organizations were hard hit. Under the old charter, choice of aldermanic candidates had been a perquisite of the district leader. Once elected, the alderman was expected to devote his time to the organization—one aldermanic president had called the Board an "assemblage of district errand boys."[31]

The City Councilman continued to render unofficial service, for few American legislators can safely ignore the voters' demands. With constituencies immensely enlarged, however, the old, intimate contact vanished. "The doorbell doesn't ring; people don't burst into the house any more," commented the wife of an ex-alderman who was elected to the Council.[32] Some of the alderman's old chores have devolved upon the Assemblyman, for the old aldermanic districts were almost identical with State assembly districts. But the void was never completely filled.

To a limited degree, the district organization's loss was the county organization's gain. With councilmen elected on a borough-wide ticket, the county leader began to exercise greater power over the selection of candidates. In some boroughs he could also request their services. Bronx County headquarters has a central filing system for "contracts" that district leaders are unable to fulfill. The City Councilmen were expected to do a share of the work.[33]

In Manhattan the borough organization suffered a crushing blow. Sadly deficient in leadership, torn by internal strife, deprived of patronage by President Roosevelt, Governor Lehman, and Mayor La Guardia, Tammany Hall had fallen upon evil days. The machine which had once run the nation's largest city became so insolvent that a bank sold its Union Square headquarters to the International Ladies Garment Workers Union. With only the courts and county offices controlled by Tammany

[31] *Proc. of Bd. of Ald., 1934,* I, 9.
[32] Interview with the Hon. Walter R. Hart, September 25, 1947.
[33] Flynn, *You're the Boss,* p. 22.

after 1934, the famine for jobs grew to such proportions that even the $5,000 salary of an alderman seemed attractive. The transition to the City Council reduced the number of Tammany placeholders in the city legislature from 22 to 2 at a single stroke. Worse still, the first P. R. election signalized the end of its dominance in municipal politics. In the first Board of Aldermen of Greater New York (1898), Tammany had controlled 35 out of 60 seats. In 1937 Brooklyn forged ahead with 9 Councilmen to Manhattan's 6. Even the Bronx caught up with Tammany in 1945, when both elected 5 City Councilmen. The outlying boroughs, bedrooms of Manhattan's hives of commerce and finance, were in the ascendent; Tammany Hall was now only one of the five county machines.

Acutely conscious of the threat embodied in P. R., the five Democratic county organizations engaged in a ten-year running battle with it. Before the 1937 election a law-suit was instituted to have P. R. declared unconstitutional. This came to naught when the Court of Appeals upheld it as an "attempt to make representative government a reality." [34]

Nothing daunted, they engineered a deal with upstate Republicans at the Constitutional Convention the following year to place on the ballot an amendment barring P. R. for any purpose in the state. It was a fiasco. Denounced by good government forces as one of the "most brazen political attacks on the principles of self-government in the history of the state," the proposition was repudiated by every political party and went down to resounding defeat at the polls. Every county in the state rejected it. In the city the proportionalists' margin of victory was even greater than in 1936—775,038 to 355,031. Of the 42 questions submitted to the city's electorate between 1931 and 1940 only two drew a greater negative vote.[35]

The next assault came in 1940. Curiously enough, the initiative-petition, written into the charter at the request of the re-

[34] *Johnson v. the City of New York et al.: Matter of Bowe v. Cohen,* 274 N. Y. 411 (1937); *Columbia Law Review,* XXXVII (1937), 1426-27; *Nat. Mun. Rev.,* XXVI, 100-1, 203-4, 262, 369-71.

[35] *The Searchlight,* XXVIII, No. 2 (1938), 7; Hallett, *P. R.: Key to Democ.,* p. 153; *Reports of Bd. of Elects., 1931-1940, passim.*

formers, was turned against their principal charter reform. Ostensibly the Bronx Chamber of Commerce led the drive; actually the Democratic machines prepared and circulated the petitions. For the third time P. R. was vindicated at the polls, although the margin was reduced to less than a quarter of a million.[36]

During the forties the Democrats tried another tack. By 1941 the Republicans, who never gained more than two or three City Councilmen under P. R., were becoming disgruntled, and the election of a Communist caused mutterings. Encouraged by these developments, a large Democratic majority passed a repealer in the City Council, but the Fusion Board of Estimate never acted on it. In 1942 the same bill died in committee. Proposals to prohibit P. R. throughout the state were introduced in the State Legislature, but never emerged from committee. Both sides were inclined to postpone the issue until the end of the war.[37]

Meanwhile there were a number of intellectual trends that favored the opponents of P. R. When the system was adopted in 1936 scarcely any P. R. literature was available, and its foes resorted, perforce, to hasty improvisation. Late in 1938 a German refugee, Dr. Ferdinand A. Hermens, attacked P. R. in a scholarly magazine,[38] and during the next decade tracts against P. R. flowed steadily from his pen. While these writings never gained mass circulation, they did provide an arsenal of arguments that were employed during the campaign for repeal.[39] The

[36] Charter, Sec. 24; *Nat. Mun. Rev.*, XXIX, 699-701, 828-30.

[37] *Proc. of Council, 1941*, II, 316-17; *1942*, I, 1067; *New York Legislative Record and Index* (Albany, 1944), pp. 14, 154; *Nat. Mun. Rev.*, XXX (1941), 736: XXXI (1942), 184-85, 361, 580; XXXIII, 153, 213-14.

[38] "The Trojan Horse of Democracy," *Social Research*, V (1938), 397-423.

[39] E. g. the Hon. Louis Cohen, Mayor O'Dwyer's assistant, who led the Democratic drive for repeal in the Bronx, consulted Hermens' *Democracy or Anarchy* early in October, 1947 and the library of the *Times* borrowed it for more than two weeks, returning it on October 24th. (Records of Municipal Reference Library.) Directly afterwards the *Times* ran a series of anti-P. R. editorials (October 27 through October 30), specifically citing Hermens' volume on the last day. The State Chamber of Commerce quoted his works frequently in a pamphlet on the subject printed during the campaign. See *P. R.: What It Is and How It Works, passim.*

Daily News, which claimed the largest circulation in the country, deserted P. R. after the first election, and the influential *Times,* which had originally given P. R. qualified support, gradually turned against it. By 1947 these were joined by the *Mirror, Journal-American* and *World-Telegram.* The *Sun* had always been unfavorable to P. R. The combined circulation of these journals far outnumbered those of the *Herald-Tribune, Post, P.M.,* and *Daily Worker,* which still endorsed it. When it is recalled that in 1936 P. R. had had almost unanimous support in the metropolitan press, it is clear that the climate of opinion was becoming hostile.[40]

What militated most heavily against P. R. was the election of two Communists. Good will towards a war-time ally had helped seat them in 1943 and 1945, but in 1947 the United States was involved in the cold war to contain Communism and the pendulum swung the other way. An investigating commission which reported to the President just before the 1947 election found a state of near-hysteria on the subject. Opponents of P. R. exploited the issue by stigmatizing P. R. as a device "straight from the Kremlin." Only under P. R., they charged, were avowed Communists ever elected to public office in the United States. (Actually several of their candidates had been elected in the Mid-West.) Those who despised Fascism were told it was responsible for the rise of Hitler in Germany and Mussolini in Italy.[41]

Some argued that extreme left-wingers controlled 18% of the Council—two outright Communists and two representatives of the American Labor Party. Although Bronx Democratic Leader Flynn publicly stated that the American Labor Party was "largely Communist controlled," this line of reasoning was not emphasized by his own party, for they had been closely involved with the left-wingers. Only two years earlier (1945), a deal with the A. L. P. had resulted in A. L. P. endorsement of the city-wide Democratic ticket and Democratic backing of Eugene P. Connolly, A. L. P. candidate for the City Council. A peculiarly inti-

40 Zeller and Bone, *op. cit.,* p. 1131.

41 *Ibid.,* p. 1133; *To Secure These Rights: Report of the President's Committee on Civil Rights* (Washington, 1947), p. 49.

mate relationship existed with Congressman Vito Marcantonio, A. L. P. Leader of New York County—the Democratic leader of his district acted as his spokesman in Tammany's executive committee. During the primary campaign preceding the mayoralty election of 1953, it was repeatedly charged that Marcantonio had brought pressure to secure the nomination of Vincent R. Impelliteri as President of the City Council. In 1945 Tammany Hall actually nominated Davis, an avowed Communist, for Councilman, although the endorsement was later withdrawn.[42]

On the other hand, some politicians were genuinely shocked by the Communists' behavior in the city legislature. When Cardinal Spellman was elevated to his office early in 1946, the two Communist Councilmen not only voted against a resolution congratulating him, but also presented a statement denouncing him. This "impertinent affront" incensed Council President Impelliteri. Watching their tactics convinced him they were more interested in "tub-thumping for un-American doctrines than . . . working for more efficient municipal government." "The radical members of the Council are not interested in getting things done, but in creating issues," declared Park Commissioner Moses. "They do not seem to know much about the city and don't seem to be interested." [43]

The campaign was skillfully managed. Ostensibly it was a spontaneous civic movement, initiated by chambers of commerce, labor councils, veterans' organizations, and taxpayers' associations. Actually it was sponsored by the city's Democratic and Republican machines. (Afterwards it was revealed that the Citizens Committee to Repeal P. R. obtained all its funds from the Democratic county organizations and that clubhouse workers were assigned to collect signatures for petitions.) A decade's experience with P. R. had provided its opponents with a variety of arguments. It was held to be too complicated, confusing, and

[42] *New York World-Telegram*, September 9, 1947; *New York Herald-Tribune*, August 24, 1947, October 3, 1950; Richard H. Rovere, "Vito Marcantonio," *Harper's Magazine*, CLXXXVIII (1944), 397; Bone, "Pol. Parties in N. Y. C.," *Am. Pol. Sci. Rev.*, XL, 274-76.

[43] *Proc. of Council, 1946*, I, 229-30; *New York Herald-Tribune*, August 28, October 30, 1947; Genevieve B. Earle, "Let's Look at the Record," Press Release of November 1, 1947 (Earle Papers in the Municipal Reference Library).

unwieldy; it was too expensive; it opened the door to fraud; it was a lottery; it destroyed neighborhood representation; it encouraged racial, religious and alphabetical voting; it was destructive of the two-party system and fostered "splinter" parties and blocs; it was undemocratic and un-American. But the trump card was the current unpopularity of Communism. P. R. was condemned as "New York's greatest gift to the Communists." [44]

The Democrats supported repeal as a matter of course, for the district system promised to restore their near-monopoly in the city legislature. The Republicans faced a more difficult decision. Conservatives among them were eager to discard a system that permitted the election of Communists and fellow-travelers. They pointed out that Republicans might easily increase their representation, for the repealer substituted 25 State Senate districts for borough-wide constituencies. In 1947 the city was represented in the Senate by 12 Republicans as against 13 Democrats. On the other hand liberal Republicans argued that the district system would virtually eliminate Republican representation in the City Council. The last state elections had taken place in 1946, the year of a Republican sweep. But City Councilmen run for office during Mayoralty elections, and in 1945 Mayor O'Dwyer had carried every Senate district. "I would rather see the Council made up of 25 Democrats," replied one dyed-in-the-wool Republican, "if that was the only alternative against the present set-up." [45]

The Republican leaders advocated repeal chiefly to consolidate their power. On the face of it there were a greater proportion of Republican and Republican-Fusion Councilmen elected in five P. R. contests than in the last five aldermanic races. But P. R. permitted the seating of prominent candidates without their leaders' endorsement. Of the three Republicans elected in 1945, two originally ran without their party's official designation.

[44] One tactic fizzled. A political off-year was selected on the theory that the machine vote would bulk larger than the independent vote. Instead there was a record turnout. *New York Times*, April 1, June 17, 1947; *New York Herald-Tribune*, October 27, 1947; Zeller and Bone, *op. cit.*, 1130, 1146; *Nat. Mun. Rev.*, XXXVI (1947), 287-88, 346-48, 360, 533-34.

[45] Letter to editor of *New York Herald-Tribune*, September 13, 1947.

With P. R. gone, insurgents would find the primaries almost an insuperable hurdle. But the party was by no means unanimous. The Young Men's Republican Club, the Young Women's Republican Club, and all the Republican Councilmen supported P. R.[46]

Substantially the same organizations that had led the revolt against Tammany and campaigned for P. R. in the thirties supported the Keep Proportional Representation Committee in 1947 —the Citizens Union, the City Club, the Commerce and Industry Association (formerly the Merchants' Association), the League of Women Voters, the Women's City Club, and the minority parties. They were joined by such newly organized groups as Americans for Democratic Action, the American Veterans Committee, and the Greater New York C.I.O. Political Action Committee. An assorted group ranging from conservative to radical, the proportionalists tried to defend P. R. on its own merits. But they found themselves fighting on ground chosen by their opponents.

When the charter was adopted, the memory of the Seabury investigation was still fresh, and the electorate accepted P. R. as a hopeful municipal reform. In 1947 the scandals of the Walker administration were fading into history and appeals for "good government" fell flat. The public mood made it easy to panic the electorate into voting down P. R. on the Red issue. In vain did the Keep P. R. Committee argue that P. R. was "as American as the hot dog, as native as baseball on a Sunday afternoon." To no avail did it quote impeccable Catholic sources to prove that P. R. was consonant with the Christian position. The Council's Minority Leader pleaded that abolishing P. R. to eliminate Communists was like burning down the whole house to roast a pig. Samuel Seabury demonstrated that those parties which purported to be shocked at the radicals elected by P. R. had themselves effected hundreds of deals with leftists on legislative candidates. With memories of the war against Fascism still fresh, in the face of the cold war against Communism, references

[46] Commerce and Ind. Assoc., "Report Concerning Election of N. Y. C. Council," pp. 11-12; Letter of Councilman Edward Rager to author, November 19, 1947.

to the Fascist Beast and the Red Menace created a powerful emotional effect.[47]

The result was a vigorous propaganda campaign, completely overshadowing contests for elective offices in that year. When the results were in, P. R. was found decisively beaten, by a majority almost as great as that which had adopted it—935,222 to 586,170. Resentment against Communism had been artfully channelled into a vote against P. R.[48]

Although good government groups and minority parties hoped eventually to restore P. R., no campaign was feasible until the Red issue subsided. Indeed, there was profound relief when the A. L. P. failed to follow through a gesture in that direction in 1948. It seemed better strategy to wait until the new City Council discredited itself.[49]

Starting with the campaign of 1949, future City Councils would be elected by the majority system from the city's 25 State Senate districts. (This was almost identical with the alternative offered by the Thacher Commission in 1936 in the event that P. R. were rejected at the polls.) Many regarded the new set-up with foreboding. Harlem leaders feared Negroes would be deprived of representation in the new legislature. Others pointed out that the use of Senatorial districts would freeze the geographic basis of representation for years to come, to the detriment of the growing boroughs. Realizing their candidates would not face borough-wide competition, district leaders would pack the City Council with "obscure nitwits," as in the days of the Board of Aldermen. No left-wingers would be elected, but neither would Liberals. Perhaps one or two Republicans would be seated. To all intents and purposes the independent voter would be disenfranchised. With the return of one-party rule the city legislature would revert to its former status as an adjunct of the Democratic machine. Important municipal questions

[47] *New York Times*, October 23, 1947; Letter of Samuel Seabury to *New York Sun*, October 31, 1947; *Nat. Mun. Rev.*, XXXVI, 587, 648; Earle, "Let's Look at the Record."

[48] *Report of Board of Elections, 1947*, p. 61.

[49] *Nat. Mun. Rev.*, XXXVII (1948), 453, 510.

would no longer be debated openly, but settled "in the mud of ward politics at its worst." [50]

Meanwhile sessions of the P. R. Council continued until the end of 1949. One immediate result of the election was a setback for the "splinter" parties. Repeal of P. R. meant the end of their representation in the city legislature. Although the election of their candidates gave the minority little power, successful campaigns for office did give their organizations a certain amount of cohesion. Smarting under its defeat, the American Labor Party, then the city's largest political minority, served notice that the coalition with Tammany was over. (The following year it supported the Wallace bid for the Presidency.) Republicans and Democrats immediately began to court the Liberal Party. Finally, Republican representation in the city was certain to be weakened, since they rarely drew their full vote in mayoralty elections. Abolition of P. R. had created serious shifts in the political balance of power.[51]

[50] Zeller and Bone, *op. cit.*, p. 1138; Comm. and Ind. Assn., "Report Concerning Election of N. Y. C. Council," pp. 19-21; Radio Broadcast of Richard S. Childs, Aug. 10, 1947; Press Release of Keep P. R. Committee, October 16, 1947.

[51] Moscow, *Pol. in Emp. St.*, p. 118; *New York Herald-Tribune,* November 5, 1947.

12. A THREE-RING CIRCUS

The darling, quarreling, billingsgate, God-awful City Council.
—FRANKLIN P. ADAMS [1]

THE NEW City Council attracted widespread interest in political, newspaper, and academic circles, not only because New York is a world metropolis, but also because of the legislature's novel and experimental features and for its uproarious and brawling initial sessions. It was only when the war began to overshadow municipal news that public interest in the City Council subsided.

The opening sessions contrasted spectacularly with the dull routine of its predecessor. A body once described as a museum was suddenly transformed into a three-ring circus. One observer found it so different from the old board that "only the fact that the Council sits in the same chamber brings any remembrance of that ancient and deposed group." In the first months of 1938 the chief cause of the turmoil was a Protean struggle for organization and control.[2]

For more than two decades the Democrats had dominated the city legislature with ease. In 1938 it was a different story. Thirteen Democrats were ranged against a coalition of thirteen—3 Republicans, 5 American Labor Party men, 3 Fusionites, and 2 insurgent Democrats. Since President Newbold Morris could cast the deciding vote in case of a tie, the coalition seemed to have a working majority.

1 Quoted by Minority Leader Earle, *Proc. of Council*, 1941, I, 4.

2 Press Release of City Affairs Committee, July 12, 1933; Tanzer, "The First P. R. Council," *The Searchlight*, XXIX, No. 1, 3; Russell Owen, "'S. R. O.' Sign out at City Hall," *New York Times Magazine*, January 30, 1938.

Then a fluke occurred. A. L. P. Councilmen Michael J. Quill was still on a protracted honeymoon when the first meeting began. His absence permitted the 13 regular Democrats to elect a vice-chairman and appoint committees. When President Morris ruled the elections improper because a majority of *all* the Councilmen was lacking, he touched off a controversy that convulsed the City Council for months.[3] The legislature became a parliamentary battleground where contending groups elected rival vice-chairmen and majority leaders, where rules of procedure and standing committees gained no more than temporary status.[4] The result was a deadlock that permitted only the most urgent and noncontroversial business to be transacted. It was not until October 18th that the Court of Appeals rendered its final decision, upholding the organization Democrats all along the line.[5]

With its minority almost obliterated, the old board's sessions had often degenerated into perfunctory performances—opposing the Tammany steamroller had seemed altogether futile. As the caliber of the legislators was elevated and its minority attained respectable size, the City Council's proceedings gained a fresh and unmistakable vitality. For the first time in decades it became a real forum for airing municipal problems. Important bills were brought to the floor of the chamber and thoroughly debated. The proceedings were even broadcast over the municipal radio station to an estimated audience of 750,000. Groton and Harvard accents mingled with Brooklynese, brogues, and a variety of intonations, as the legislative sessions became one of the most popular programs on the air. No one appreciated the vigor of the new assemblage more keenly than Newbold Morris. Few men in public life have been exposed to the abuse he en-

[3] Section 34 of the Charter reads: "No local law or resolution shall be passed except by at least the majority affirmative vote of all the Councilmen."

[4] The Fusion alliance chose James A. Burke, insurgent Democrat from Queens, Vice-Chairman and B. Charney Vladeck, of the A. L. P., Majority Leader. The regular Democrats elected John B. Cashmore Vice-Chairman.

[5] By this time the regular Democrats actually controlled the Council, Councilmen Burke and Conrad having re-entered the Democratic fold. *Nat. Mun. Rev.*, XXVII, 115-16, 558-59; *Morris v. Cashmore,* 278 N. Y. 262, 278 N. Y. 732 (1938).

dured as presiding officer. Speaking from the floor, political opponents baited him mercilessly.[6]

There were signs that the City Council was beginning to look beyond narrow district boundaries and to consider the welfare of the entire city. In place of countless permits for street stands and designation of individual play streets, it became interested in city-wide issues, such as housing, regulation of consumer commodities, and civil service reform. The general police power was employed more vigorously, and greater interest was displayed in reforming the city government.[7]

Nevertheless the City Council was not transformed into an effective legislature in a single term. Nothing drastically objectionable emerged, but on the other hand there were no bold solutions to the city's problems. Aldermanic "privilege," which had dictated automatic consent to members' proposals affecting their own communities, reappeared in an odd form. Councilmen just didn't seem able to resist their constituents' requests on place names—more than half the local laws of 1938 related to the naming of streets, parks, or squares. Financial powers were still regarded as a convenient weapon for belaboring a Fusion administration, rather than an opportunity for framing municipal policies.[8] As the City Council convened for its second term, it was admonished by its presiding officer:

> A legislative body which neglects the powers vested in it by the people, preferring to fritter its time away with non-legislative activities, can hardly command respect. The naming and renaming of streets, parks, and other public places, the consideration of endless "request" resolutions to city departments over which we have no control . . . hardly seem to instil confidence in the people. Such activities are pointless and serve only to voice the question of the need for a local legislative body at all.[9]

[6] Asher William Schwartz, "A Study of the New York City Council" (typewritten manuscript in Municipal Reference Library, September 1, 1941), p. 12; Morris, "Advantages of the City Council over the old Board of Aldermen," *Flatbush Magazine,* XVI, No. 9, 1; Rovere, "Good Citizen," *The New Yorker,* XX, No. 37, 30-31.

[7] Charles Belous, "A Year Gone By: Being a Report on the Work and Progress of the New York City Council" (November, 1938), 5; Schwartz, *A Study of the N. Y. C. Council,* p. 25 ff.

[8] Schwartz, *op. cit.,* pp. 35-39, 51-52; Prince, *N. Y. C. Council,* p. 96; *The Searchlight,* XXIX, No. 1, 13-15; Lazarus, *The Council,* p. 7.

[9] *Proc. of Council, 1940,* I, 11-12.

There were some bright spots. The house ratified the administration's program of financing relief on a pay-as-you-go basis, and passed the Vladeck Low Rent Housing Law. But on the whole the first City Council scarcely acquitted itself better than the average do-nothing Board of Aldermen. The most glaring failure was in connection with county offices, once described as "nests of the spoils system, reeking with incompetence and favoritism, and expensively operated by gentlemen of obvious unfitness." After ten months of tireless efforts Councilman Genevieve B. Earle succeeded in discharging from committee a series of county consolidation bills. They were considered at a meeting which consumed twenty hours, as the Democrats attempted to wear out the minority. In the end, two Republicans voted with the Democrats to defeat the measures. The organization had saved the county jobs for the faithful, but the defeat of the reorganization bills helped produce two years of stalemate.[10]

Some of the onus could be imputed to the majority, which seemed more eager to criticize and obstruct the city administration than effect a constructive legislative program. Anti-Tammany elements believed the majority's strategy was to bring the new City Council and P. R. into disrepute.[11] A Citizens Union observer stated:

> Members of the old guard . . . have done their best, directly and indirectly, to make the Council look silly, hoping in that way to discredit P. R. It almost seemed as if some of the majority members, instead of trying to make records for themselves, were sitting back and waiting for opportunities to keep the entire Council from making any sort of record in the hope that by so doing the old Board of Aldermen might by some miracle be brought back to life.[12]

The majority derived a singular advantage from their background of parliamentary experience. Re-enacting the rules of the old Board of Aldermen, which were well suited to their pur-

[10] Seidman, *Investigating Mun. Admin.*, p. 110; "The City Council—Its First Year," City Affairs Committee Bulletin, February, 1939; *The County Reorganization Amendment,* City Aff. Comm. Bull., September, 1940; *The Searchlight,* XXIX, No. 1, 4-6.

[11] Belous, "A Year Gone By," p. 8; "The Councilmanic Race—1939," City Affairs Committee Bulletin, September, 1939.

[12] *The Searchlight,* XXIX, No. 1, 3.

poses, enabled them to restrict the minority yet permit themselves the widest latitude. When the majority wanted to take the opposition by surprise, a committee report was pulled out of a hat and introduced without prior notice on the calendar. If the minority desired to discharge a measure from committee, however, it was virtually powerless, for it required the consent of a majority of all the members. Charles E. Keegan, the Beau Brummel of the City Council, was particularly adept at entangling the minority in procedural snarls—or needling Newbold Morris.[13]

The deviltry of the majority was not the sole reason for the Council's disappointing record. The long period of legal wrangling over organization permitted few decisive issues to crystallize the first year. Again, with the conspicuous exception of Joseph Clark Baldwin, who had served as State Senator and Minority Leader in the Board of Aldermen, and B. Charney Vladek, former leader of the "minor" minority in the Board of Aldermen, the entire minority were freshman legislators. Good government advocates hoped they would grow in effectiveness as they gained in experience. (At the end of a decade, however, Minority Leader Earle confided that many in her group believed in good government, but did not know how to get it. Compared to the professional politicians on the Democratic side of the aisle, the minority was amateurish and adolescent.)[14]

In addition, some of the body's newly found energies were expended in dubious ventures. President Morris once rebuked it for "guerrilla excursions organized for political purposes under the guise of 'investigations.'" Like aldermanic majorities of yore—both Fusion and Democratic—the majority sallied forth to harass a hostile Mayor with probes of his administration. But where the aldermen had rarely used their power, the City Council seemed ready to investigate at the drop of a hat. In a single term twenty such inquiries were authorized. Fortunately, perhaps, little emerged from these expeditions. In one instance it

[13] *Ibid.*, XXIX, No. 2, 11; Schwartz, *op. cit.*, pp. 47-48; Belous, *op. cit.*, pp. 8-9; *Manual of the Council, 1938-1939* (New York, 1939), p. 11.

[14] *The Searchlight,* XXIX, No. 2, 9; Earle, *Reminiscences,* pp. 69, 76.

was learned that Brooklyn College lacked a flagpole for displaying the stars and stripes. Before a legislative committee could capitalize on the issue, the campus acquired a flagstaff.[15]

In later sessions the Democrats recovered from their outraged shock at finding a substantial and articulate opposition and buckled down to serious work. Even during the stormy initial sessions, Majority Leader John Cashmore gave the administration grudging cooperation, yielding enough votes to pass essential measures. In Mayor La Guardia's last year of office (1945) the majority leader boasted that his party had always supplied the votes needed for administration legislation that was obviously in the city's welfare. After Pearl Harbor, Majority Leader Joseph T. Sharkey restrained his more belligerent adherents with the result that "needless controversy and nagging contention" gave way to a more orderly procedure. (Years later Sharkey recalled the decorum at the opening sessions with a pang of regret.) One promising reform was the amendment of the rules to permit greater minority participation in the Council's work. As time went on the minority found it possible to make constructive recommendations on pending legislation with the assurance that they would gain a fair hearing and that their suggestions might be incorporated into the final draft.[16]

There were some Councilmen, particularly among the minority, who gave serious attention to basic civic issues. When Mrs. Genevieve B. Earle was elected minority leader, she offered the following legislative program: county reorganization, tax reform, reorganization of city employees' pension systems, slum clearance, low income housing, traffic safety, consumer protection, improvement of labor standards, and solution of the problems of youth. As long as La Guardia remained Mayor, however, the City Council failed to grapple with vital municipal problems. In areas such as consumer protection, local laws for licensing ice

[15] *Proc. of Council, 1939,* I, 59; *1940,* I, 12; *The Searchlight,* XXIX, No. 1, 4, 10-11; Schwartz, *op. cit.,* pp. 40-43; Interview with the Hon. Stanley M. Isaacs, September 9, 1947.

[16] Newbold Morris, *Reminiscences* (Oral History Project, Columbia University, 1950), pp. 41, 72; *Proc. of Council, 1944,* I, 8; *1945,* I, 3; *The Searchlight,* XXXIII, No. 1 (1943), 13; *New York Herald-Tribune,* March 23, 1947.

and poultry dealers or prohibiting service charges exceeding $1.00 on transportation tickets comprised a fragmentary and oblique approach, but there was no frontal attack on the larger problem.[17]

During the La Guardia administration (1938-45)[18] the house's legislative record was spotty. Perhaps one or two outstanding laws were enacted in each session. When the first City Council accepted the Mayor's relief tax program, New York became one of the few cities in the country to develop new sources of revenue for unemployment relief. The Vladeck Housing Law led to the country's first municipal slum clearance program in conjunction with the federal government. The second Council (1940-41) set up a sound actuarial system for policemen and firemen and passed bills to eliminate the obsolete county offices. (Action on this issue, however, came only after a petition of 92,000 voters placed the question on the 1941 ballot for a referendum. At that, the City Council's bill was rejected at the polls in favor of the more drastic proposals of civic organizations.) As the reform administration drew to a close, President Newbold Morris listed forty-nine of its more notable enactments. But most were of minor import. To advance the war effort, for example, the City Council had voted to require obedience to air raid wardens' signals, to prohibit smoking on docks, and to prescribe fire protection equipment for buildings. In 1945 Morris candidly informed the house, "we have not approached the performance the public had a right to expect of us."[19]

During the first administration of Democratic Mayor O'Dwyer (1946-49) the Council addressed itself more vigorously to the solution of municipal problems. When Congress relaxed rent controls in 1947, gouging of tenants and wholesale evictions were feared. In this crisis, New York was one of the first cities to act. Majority Leader Sharkey guided through the City Council a

17 *Proc. of Council, 1940,* I, 13-15; Rebecca B. Rankin (ed.) *New York Advancing: Victory Edition* (New York, 1945), pp. 271-73.

18 The Board of Aldermen was still functioning during La Guardia's first term (1934-37). The City Council's first session was held at the beginning of his second term.

19 *Nat. Mun. Rev.,* XXIX, 143, XXX, 604; Rankin, *N. Y. Advancing: Victory Ed.,* pp. 271-73; *Proc. of Council, 1945,* I, 2.

series of emergency measures to plug up holes in the Federal statute, limiting rent increases and tightening grounds for eviction. A black market in hotel rentals the following year was countered by new laws providing further protection. The enactment and implementing of these measures gained widespread approval. "The Sharkey rent laws have made New Yorkers more secure in their shelter in this year of weak rent control," wrote a consumer page editor. H. T. Webster, a noted newspaper cartoonist, portrayed an apartment-seeking family exulting at the news that a renting agent had been sent to the workhouse. The principal Sharkey law succumbed in early court tests,[20] but the state legislature speedily validated it, and it survived later decisions.[21] So popular did the Democratic local laws prove, that a Republican candidate for reëlection to the State Senate used the campaign argument that he had introduced the curative statute.[22]

Its forthright handling of rent control and passage of laws to regulate garages, parking spaces, and fire safety in multiple dwellings convinced Samuel Seabury that the last P. R. Council (1946-49) was the "best legislature we have had so far." Later this same Council tackled the difficult problem of traffic congestion, setting up a central Traffic Commission, and enacted a Smoke Control Bill. The latter earned Majority Leader Sharkey an award from the Outdoor Cleanliness Association. Attacking problems of prime importance gave this Council a stature the Board of Aldermen could never approach.[23]

Why did the last Council produce a more substantial record than its predecessors? Often the key to a modern legislature's actions lies in its relations with the executive. A study of the

[20] Local Law 66 of 1947 in *Tartaglia v. McLaughlin,* 190 Misc. 266, 273 App. Div. 821 (1948).

[21] Based on L. 1938, C. 4. See *Molnar v. Curtin,* 273 App. Div. 322 (1948). Incidentally, the state law led to a judicial reversal of *Tartaglia v. McLaughlin* in 297 N. Y. 419 (1948).

[22] *Nat. Mun. Rev.,* XXXVI, 577-78; *New York Herald-Tribune,* October 23, 1948; *P. M.,* March 28, 1948; *New York State Legislative Annual, 1948* (New York, 1948), pp. 222-23; Handbill for Senator Irwin Pakula, 1948.

[23] Samuel Seabury, "P. R. Should Not Be Abolished," Radio address over Station WNBC, October 8, 1947; *New York Herald-Tribune,* May 27, 1949.

bills passed in the Council in its first three years (1938-40) indicates that the legislators undertook very little on their own responsibility. There were 191 laws dealing with trivial subjects, such as the naming of streets or authorization of inter-departmental property transfers. Ninety-eight building code changes were drafted by outside experts and building interests and approved first by the Department of Housing and Buildings. Of the remainder, 92 were requested by the administration; only 21 originated in the City Council itself. It would appear that the house's relations with the Mayor were of paramount importance.[24]

Significantly, the first four Councils (1938-1945) were dominated by Democratic majorities while the administration was Fusion. Mayor La Guardia felt that the house harassed him to the point of unjustifiable abuse. Violent denunciations of his administration were frequent and the threat of investigations was regularly used as a club. Fourteen years' experience in Congress, however, left the Mayor quite philosophical about these ructions. "I have handed out too much legislative punishment in my time to be permitted to complain that I am on the receiving end this time," he declared. Nevertheless, persuading the City Council to accept his legislative proposals was no easy matter. Sometimes little deals were arranged through the county leaders, sometimes he tried cajolery, sometimes threats. "I thrive on opposition," he once informed the legislators. "Don't give me the ammunition." In practice the Democrats supported the bulk of his requests. Often they had little alternative. As a responsible majority they would bear the onus if the city government broke down through failure of the City Council to enact necessary legislation. But if they coöperated with the administration in emergencies, it was hardly in the interest of the Democratic majority to promote a Fusion mayor's record.[25]

The threat of legislative opposition exasperated Mayor La Guardia, but it probably exerted a wholesome influence on mu-

[24] Schwartz, *op. cit.*, p. 69.

[25] *Nat. Mun. Rev.*, XXIX, 274; Earle, *Reminiscences*, pp. 60-61, 99-100; *Proc. of Council, 1940*, I, 19; *1941*, I, 46; Flynn, *You're the Boss*, p. 139.

nicipal government. There was a streak of Caesarism in La Guardia's temperament, which was restrained by the prospect of Councilmanic criticism. Instead he turned on his own cabinet, often treating his commissioners "as if they were feeble-minded office boys." In his frenetic rage, he drove several superb administrators, whom he himself had installed, out of the municipal government. Oddly enough, he parted on friendly terms with the legislators. In his final public report he lashed out against the state legislature and courts, but praised the City Council for its "full cooperation and help." [26]

In Mayor O'Dwyer's first administration (1946-49) it was a different story. With city administration and city legislature controlled by the same party, no one could seriously expect the City Council to investigate the executive departments. Once a Councilmanic committee had been greatly agitated because Mayor La Guardia had permitted the appointment of 5,000 provisional employees in the civil service. This was in 1940, when the city was rapidly losing workers to war industries. In 1949, with no scarcity of manpower, the mayor estimated the number at more than 25,000. Needless to say it was suspected that some positions were being filled by clubhouse favorites. This time efforts by the minority to probe the situation were thwarted.[27]

Under Mayor O'Dwyer the whole atmosphere was transformed. Bills sponsored by the administration might be amended, but passage was assured. When Mayor La Guardia requested "nuisance" taxes for home relief, the Democrats refused to sponsor them and subjected them to withering criticism before supplying their votes. When the Majority Leader introduced the identical bills at the request of Mayor O'Dwyer, they were praised on the floor of the City Council and went through with ease. The last P. R. Council (1946-49), as we have seen, achieved the most impressive record. Of course legislation to control rents and summary evictions, to reduce air pollution and

[26] Henry F. Pringle's review of *The Making of an Insurgent,* by Fiorello H. La Guardia in *New York Times Book Review Section,* May 23, 1948; Limpus and Leyson, *This Man La Guardia,* p. 385; Earle, *Reminiscences,* pp. 114-15; Rankin, *N. Y. Advancing: Victory Ed.,* pp. xv, xxix.

[27] Earle, *Reminiscences,* pp. 99-100, 108-110.

deal with traffic congestion cast luster upon the administration. The legislative machine seemed to operate more smoothly when a Democratic majority cooperated with a Democratic Mayor.[28]

Like all legislative bodies, the City Council had its dreary and barren stretches. The more responsible members deplored the hopeless proposals introduced only to gratify constituents, the foolish and frivolous laws that slipped through. At one time the body was considering twin bills for naming a park in Brooklyn. One called it Callahan-Kelly, to satisfy local Irish residents, the other Amerigo Vespucci, for the benefit of the Italian neighbors. Both passed; Mayor La Guardia vetoed both. All too often the City Council wandered far afield. In 1947 it passed resolutions urging President Truman to solve a meat shortage by seizing cattle and distributing the meat to the public, and advising him how to instruct American delegates to the United Nations.[29]

Many Councilmen insisted that the body could never play a vital rôle in the city government because its authority was too trivial. A Fusionite complained that when he had campaigned for the new charter in 1936 he had believed the city would gain a vigorous legislature. After his election he discovered that 90 to 95% of the legislation was subject to the approval of the Board of Estimate, the mayor, or the electorate. One critic called the legislators "fiscal eunuchs." In 1940, however, the Minority Leader opined that the Council had yet to demonstrate it deserved broader powers, for it had never adequately exercised those it possessed.[30]

Curiously enough, both proportionalists and their opponents agreed that the City Council could never become an effective legislature. Like the Councilmen, the former maintained that its powers were too limited. On the other side it was argued that P. R. had "acted as an instrument of disintegration, fragmentizing the electorate by emphasizing areas of disagreement rather

28 *Ibid.*, pp. 97-98.

29 *Ibid.*, pp. 56-57, 86, 89; Rovere, "Good Citizen," *The New Yorker*, XX, No. 37, 29; *City Council Record*, XXIII, No. 9 (1947), 39, 50.

30 Belous, *op. cit.*, pp. 5-7; *Proc. of Council, 1940*, I, 14-15.

than agreement." Hence it promoted chaos and prevented the formation of a workable majority.[31]

To Minority Leader Earle, this reasoning seemed "pure buncombe." Her research disclosed that the entire minority voted with the majority on 267 out of the 305 measures passed in 1940. Eighty per cent of the local laws of 1946 and 1947 gained unanimous approval; some of the remainder were enacted with only a single dissenting vote. "There is no stalemate in our legislative effectiveness," she declared. Most measures obtained overwhelming approval because suggestions of the minority had been accepted by the majority. The minority could hold up egregiously bad bills, but it could hardly block legislation in the welfare of the city, even if it wanted to do so.[32]

Normally the majority leader succeeded in obtaining agreement on pending measures before the roll call. If difficulties arose, Sharkey would whip recalcitrant members into line at a party caucus. Intra-party disputes stemmed from two sources—borough jealousy and clashing political philosophies. Like the Brooklyn aldermen at the turn of the century, the legislators from Queens believed their borough was not obtaining its fair share of offices. (This grievance was not related to P. R., for the Queens Councilmen nourished their resentment even after the district system of elections had been restored.) Again, in the New Deal and Fair Deal era the municipal machine gained fresh vitality by aligning itself with the forces of liberalism. The Queens Councilmen, however, stood far to the right of center, and Sharkey was frequently obliged to oppose their proposals for censorship of billboards, theatre posters, and public school texts.[33]

To prove that P. R. facilitated cooperation between the minority and better elements among the majority for good government, the proportionalists sometimes highlighted revolts in the

[31] Richard S. Childs, "The Ballot Is Still Too Long," *Nat. Mun. Rev.*, XXXV, 70; Geo. H. Hallett, "The Case for P. R.," *The American Scholar*, XII (1943), 167; *New York Times*, April 2, 1947; *New York Daily Mirror*, November 3, 1947.

[32] Earle, "Let's Look at the Record," *Proc. of Council, 1941*, I, 3-4.

[33] Earle, *Reminiscences*, pp. 50-51, 82-84; *New York Herald-Tribune*, December 11, 1950; Irwin Ross, "Big City Machines and Liberal Voters," *Commentary*, X (1950), 301-6.

Democratic fold.[34] Uprisings of this nature, however, rarely occurred after the hectic first Council. Party discipline was too strong and the Democrats too shrewd to permit their majority to be dissipated at the option of a few dissidents. In later sessions the regular Democrats usually took their cues from the majority leader. If a caucus on an important measure was required, the decision was binding on the Democratic delegation.[35] Mayor La Guardia, whose experience as Aldermanic President had given him an insight into such matters, recognized the Democrats as the responsible majority and asked the majority leader to sponsor important administration bills. Although the Fusion minority were his natural allies, he rarely conferred with Minority Leader Earle on legislative matters.[36]

For sparring purposes, all non-regular Democrats were combined into the opposition. In the beginning it was merely outnumbered; later it became hopelessly divided. During the first four years, when they regarded themselves as part of the reform movement that had swept Tammany out of the city administration, they worked as a team. Before every meeting they conferred at the luncheon table or in the minority leader's office to define their position on pending legislation, and in Council sessions they usually voted as a unit, particularly on administration proposals. After 1942, however, they degenerated into a "Falstaffian rabble." In the third Council's coalition (1943-44) there were conservative Republicans who would not sit in the same room with the newly elected Communist; he, in turn, eyed them askance. The American Labor Party had split into left wing and right wing (later the Liberal Party), who were scarcely on speaking terms. Holding a meeting of such disparate groups was out of the question. It was necessary, in fact, physically to separate them. The Republicans remained in the Minority Leader's office, while the Liberals, Laborites, and Communists established

34 Letter of Samuel Seabury to *New York Times,* November 1, 1947; William R. Woodward and George H. Hallett, Jr., "Proportional Representation Works!" *Forum, CVII* (1947), 100.

35 Occasionally local interests were strong enough to overcome party regularity. The Councilmen from Queens, a borough of small homes and small landlords, did not always vote for the Sharkey rent laws.

36 Earle, *Reminiscences,* pp. 60, 75-76.

separate headquarters in the basement. "The minority jumped on horseback and went off in all directions," sadly commented the minority leader.[37]

Actually it mattered little whether the minority acted unanimously or split. The Democrats had the advantage of numbers, and no minority proposal could pass without their leaders' consent. The American Labor Party, for example, succeeded in enacting one local law (the Vladeck Program for slum clearance) in the Council's first three years.[38] In ten years as minority leader, Mrs. Earle could not get a single important measure through the Council. As we have seen, both a Fusion mayor and a Democratic mayor entrusted their vital legislation to the Democratic majority leader. The minority was given the bills the Democrats regarded as too trivial or too unpopular to handle. One minority member saw all his motions tabled, defeated, or emasculated. Among them was a resolution demanding the abolition of the six day week for civil servants. Shortly thereafter the majority leader put an almost identical measure into the hopper. This time it passed. (A minority Councilman could get good legislation enacted if he permitted the majority to take the credit.) In the last few years of P. R. the minority leader concentrated on improving and amending the majority's proposals rather than introducing her own.[39]

How effective were the two Communists whose election turned public opinion against P. R.? Between them over two hundred proposals were introduced. None became law. None of Cacchione's resolutions ever passed. A handful of Davis' resolutions dealing with such subjects as lynching in Georgia, George Washington Carver Day, and Negro History Week, went through.

[37] *Ibid.*, pp. 58-60, 72-73, 123-25; Letter of Robert Moses to *New York Times*, November 3, 1947.

[38] Five of its proposals also passed. These were in the form of petitions, however, and had no force in law. In a strict sense resolutions dealing with such subjects as a federal anti-lynching law were outside the scope of municipal legislation.

[39] Benjamin Fielding, "A Brief Review of the ALP in 1938-1939-1940 at City Hall and the 'Twelve Point' Program for 1941" (Press Release of American Labor Party, January 15, 1941); Earle, *Reminiscences*, pp. 67-68, 77, 113; Powell, *Marching Blacks*, p. 156; *Proc. of Council, 1945*, I, 5.

Cacchione and Davis influenced the minority only slightly and the majority not at all. City Hall reporters ignored them. Nevertheless their presence was a godsend to the Democratic machine in its anti-P. R. campaign.[40]

If the Fusion coalition could not enact its legislation, what purpose did it serve? For one thing, a substantial minority could influence the City Council's relations with the city administration. Throughout Mayor La Guardia's first term, he faced a hostile Board of Aldermen. With a three-fourths majority they could slash his budget and override his veto, regardless of how the minority voted. After P. R. had reduced their numbers, the Democrats were still eager to bedevil the Mayor by hacking at his appropriations. But now some minority support was needed. In 1943 three Fusion Councilmen joined the Democrats to overrule the mayor's budget veto. Non-partisan civic groups applauded their discriminating votes, for they had upheld the Mayor on items deemed essential and eliminated unnecessary appropriations. Moreover they had rebuked a mayor who was becoming autocratic in the exercise of executive power. Incidentally, since the consolidation of the city, no Board of Aldermen had asserted itself to the extent of overriding a budget veto.[41]

When William O'Dwyer became mayor, the minority became watchdogs of the administration. Criticism assumed a variety of forms. One Republican introduced hosts of resolutions to investigate—to investigate the Long Island Railroad, liquor officials, the numbers racket, and countless other matters. The City Council never acted on them, but he obtained scads of publicity. A more effective technique, developed by a Harlem Councilman in the La Guardia régime, was to concentrate on a specific area. A. Clayton Powell once sponsored an investigation of the exclusion of Negro women from nurse's training schools in city hospitals. It did not pass, but in time he had the satisfaction of seeing Negro women training in city hospitals. A new source of

[40] *City Council Record,* XIX-XXV (1943-49), *passim.*

[41] Lillian Ross, "$1,031,961,754.63," *The New Yorker,* XXIII, No. 12 (1947), 31; *Nat. Mun. Rev.,* XXXII, 409-10.

employment had been opened for his constituents. Councilmen Earle and Isaacs usually acted on broader issues, focusing attention on possible administration abuses. In 1948 they requested a reduction in the number of provisional civil service employees. So incensed was Mayor O'Dwyer at this resolution that he shook his fist in Councilman Isaacs' face. Nevertheless the number of provisionals was drastically reduced.[42]

The most immediate and significant influence of the minority was the regeneration of the City Council itself. P. R. had provided a substantial opposition, capable of keeping the majority on its toes. The dispirited and perfunctory committee hearings of the Board of Aldermen gave way to well attended meetings where issues were vigorously threshed out. Matters that would have quietly slipped through the old Board came under public scrutiny, as vital issues were thoroughly debated on the floor of the City Council. If the minority was unable to control the body, it could act as a brake upon the majority, drawing attention to bad legislation and participating in the framing of desirable bills.[43]

The feverish initial sessions of the new legislature were accompanied by a sharp increase in public interest. Tiresome even to its members, the Board of Aldermen's dreary sessions had been virtually ignored by the public. Even City Hall reporters had passed them by. Now the electorate began to take notice of its governing body. Attendance at hearings for important bills and committee meetings zoomed. The violent struggle for control, stormy meetings, and radio broadcasts of its debates made the new legislature a public theatre. But increased publicity did not always enhance its reputation. A hard-working member of the minority complained that the press ignored the City Council's intelligent and constructive work in favor of spectacular and bizarre incidents. After a session devoted to intelligent, even scholarly debate, a metropolitan newspaper featured a brief out-

[42] *City Council Record,* XXIV (1948), No. 7, 59; Powell, *Marching Blacks,* p. 157; Earle, *Reminiscences,* pp. 108-110.

[43] Genevieve B. Earle, "P. R. Has Achieved Its Purpose and Prevents Landslides" (Press Release of 1946, from the Earle Papers in the Municipal Reference Library); Commerce and Ind. Assoc., "Report Concerning Election of N. Y. C. Council by P. R.," p. 19.

burst in which one legislator called another a liar. The result was a field day for critics who regarded the Council as a source of "ribald amusement." The most respectable journals yielded documentary evidence of the body's delays, its horseplay and childish antics, and its excursions into national and international affairs.[44]

Even after the struggle over organization had ended and the City Council had settled down to humdrum business, public interest persisted. Hearings on controversial bills were well attended—350 people crowded into the Council chamber and half as many more were turned away from a public session of the Committee on General Welfare on one of the Sharkey bills. Forty-five speakers appeared to debate the merits of the air-pollution bill. Hundreds of communications poured into the City Council on important measures. In a single week Majority Leader Sharkey received almost 4,000 letters on one of his rent laws. Once the League of Women Shoppers joined forces with coöperatives and consumer groups to dramatize the high price of milk and demand a legislative inquiry. Thereupon Walter R. Hart, Chairman of the Rules Committee, was bombarded by a mass mailing of empty milk cartons. Lobbyists for private interests sometimes exerted a powerful, but subtler influence. Often these pressures were reflected in the final draft of a law. Newspapers followed the deliberations of the City Council more closely than the old Board of Aldermen. When Councilman Cunningham sponsored a local law to authorize the Commissioner of Licenses to censor theatre performances and advertising, it was denounced in editorials as "mischievous and unwarranted." Such vehemence indicates that the City Council's actions were being taken seriously.[45]

No living New Yorker could remember a city legislature as highly esteemed as the City Council. The President of the Na-

44 Owen, "'S. R. O.' Sign Out At City Hall," *New York Times Magazine*, January 30, 1938; Belous, *op. cit.*, pp. 1-2, 4; Moses, *Theory and Practice in Politics*, p. 40.

45 Moscow, *Pol. in Emp. St.*, p. 211; *New York Herald-Tribune*, August 6, 1947; April 6, October 22, 1948; August 25, 1949; *New York Star*, October 28, 1949. On the Cunningham bill, see editorials in *New York Times*, April 13, 1948, *New York Sun* and *P. M.*, June 14, 1948, and *New York Herald-Tribune*, June 15, 1948.

tional Municipal League, who had once informed the aldermen they were "brainless," observed that no one would dream of addressing the Council so contemptuously. Theodore Roosevelt had believed in stripping the Board of Aldermen of authority to ratify the mayor's appointments; at least one reputable organization has proposed restoring the City Council's power to confirm appointments to the Board of Education.[46] For generations no legislation emanating from the Board of Aldermen was important enough to justify debate in a political campaign (unless it involved legislative malfeasance). In 1949 the Sharkey rent laws became a major issue in the mayoralty campaign. The City Council had earned a respectable place in the municipal government.[47]

[46] The purpose of this suggestion was to give the public an opportunity to check on the caliber of appointees through hearings in the Council. Letter of Harry Winton, Executive Secretary of the United Parents Associations, to author, October 8, 1948.

[47] Broadcast of Richard S. Childs over Station WJZ, August 10, 1947; Circular letter of David I. Ashe, President of United Parents Associations of New York City to Presidents, Legislative Chairmen, and Bulletin Editors of affiliated Parents Associations, October 7, 1948, October 8, 1949; *New York Times,* August 12, 1949; *New York Herald-Tribune,* September 22, 1949.

13. SUMMARY AND CONCLUSIONS

It remains . . . now for the City Council to carve its place into the government structure of the City of New York.—NEWBOLD MORRIS, *First President of the Council, January 26, 1938* [1]

IT BECAME FASHIONABLE in the 1930's to condemn New York's charter as a relic of the horse car era. "I know of nothing in the city that is as old as the charter," reflected ex-Governor Smith in 1932, "unless it be the Criminal Courts Building, the city prison, the City Hall, and the sewer system." It cannot be gainsaid that portions of the document were obsolete—certainly provisions for regulation of tricycles, stage coaches, and horse trolleys by the Board of Aldermen were outdated.[2] But the real trouble with the city legislature went deeper. A decade after the Greater New York Charter was adopted an authority had diagnosed the situation:

New York has [not] made any improvement in its government through elevating the character of the local legislature. Little, if any, thought and no effort worth mentioning has been bestowed . . . upon this method of bettering the conduct of local affairs. . . . The legislature of its own motion and at the suggestions of residents of the city was habitually modifying, revising, or repealing this or that provision of the huge congeries of statutes under which the city government was conducted. Nothing was final. The city government at any given time was simply one of a series of legislative experiments. . . . Under these conditions it is not surprising that the bettering of city government in New York through the elevation of the character of the aldermen was not seriously attempted nor even seriously considered.[3]

[1] Radio Address over Station WHN, "Municipal Home Rule Under the City Council."

[2] *Seabury Minutes,* p. 9638; "Absurdities in the Charter and in the Code of Ordinances" (Earle Papers in the Oral History Project at Columbia University; mimeographed); Charter of 1901, Secs. 49-50.

[3] Deming, *Govt. of American Cities,* pp. 89-90.

The result was a city legislature that fell into an "abyss of disrepute." The penalty for past misdeeds had been loss of its most vital authority. What powers it retained it neglected. Failure to enact ordinances of general interest, ineffectiveness as a forum for considering civic problems, and impotence of minority parties in the Board of Aldermen gave it a reputation as a "civic mummy." In its latter years it was resurrected only to make life miserable for a reform mayor.[4]

The Board of Aldermen failed the public, but not the city's political leaders. For them it ground out statutes on request. "The easiest thing Tammany now does is to keep the Board of Aldermen in the boss' or bosses' vest pocket," declared two authorities in 1932. Important decisions were made on a higher level and orders passed on to the city legislature. There, voting had degenerated into a reflex action.[5]

For sixteen years—1918 through 1933—the Democrats controlled every branch of the city government. During this period the Board of Aldermen meekly acquiesced to the demands of the mayor, Board of Estimate, and leaders of the dominant political party. "Today the Board functions mechanically, like a nicely fitted unit in a well controlled machine," stated one observer in 1930. As opposition in the house dwindled to microscopic size, the last voice of criticism in the municipality was stilled. Even the second major party failed to gain effective representation, and virtually a one-party system prevailed. The city was ruled by a "totalitarian government in which a token representation of the opposition was tolerated." [6]

Why did the citizens submit to the iniquities of a boss-ridden legislature that had become a useless appendage to the city government? The average citizen had only a vague picture of mu-

[4] Statement of George H. Sibley, former President of the Association of Young Republican Clubs in press release of Keep Proportional Representation Committee, October 16, 1947; Johnston, "Courtroom Warrior," *The New Yorker,* VIII, No. 4, 22.

[5] Thomas and Blanshard, *What's the Matter with New York,* p. 304; Garrett, "One of the Boys," *The New Yorker,* II, No. 10, 22.

[6] *The Searchlight,* XX, No. 1, 7; "Report of Special Committee on Proportional Representation to the Board of Directors, Commerce and Industry Association of New York" (September 17, 1947), p. 21.

nicipal government, particularly of the Board of Aldermen, whose sessions were of little interest even to its own members. He knew his alderman, if he knew him at all, principally as a clubhouse worker, eager to gratify the voters with an endless stream of small favors. The aldermen themselves justified their salaries not on their performance as legislators, but on their unofficial assistance to their constituents. With a few conspicuous exceptions the City Fathers were party hacks who did not pretend to be Solons. Rarely did they see beyond the boundaries of their neighborhoods, and civic welfare was subordinated to district needs.

It was futile to expect reform to originate in this milieu. There were a few perceptive young men among the majority who recognized the Board of Aldermen as a burlesque of a legislature, but soon realized that any protest would instantly put an end to their political careers. The minority was powerless. In the municipal campaign of 1933 several anti-Tammany candidates promised sweeping changes. "If nominated and elected alderman," vowed Republican Lambert Fairchild, "I shall make it my first duty to work toward the entire elimination of the worthless and expensive office which I shall then occupy." Once installed, Alderman Fairchild never troubled to introduce proposals for change. A Fusion candidate with a background of similar promises made an expansive gesture with a charter amendment to reduce the number of aldermen and elect them by P. R. The committee to which it was referred promptly buried it. These circumstances vindicated Judge Seabury's assertion that no serious charter revision would ever be initiated by the Board of Aldermen. "Governing bodies rarely commit suicide," he wrote.[7]

Judge Seabury's disclosures of sordid misgovernment provided the stimulus needed for charter reform. An angry and indignant electorate drove Tammany out of the city administration and lent a sympathetic ear to pleas for recasting municipal government. By obstructing charter reform for several years

[7] *New York Times,* March 15, 1928, September 15, 1933; Pratt, "Men Are Bad Housekeepers," *Harpers Mag.,* CLIV, 684; *Mun. Ass. Rec.,* X-XI, *passim;* Seabury, *Final Report,* p. 12.

the dominant party succeeded in maintaining its clutch on the city legislature. Eventually it yielded and authorized Mayor La Guardia to name a charter commission.

Since the consolidation of the city, the executive branch had been installing such improvements as modern accounting methods and centralized purchasing. Reform of the city legislature was long overdue. It would have been difficult to find a group as well qualified as the Thacher Charter Revision Commission or as able a staff as that headed by Professor Joseph D. Chamberlain and Lawrence A. Tanzer to perform the task. Simplifying the unwieldy and almost incomprehensible municipal charter that had developed haphazardly over a generation has been called "the most difficult and complex assignment to face any student of government, municipal or otherwise, in recent history." Some political scientists believed the new charter embodied the best features of municipal government of the day. Its principal innovations grew out of an effort to correct the defects of the two municipal deliberative chambers. Log-rolling by local interests in the Board of Estimate was to be eliminated by a city-wide Planning Commission. For the single-voiced, boss-ruled, do-nothing Board of Aldermen, a majority of the Commission favored P. R. (Incidentally, New York was the first American city to adopt P. R. without the manager plan.)[8]

Subsequent controversy has obscured the Commission's decisions. It gave P. R. no blanket endorsement for national, state, or even municipal legislatures. Professor Joseph P. Chamberlain, Counsel to the Commission, repeatedly told the author that a majority would never have approved of P. R. for Congress or the New York State legislature. Technically they did not even recommend P. R.—they only followed the mandate of the state legislature to present a new charter and a separate P. R. option. (The Smith Commission had made the same decision, although most of its members opposed P. R.) But given the situation then existing in New York, a majority of the Thacher Commission personally believed P. R. would produce a vigorous opposi-

[8] *New York Herald-Tribune,* November 13, 1950; W. Seward Salisbury, *New York: The State and Its Government* (New York, 1942), p. 47.

tion, capable of destroying one-party dictatorship in the city legislature and providing a valuable check on the administration. As they saw it, boroughwide constituencies would elect men of broad vision rather than neighborhood spokesmen. Sparked by enthusiastic civic associations, the campaign for charter ratification met with overwhelming approval.

Proportionalists pointed with pride to the first P. R. election. An editorial from the *New York Herald-Tribune,* summarizing its outcome, has become a favorite quotation: "P. R. in fact operated magnificently then. It raised tremendously the character of representation in the Council, as contrasted with the horizontal statesmen of the old Board of Aldermen, and gave it a political division in reasonable accordance with the real sentiment of the city." [9]

Undoubtedly the stature of the City Fathers was elevated. The minority now contained men and women of responsibility and perspective; the majority was compelled, perforce, to eliminate its least capable legislators. "The pot-bellied alderman has been replaced by the paunchless Councilman," remarked a publicist.[10] What distinguished the City Council from the Board of Aldermen was the number of unbossed lawmakers, the public-spirited members who used their position to maintain municipal standards at a high level. Elected without organization support, legislators like Genevieve B. Earle, Stanley M. Isaacs, and Robert K. Straus offered a yardstick for gauging machine candidates. They could hardly have been seated under the single-member district system. P. R. offered the voters fuller and freer expression than the majority system.

Were P. R. elections lotteries or did they give each party equitable representation? A review of five P. R. elections indicates that they rendered substantial justice to all parties large enough to amass the required quota. Under P. R. alert and well disciplined parties could squeeze out an extra seat or two, while loose organizations, such as the Fusionites, lost out in the vote

[9] *Proportional Representation ("P. R.")*, Leaflet No. 5, Proportional Representation League (1939). See also Hallett, *P. R.: Key to Democracy,* p. 151.

[10] Warren Moscow, "Exit the Boss, Enter the 'Leader,'" *New York Times Magazine,* June 22, 1947.

transfers. But P. R. never permitted the gross distortions produced by the district system—the last aldermanic election (1935) gave the minority a mere 5% of the seats with 36% of the votes, and after the district system was restored, the first Councilmanic election (1949) gave them 4% of the seats with 47% of the vote![11]

As a result the Council obtained a militant and articulate minority that never comprised less than one-third the membership. (The last Board of Aldermen with a comparable opposition had been elected in 1919.) For eight years they supported a reform mayor's programs; when Tammany returned to power they kept ceaseless watch over the administration. In the latter period the Democratic majority could ward off full-dress investigations, but it could not muffle criticism. When Al Smith was President of the Board of Aldermen he once declared, "A good, healthy, vigorous minority is the necessary check on great power."[12] That was precisely what P. R. guaranteed.

It was generally recognized that P. R. created a self-adjusting mechanism which automatically reapportioned the voting districts for each election. After the last aldermanic campaign (1935) the average alderman from Manhattan represented 69,000 people, from Queens 240,000. The first P. R. election seated one Queens Councilman for every 87,000 voters and one Manhattan Councilman for every 90,000. In that very election (1937) a number of districts in Manhattan elected state Assemblymen with less than 15,000 votes apiece, while more than 95,000 votes were cast in some Bronx and Queens districts. At one stroke P. R. created a fair basis for representation. At the same time, as the election district was extended to include the whole borough, the possibility of gerrymandering disappeared.[13]

Critics of P. R. contended that the presence of several splinter parties in the city legislature produced disintegration and destroyed party responsibility. This concept had grown out of

[11] *Nat. Mun. Rev.*, XXXVIII (1949), 566.

[12] Hapgood and Moscowitz, *Up from the City Streets*, p. 149.

[13] *Prop. Rep. for N. Y. C.*, p. 4; *Probs. Rel. to Leg. Org. and Powers*, p. 250; *Prop. Rep.: What It Is and How It Works in N. Y. C.*, p. 41.

Professor F. A. Hermens' studies of P. R. in European parliaments.[14] Did it apply to the City Council?

A review of European legislatures elected by P. R. is outside the scope of this volume. But a comparison between the American Congress and the New York City Council may prove instructive. In 1949 the Democrats seemed to have safe control of both houses of the national legislature, with a margin of 12 in the Senate and 91 in the House of Representatives. Yet they were unable to redeem pledges made in the campaign of 1948 because Dixiecrat legislators, who were nominal Democrats, allied themselves with Republicans to defeat vital legislation.[15] That same year, with a majority of one, the Democrats in the City Council put through every important measure their Majority Leader introduced. Most legislation, in fact, passed unanimously, with the minority participating in the drafting of important bills. The majority system is said to promote cohesion and party responsibility; yet the Congressional majority elected under this system in 1948 fell apart, and on many crucial issues real control was vested in blocs and informal coalitions. P. R. is supposed to promote chaos and fragmentation, but the Democrats elected by P. R. maintained their control in the municipal legislature in 1949 with a bare majority. The City Council's firm majority and Congress' unstable majority were not due to the way they were elected but to the character of the American party system. The leading parties have strong local control, but weak central organizations. The force that holds a legislative majority together is not the electoral system, but party discipline and cohesion.[16]

P. R. elections entailed a number of distinct disadvantages; Minority Leader Earle believed the complications contributed to their abandonment.[17] Sometimes the number of candidates was

[14] For a succinct statement of his theories see F. A. Hermens, *Democracy and Proportional Representation* (Chicago, 1940).

[15] Hubert N. Humphrey, "The Senate on Trial," *American Political Science Review,* XLIX (1950), 659.

[16] Even Prof. Hermens conceded that the hypothetical process of disintegration had "slowed down" in the City Council. See his letter to the editor of the *New York Times,* October 22, 1947.

[17] *New York Herald-Tribune,* August 25, 1949.

bewildering—the Brooklyn ballot never contained less than 25 names, and once it was 99. At best the count was unwieldly, cumbersome, and open to manipulation. The first election revealed ballot-tampering and concrete evidence of fraud. Wherever paper ballots are used irregularities are likely. P. R. elections were easily as honest as most primaries, but voting machines (which were never used for P. R.) have proven the best preventive for fraud.

Opponents charged that P. R.'s "trick" ballot meant "voting in the dark, firmly blindfolded." This was an overstatement, but even supporters of P. R. found a high proportion of invalid ballots. If the electorate is to master the system, continuous education is required. After the campaign of 1937, missionary work tapered off, with the result that fewer ballots were properly marked. There was a higher proportion of invalid ballots in the last two P. R. elections than in the first and second.[18]

P. R. elections were scored as extravagant and wasteful, particularly when the city was struggling for fiscal solvency. Even after the inefficient procedures of 1937 were eliminated, at a saving of almost a half million dollars, a hard, irreducible core of $200,000 remained. Was it worth the price? The Seabury investigations revealed that scores of officeholders had stowed that sum in their personal tin boxes. P. R. provided low cost municipal insurance—at an annual premium of one cent per capita—to provide a vigilant minority, capable of checking administration abuses.

Did P. R. stimulate voting along racial or religious lines? The vote transfers of P. R. ballots demonstrate beyond all doubt that the electorate was influenced by race and religion. The same motives will operate, however, under any system of voting. This was illustrated when New York State was reapportioned in 1943. At the instigation of Harlem leaders a Negro district was carved out in Manhattan to assure the election of a Negro Congressman—a perfect example of racial politics under the majority system. But racial and religious motivations are only part

[18] Letter of State President of Affiliated Young Democrats of New York to *New York Times,* August 25, 1947; Comm. and Ind. Assn., "Report Concerning Election of N. Y. C. Council," p. 8.

of a larger picture. The electorate does not merely vote as Negroes or whites, or as Catholics, Protestants, and Jews; they also vote as veterans, as civil service employees, as devotees of a political party, or admirers of a particular candidate. Under the majority system political managers endeavor to offer a "balanced" ticket, appealing to as many interest groups as possible. Under P. R. the voter is at liberty to choose any candidate who offers the principles he wants; if his favorite is eliminated, his vote can then be counted for his next keenest interest. The majority ticket offers the voter a package embodying some things he wants and some things the party leaders persuade him to accept. P. R. offers a free choice. That is why the politician has fought P. R. tooth and nail wherever it has appeared.[19]

P. R. had been proposed as a means of destroying Tammany's stranglehold on the city legislature. To the chagrin of the Democratic leaders, this purpose was achieved. They managed to maintain a majority in the City Council, but the margin of superiority was always smaller than in the Board of Aldermen. The new system was particularly galling to Bronx Leader Flynn. From 1923 to 1937 every Democratic candidate for alderman from the Bronx save one was elected; under P. R. less than 60 per cent of the Bronx Councilmen were Democrats. Little wonder that the county leaders took a dim view of P. R.!

If anything, the district leaders were even less enthusiastic about the Councilmen. The old-time alderman was a humble creature, who cheerfully performed the petty tasks his leader assigned. The new Councilman was more independent. In Queens one candidate consented to run on condition that the bosses claim no lien on his services. After his election he considered himself under no obligation to run political errands. In the "good old days", Alfred E. Smith himself was not exempt from clubhouse duties, even when he became floor leader in the State Senate.

The new Councilmen were not inclined to take orders from clubhouse worthies without demur. Some were successful pro-

19 Powell, *Marching Blacks*, pp. 160-61; Oxie Reichler, "The Politician Hates P. R.," *Nat. Mun. Rev.*, XXXVI, 318-19.

fessional men, some national celebrities. Benjamin J. Davis, Jr., member of the national board of the Communist Party, gained nation-wide attention when he and ten fellow-radicals were convicted for conspiracy against the federal government. A mere district leader would never find his name in newspaper editorials as often as Councilman Quill, international president of the Transport Workers Union. Four Councilmen (and no district leaders) were mentioned in John Gunther's best-seller, *Inside U. S. A.* But this was not an unmixed blessing. Public figures like Quill found their primary careers demanding the lion's share of their time. Sometimes a committee meeting lacked a quorum because an engineer was supervising a contract or a lawyer was in court. One of the Sharkey rent laws was defeated in its first floor test because two supporters were absent. The old time alderman was a full time alderman. But normally he spent most of the week as his district leader's handyman. Few aldermen took their jobs as lawmakers seriously. Fewer still were equipped to deal intelligently with the broad problems of a metropolis. They were good Samaritans rather than legislators.[20]

Republican leaders also resented the "big shot" Councilmen who considered themselves too high and mighty to act as district errand boys. There was no solace in the fact that P. R. elections seated a larger proportion of Republicans than district elections for the old Board, for some Republicans defied the machine and gained office as independents. The elimination of primaries made it easy to get on the ballot, and in a P. R. campaign a candidate with a distinguished record was likely to defeat an obscure machine designate.

Publicity, not docility, was the Councilman's crying need. Borough-wide constituencies under P. R. eliminated "safe" districts in which party regularity was the prime qualification for nomination. There was even competition among candidates of the same party within boroughs. With no assurance of automatic election, candidates found it more profitable to "sell" themselves to the public than work for the district machines.

[20] *The Nation,* CLXVII (1948), 534; *The Searchlight,* XIX, No. 2, 11; A. H. Raskin, "Presenting the Phenomenon Called Quill," *New York Times Magazine,* March 5, 1950; *New York Herald-Tribune,* September 9, 1949; John Gunther, *Inside U. S. A.* (New York, 1947), pp. 554 ff.

Party managers viewed these developments sourly. The secret of their control over the old Board of Aldermen had been the designation of subservient hacks for an inconspicuous office. Drawing attention to the legislators' achievements promoted the fortunes of unbossed Councilmen, Democratic and non-Democratic alike. This was why the majority leader attempted to end broadcasts of the first Council's proceedings. So great was the lawmakers' need for publicity, however, that the Democrats revolted—the first *putsch* on the Democratic side of the aisle since the turn of the century! The election of 1939, however, gave the Democrats a two-thirds majority. This time their leaders cracked the whip and the Councilmen fell into line.[21] Some authorities regretted the passing of a valuable experiment in municipal education. Never before had so many New Yorkers learnt so much about their city legislature or their representatives at City Hall. In this instance, the public welfare was sacrificed to party expediency. Interestingly enough, when Mayor O'Dwyer inaugurated television broadcasts for the executive branch of the municipal government some years later, no objections were raised. It is in the interest of the dominant party to keep the city's chief executive in the limelight. It is not in the organization's interest to give publicity to the minor local offices.

From the beginning the party leaders realized that airtight control of the municipal legislature could be restored only by abolishing P. R. They tried every legal means—court tests, constitutional amendment, local law, and the initiative-petition. After ten years the magic formula was discovered—the Red Menace. Where municipal issues had failed, the political parties and the civic organizations they subsidized found the most potent theme for discrediting the electoral system was Communism. P. R. was a casualty of the cold war.

Did P. R. effect any improvement in the legislature itself? The discredited Board of Aldermen was transformed into a house that compared favorably with any local legislature—this was the verdict of Minority Leader Earle. An alert and aggressive minority injected new life into a moribund body. Perfunctory com-

21 *The Searchlight,* XXIX, No. 1, 14; Schwartz, *op. cit.,* pp. 12-13.

mittee meetings gave way to vigorous, well-attended sessions. Matters that had once quietly slipped through the Board of Aldermen were forced into the open by a vigilant opposition. Few people had known the old Board of Aldermen existed; Mrs. Earle believed New Yorkers followed the proceedings of the City Council more closely than those of Congress.[22] What is more, they participated in the legislative process—hearings on controversial matters occasionally drew throngs, and many of the speakers' suggestions were adopted. The legislative branch had earned a new and respectable place in the city government.

But the acid test of a legislature is its performance. Midway in the P. R. Council's career a survey by a civic association disclosed that its legislative record was statesmanlike compared with its predecessor's.[23] This was scarcely a commendation. Any body that did no better than the Board of Aldermen would be a sorry excuse for a legislature. By and large, no Council came to grips with vital municipal problems save the last. Local laws dealing with rent control and summary evictions, garages and parking space, air pollution, and traffic control made this Council's achievements outstanding.

This record was partly due to human frailty. In the beginning the majority was only too ready to bait the administration, to hamstring the minority, and to discredit P. R. itself. Later the Democrats became reconciled to the City Council. Majority Leader Sharkey enforced civil behavior on his side of the aisle and treated the minority with courtesy and fairness. But politics were never quite forgotten. If the Democrats did not vex Mayor La Guardia after Pearl Harbor as impishly as before, they were not disposed to glorify his Fusion administration with a brilliant legislative record. During Mayor O'Dwyer's first administration the reverse was true, and the P. R. Council whose majority was of the same political persuasion as the city administration made the most creditable showing.

But no City Council, no matter how able or sincere, could play a decisive part in the city's affairs. The work of a city govern-

[22] Earle, *Reminiscences,* p. 86.
[23] *Nat. Mun. Rev.,* XXXIII (1944), 264.

ment is more akin to that of a business corporation than a purely political unit. Hence the Board of Estimate, which makes the principal administrative and financial decisions, is easily the more important body. Municipal councils that are confined to policy-making perform only minor functions, for there is not much legislative work to do, even in a big city like New York. What is more, all important measures originating in the City Council require the concurrence of the Mayor, the Board of Estimate, or the electorate.

Even in the sphere of policy determination, the City Council labors under a handicap common to all modern legislatures. Before the industrial revolution, when the population was small, almost any alert and reasonably educated citizen could understand most municipal issues. Today the municipal corporation is necessarily administered by experts, trained to cope with its complex and multifarious problems. Hence the mayor and the executive organs are far more familiar with the needs of the metropolis and the legislation it requires than the Councilmen. As we have seen, most important legislation was drafted by the city administration rather than the City Council itself.

Finally, all branches of the municipal government are seriously circumscribed by the Home Rule Law. "I have to come to Albany not on my knees with my hat in my hand, but *crawling*," growled Mayor La Guardia. New York is not unique in this regard. "Every city sits in a legal straight-jacket designed by representatives of the state," declares one authority. "It cannot move except when the legal jacket is loosened according to the whims of its members." Newbold Morris, President of the City Council for eight years, believed the house would attain real stature only after the city obtained a more liberal grant of power.[24]

What improvements could have been made in the P. R. Council? Several proposals have been made concerning P. R. itself. One political scientist noted that it had improved New York's governing body, but that the Hare System entailed certain dis-

24 "Mayor La Guardia's New York," *Fortune Magazine*, XX, No. 1 (1939), 202; Charles S. Rhyne (ed.), *Municipalities and the Law in Action: 1948* (Washington, 1948), p. 165; Rankin, *New York Advancing: Victory Ed.*, p. 275.

advantages—constitutional difficulties, a more complex ballot for voters, and an expensive and time-consuming count. All these could be obviated by the list system, which gives every organized party a number of legislators proportionate to the vote it polled. If a minority is essential to the New York Council, argued an opponent of P. R., why not give the strongest party in an election fifteen seats and the runner-up ten? [25] Regardless of their merits, these alternatives stood no chance of adoption. The principal boosters of P. R. in New York were thoroughly committed to the Hare System, which gives the independent voter the greatest freedom of choice. Without their support no system could seriously be considered.

One of the advantages of the party list system would have been the use of the same voting machine for P. R. as other offices. On the other hand there were special machines devised for the Hare system, capable of holding the names of 143 candidates—far more than the number of nominees in any county in New York's five P. R. elections. The voter simply pulled down his preferences serially, while little numbers popped up to indicate the sequence of his choices. Undoubtedly they would have eliminated invalid votes, permitted the returns to be known the day after elections, and insured strict accuracy. Wherever paper ballots are used the possibilities of fraud increase. Would P. R. machines have been more economical? In 1937 an officer in the Department of Accounts estimated their cost at $2,000,000. Whether the overhead expense would have offset the costs of P. R. elections was never definitely settled.[26]

The City Council itself would have benefitted from expert assistance. No one could expect every Councilman to master the budget, tax bills, the building code, and all the complicated issues that confront a modern legislature. Without technical advisers, he had to turn to lobbyists, pressure groups, administrative officials, or the staff of the President of the Council (which was

[25] Harold F. Gosnell, "A List System with Single Candidate Preference," *American Political Science Review,* XXXIII (1939), 645-50; Hermens, *Democracy and Proportional Representation,* p. 29.

[26] *Probs. Rel. to Leg. Org.,* pp. 260-61; Sophia A. Olmstead, "Remarks on the P. R. Election," Radio Address over Station WEVD, December 1, 1937.

hired by the city for the presiding officer, not the City Council). Fortunately, the Municipal Reference Library, which may be compared in a modest way to the Library of Congress, was located across the street. Its efficient and courteous staff was always ready to assist Councilmen in making use of its resources.[27] But a legislator who undertook an extended or technical research project had to perform the work himself or hire assistants at his own expense.

Of all phases of the City Council's work, probably the Building Code is the most specialized. Except for occasional members who happened to be in the building construction business, most Councilmen understood precious little of it. In view of the slight scope for non-expert discretion, some observers have suggested transferring the preparation and amendment of the Building Code to an administrative agency. The Sanitary Code has fallen under the jurisdiction of the City Board of Health and the promulgation of traffic rules under the Police Department for this very reason. It is not easy to believe, however, that the City Council would readily relinquish this authority, particularly since it helps win the Buildings Committee grateful friends with odd jobs for deserving constituents. Fortunately, for the greater part of its life the P. R. Council's Buildings Committee was headed by Councilman Hugh Quinn, who enlisted the coöperation of experts—prominent engineers, architects, builders, and professors of engineering—in a continuous process of study and revision. Professional men praised Quinn for performing an impartial and meritorious job and for staunchly resisting all outside pressures. Not all changes in the city's administrative code have been introduced into the City Council with the scrupulous regard for the public interest exhibited by Quinn.[28]

One of the most difficult of all the legislator's tasks is bill drafting. Like the Board of Aldermen, the City Council has

[27] E.g. in 1947, at the request of Minority Leader Earle, Miss Rebecca B. Rankin, head of the Municipal Reference Library, surveyed the principal city legislatures of the United States to ascertain what clerical and technical assistance each employed. (From the files of the Minority Leader.)

[28] Letters of Councilman Quinn to *New York Sun,* June 11, 1948, May 6, 1949; Earle, *Reminiscences,* pp. 78-79.

passed scores of defective measures. In one instance a bill to exempt materials for exhibits at the World's Fair from emergency relief taxes inadvertently repealed the tax itself. It passed both City Council and Board of Estimate; not until it reached the mayor's office was the offending clause detected. Some authorities suggested a bill drafting bureau, akin to the Congressional Office of the Legislative Council, to save the public and courts valuable time and money.[29]

The problem was largely solved by the efforts of Minority Leader Earle. In 1947 she convinced the City Council of the necessity for providing a modest staff. Today the offices of both Majority Leader and Minority Leader employ a secretary and legal assistant. Moreover the city's Law Department has freely offered its services to all Councilmen. (But the Corporation Counsel's Office did not always command the confidence of the legislators. When La Guardia was Mayor the Democratic majority distrusted his appointees. Even when the Democrats returned to power Democratic representatives of one county were reluctant to entrust their bills to lawyers from another county.) Ultimate responsibility, however, lies with the individual Councilman. They are better educated today than the old aldermen —a majority of those elected in 1949 were lawyers. Proper use of available legal facilities, together with study, diligence, and painstaking care on the part of the sponsors will assure technically foolproof bills.

The City Clerk plays no part in the legislative process, but he is appointed by the Council. The Fusion minority, which tried to organize the first Council, believed that jobs in the City Clerk's office were being awarded as small prizes to clubhouse workers. They intended to reduce the personnel and bring them under civil service. As we have seen, the Fusion coalition lost control, and their plans were never consummated.

[29] Maurice J. Levin, *A Bill Drafting Bureau for the City Council* (New York, 1938), *passim*.

EPILOGUE

How did the City Council fare in the 1949 elections under the majority system? Predictions that the city legislature would revert to a one-party régime proved only too accurate. The campaign manager of the Keep-P. R. forces in 1947 had foretold the precise results, 24 to 1.[30] Had the Liberals not endorsed Republican candidate Stanley M. Isaacs, the Democrats might have made a clean sweep—with a bare majority of the vote. The following table indicates the results:[31]

	Percentage of Votes	*Percentage of Seats Won*	*Seats in Proportion to Votes Cast*	*Seats Won*
Democratic	52.6	96	13.2	24
Republican	21.6	4 [b]	5.4	1 [b]
Liberal	13.7	0 [c]	3.4	0 [c]
American Labor	11.9	0	3.0	0
	99.8 [a]	100	25.0	25

[a] Does not include the 20,000 votes cast for Communist Councilman Davis.

[b] One coalition candidate was endorsed by Republicans, Democrats, and Liberals. During his incumbency he sat with the Democrats and was referred to as a Democrat in the press.

[c] Five candidates endorsed by the Liberal Party gained seats—three Democrats, one Republican, and one coalition nominee. In practice they acted as four Democrats and one Republican.

The return of the district system rounded out a full cycle. A single party again enjoyed a near-monopoly in the city legislature; once again a large segment of the electorate was unrepresented. Choice of candidates once more became the perquisite of the district leaders.[32] Although State Senate districts had been reapportioned only six years before, representation was no longer equal. In 1949 Brooklyn elected one Councilman for every 88,000 voters, Queens one for every 118,000. Differences

[30] Letter of the Hon. John J. Lamula to the *New York Herald-Tribune,* November 14, 1949.

[31] *Nat. Mun. Rev.,* XXXVIII, 566-67; *Annual Rep. of Bd. of Elects., 1949,* pp. 78-86, 93.

[32] When the Board of Aldermen contained 65 members almost every district leader named his own alderman. Now that the Council has been reduced to 25, some horse trading is necessary. Within each Senate district the district leaders parcel out the available appointive and elective offices, including the Councilmanic nomination, on the basis of mutual agreement.

between individual districts were even more marked. In one Queens constituency 157,000 votes were cast for Councilmanic candidates; 72,000 were polled in a Brooklyn district that same day. Such inequalities might very well increase before the next redistricting—the state had waited 26 years for the reapportionment of 1943. Once again a single man comprised the whole minority. Recalling the experience of Joseph Clark Baldwin, who had been outnumbered 64 to 1 in the Board of Aldermen, Stanley M. Isaacs realized only too well the difficulties he confronted.[33]

Would the clock be turned back to the days of the disreputable old Board of Aldermen? Fortunately the new Council (1950-1953) did not turn out as badly as the proportionalists had feared. There was no perceptible decline in the quality of the membership—about 40 per cent were recommended by the Citizens Union. The Negro community, which had expected a clubhouse nonentity, elected Earl Brown, successful coalition candidate against Communist Councilman Davis. Harvard trained, a one-time college instructor and editor of the *Amsterdam News,* Brown was exceptionally well qualified to represent Harlem. The present City Council, moreover, is limited to 25, a size that makes for greater efficiency than the cumbersome 65-man Board of Aldermen.[34]

Nor was the minority altogether helpless. The majority promised that Councilman Isaacs' motions would be seconded, and the Council rules were amended to make him a real member of every committee, with the right to make motions, to move to discharge, and to amend. (Past minority leaders had been merely ex officio members of all committees.) Few men had his qualifications to act as sole minority member. Conscious of his intimate knowledge of city affairs, majority Councilmen would think twice befor introducing nefarious or defective legislation. Isaacs could deliver scathing criticism from the floor or persuade leading

[33] *Report of Bd. of Elects., 1949,* pp. 78, 80; *New York Times,* November 18, 1949; *Nat. Mun. Rev.,* XXXVIII. 566-67.

[34] *Across from City Hall,* V, No. 4 (1949); *New York World-Telegram and Sun,* February 12, 1951.

metropolitan newspapers to print scorching editorials on pernicious bills. On the other hand he knew how to gain the confidence of his majority colleagues by supporting constructive legislation, by offering to revise faulty bills in committee, or even by helping the majority leader maintain discipline in his own ranks. (Sharkey and Isaacs, liberals both, saw eye to eye on most issues, and the minority leader could in all sincerity extol most measures sponsored by the Majority Leader.) In return Isaacs obtained majority support for some of his own projects.[35]

Former Minority Leader Earle predicted, in fact, that Isaacs would attain surprising success. Fighting "courageously, unaided, unheralded, and unsung," he won a number of notable, temporary victories. After a brilliant investigation of taxi companies' finances in 1950, he persuaded the majority to shelve an administration-sponsored bill to increase taxi fares. More spectacular was the defeat of a proposal to increase the city's share of police and firemen's pensions. Some suspected that the City Council passed it, 24 to 1, shortly before the 1950 elections to embarrass Acting Mayor Impellitteri, an anti-Tammany mayoralty candidate. As a member of the Board of Estimate, Impellitteri would have to pass on the controversial measure just before election day. When it appeared on the Board of Estimate's calendar, Isaacs personally appealed that it be laid over. John P. Crane, President of the Uniformed Firemen's Association, was enraged—he had obtained advance commitment on the bill from every Councilman save Isaacs. (Later it was revealed that $175,000 was missing from the firefighters' association funds, and Crane testified under oath that he had given public officials thousands of dollars to obtain "good will" for firemen's legislation.) Nevertheless Isaacs persuaded the press and civic associations to denounce the bill. The taxi bill and pension bill eventually passed, but Isaacs had fought a gallant rear guard action almost single-handed.[36]

[35] Letter of Minority Leader Earle to *New York Herald-Tribune,* October 24, 1949; Isaacs, *Reminiscences,* pp. 238-46; Speech of Councilman Isaacs at Federal Club, April 30, 1951.

[36] Earle, *Reminiscences,* pp. 125-26; Letter of John Ellis to *New York Herald-Tribune,* October 24, 1949; *New York Times,* March 22, 1951; Speech of Council-

Isaacs was almost physically assaulted by members of the police organization, but he did help enact a measure to compel policemen to testify at public hearings. When District Attorney Miles F. McDonald was investigating alleged links between a gambling syndicate and law enforcement agencies in Kings County, he found it virtually impossible to obtain the testimony of police officers. Rather than waive immunity, as the state constitution required of all city officials, they would retire on pension. A bill was introduced requiring thirty days' advance notice, on pain of forfeiture of pension rights. The City Council passed it, but with an amendment that emasculated it. Majority Leader Keegan was having difficulty with his followers, but Isaacs supported him. The minority leader mobilized public opinion—Police Commissioner Murphy and Bronx Leader Flynn came out against the crippling amendment, while newspaper editorials denounced it. Ultimately the Council reconsidered, and the original proposal passed. All alone, Isaacs accomplished almost as much as the assorted and divided minority of ten in the last P. R. Council.

If the majority treated the sole surviving member of the minority with the utmost respect, they no longer blindly followed their own leaders. In 1949, when the Democrats enjoyed a majority of one in the P. R. Council, they readily understood the necessity for tight discipline. With an overwhelming preponderance of votes in the 1950-1953 sessions, they were more difficult to keep in line. When Mayor Impellitteri wanted to assure passage of his tax proposals, which he needed to balance the city's 1952-1953 expense budget, Majority Leader Sharkey was obliged to caucus, to threaten and cajole. Such scenes were unheard-of in the old Board of Aldermen, where assent to administration proposals was almost automatic.[37]

This trend could not be ascribed entirely to the legislators' in-

---

man Isaacs at Federal Club, April 30, 1951; *Third Interim Report of the Special Committee to Investigate Organized Crime in Interstate Commerce Pursuant to Senate Resolution 202,* May 1, 1951, pp. 140-41.

[37] *New York World-Telegram and Sun,* March 31, May 26, December 6, 1950; *New York Herald-Tribune,* December 11, 1950, April 30, 1952; Isaacs, *Reminiscences,* pp. 239-40.

dividualism. The majority was seriously split by intra-party differences. In the 1950 Mayoralty campaign, Council President Impelliteri defied the regular leaders and was elected Mayor as an "independent."[38] It was an amazing *coup,* but it created an internecine struggle within Tammany Hall. Consequently the Manhattan Councilmen responded to the promptings of Tammany Leader Carmine G. De Sapio rather than the Mayor, who belonged to the opposing Tammany faction. The Queens delegation, which demanded a greater share of public offices for their borough, also threatened to act as free agents in the Council.

When important bills were pending, it was sometimes necessary for the county leaders themselves to "persuade" the Councilmen from their boroughs to vote with the organization. Naturally the Councilmen acquiesced, but with some grumbling about being "just rubber stamps."[39] Outsiders had frequently called the old Board of Aldermen just that, and thoughtful members realized that the critics were right. Minority aldermen might openly say so, but the Democratic majority knew how dangerous it was publicly to complain about it. In its hankering for independence, the Council faintly resembled the city legislature before 1888, when the majority leader was unable to "deliver" the vote. But no one could make a direct comparison with the "Boodle Board," which negotiated directly, almost openly, with pressure groups for the city's favors.

Given an able and public-spirited minority, the Council would probably play a useful, but highly limited rôle in the city government.

[38] Actually Impelliteri was a member of Tammany's Sampson faction. It was Frank J. Sampson, leader of Tammany Hall from 1947 to 1948, who persuaded Impelliteri to run. Sampson had been fighting a running battle with Tammany Leader Carmine G. De Sapio, who held on to his position despite the defeat of his own candidate, Ferdinand Pecora, in the 1950 Mayoralty elections.

[39] *New York World-Telegram and Sun,* February 22, 1952, April 10, 1953; *New York Herald-Tribune,* April 30, 1952.

Appendix A. CHRONOLOGICAL LIST OF IMPORTANT DATES PERTAINING TO THE NEW YORK CITY LEGISLATURE

1851 Board of Aldermen grants first trolley franchise.
William M. Tweed elected to the Board.

1852 Board of Aldermen earns the name, "The Forty Thieves."
Tweed a ringleader.

1871 Simon Sterne publishes *On Representative Government and Personal Representation,* first American treatise on proportional representation.

1872 State Commission drafts a charter with a plan of proportional representation for the Board of Aldermen.
Governor Hoffman vetoes it.

1873 New city charter provides a crude system of proportional representation called "limited voting" for the Board of Aldermen.

1880 State Legislature enacts a new charter for the City of Brooklyn, to go into effect in 1882, centering the government in the hands of the Mayor.

1882 Limited voting for Board of Aldermen discarded in favor of single-member district system.

1884 The "Boodle Board": All but two aldermen involved in a franchise scandal.

1893 Founding of the Proportional Representation League.

1894 National Municipal League founded.

1896 State Legislature passes a law to consolidate Greater New York.
Charter Commission appointed by the Governor.

1897 State Legislature ratifies report of Charter Commission for Greater New York.
New charter creates a bicameral municipal legislature—a Board of Aldermen (with two-year term) and a Council (elected for four years).
First elections for the government of Greater New York.

1898 Government of Greater New York goes into operation.
First meetings of Municipal Assembly.

1899 Mazet Committee investigates corruption in the city. Its revelations help turn Tammany out in the 1901 elections.

1900 Governor Theodore Roosevelt appoints Charter Revision Commission to remedy defects of the original Greater New York Charter: a unicameral Board of Aldermen recommended.

1901 Report of Charter Revision Commission adopted by State Legislature; becomes new city charter.
First elections for unicameral Board of Aldermen.

1902 First sessions of a single-chambered legislature of Greater New York.

1905 Pennsylvania Railroad capitulates to Board of Aldermen and grants profitable trucking contract to obtain consent for a Manhattan terminal. As a result, the State Legislature practically strips the aldermen of franchise-granting power. Board of Estimate and Apportionment becomes the most powerful governing body in the city.

1912 Henry H. Curran heads aldermanic committee to investigate the Police Department.

1913 Aldermanic committee investigating Police Department reports; many of its recommendations adopted.

1914 – 1915 The "best Board of Aldermen" of Greater New York: Reform of procedure, new building code, new code of ordinances enacted.

1916 Ashtabula, Ohio, becomes the first American city to adopt P. R.

1923 State constitutional amendment authorizing Home Rule passes. Baldwin Commission recommends P. R. for the Board of Aldermen.

1924 Legislature passes Enabling Act to permit Home Rule for cities. Municipal Assembly (Board of Aldermen and Board of Estimate and Apportionment) set up as New York's Home Rule legislature.

1926 President Joseph V. McKee reforms parliamentary procedure in the Board of Aldermen.

1927 The Queens sewer scandal breaks. George U. Harvey, "The Fighting Alderman," ostensibly leads the fight against the malefactors.

1930 Ten assistant sergeants-at-arms assigned to guard the sole entrance to the Aldermanic Chamber.

1931 Committee of One Thousand organized.
Judge Seabury begins investigation of Magistrates' Courts and of New York County's District Attorney. Joint Legislative Committee Investigating Affairs of the City of New York appoints him Counsel.
Staff of President of Board of Aldermen implicated in school site scandal.
64 Democrats and a single Republican elected to the Board of Aldermen.

1932 Judge Seabury reports to the State Legislature.
Governor Franklin D. Roosevelt's last message to the Legislature pleads for charter revision.

1933 Civic associations campaign for charter revision.
State Legislature kills all proposals for charter revision.
Charter Commission appointed by Mayor O'Brien finds little fault with the Board of Aldermen.
Referendum permitting Mayor O'Brien to name a Charter Commission rejected at polls.

1934 State Legislature names Smith Commission to revise city charter.
Smith Commission breaks up in disagreement.
Special session of Legislature authorizes Mayor La Guardia to name a new Charter Revision Commission.

1935 Mayor La Guardia appoints the Thacher Commission, which studies the city government and prepares the first draft of the new charter.

1936 Thacher Commission holds public hearings on preliminary draft of city charter; revises its draft in the light of the hearings.
Effort to wipe charter and P. R. proposal off ballots fails in the courts (*Mooney v. Cohen*).
Electorate offered new charter with option of majority elections to Council by State Senate districts or P. R. by boroughs. Both charter and P. R. win out at the polls.

1937 First P. R. election to the City Council: 13 Democrats, 3 Republicans, 3 Fusionites, 2 independent Democrats, and 5 members of the American Labor Party seated.
P. R. declared constitutional by the Courts (*Johnson v. the City of New York et al.: Matter of Bowe v. Cohen*).
Board of Aldermen holds its last session.

1938 New charter goes into effect.
Opening sessions of the City Council: struggle for control between the Fusion coalition and Democrats until the Court of Appeals rules in favor of the Democrats (*Morris v. Cashmore*).
Constitutional convention extends powers of city councils: State Legislature may now pass a special law affecting a city only after a request by Mayor and Council of city affected or by two-thirds of the Council. Local laws may supersede special state legislation passed since 1924.
Constitutional amendment to prohibit P. R. in any election in the state drawn up by convention: rejected at polls.
Power of Council to pursue independent investigations of executive department vindicated in the courts (*In the Matter of Radio Station WNYC*).

1939 Second P. R. election to the Council: 14 Democrats, 2 Republicans, 2 Fusionites, 1 independent Democrat, 2 members of the American Labor Party elected.

1940 Referendum petition to eliminate P. R. beaten at the polls.

1941 Local law to abolish P. R. passes City Council; dies in Board of Estimate.
Third P. R. election to Council: 17 Democrats, 2 Republicans, 3 A.L.P. candidates, 3 Fusionites, 1 Communist seated.

1943 Fourth election to Council: 10 Democrats, 3 Republicans, 2 American Labor Party members, 2 Communists gain office.

1945 Term of City Council extended to four years.
Fifth P. R. election to Council: 14 Democrats, 3 Republicans, 2 American Labor Party members, 2 Communists, 2 Liberals elected.

1947 Campaign to eliminate P. R. succeeds.

1949 First election to Council under the majority system: 24 out of 25 seats won by Democrats with 52.6% of the vote.

1953 Second election to Council under the majority system. Democrats win 23 out of 25 seats with 51.7% of the vote.

Appendix B. DIGEST OF PRINCIPAL LAWS AFFECTING NEW YORK'S MUNICIPAL LEGISLATURE

The Charter of 1873 introduced the "limited vote" for elections to the Board of Aldermen. Under this system several legislators are elected for a single district, but each voter ballots for a number less than the whole. The election law which governed the city from 1873 to 1882 provided that each of the city's electors vote for two aldermen from his district and four aldermen at large. Three aldermen were seated from every district and six at large. This crude system was the city's first experience with proportional representation.

The First Greater New York Charter, which went into effect in 1898, provided for a bicameral legislature, a Council (elected for four years), and a Board of Aldermen (elected for two). Nominally the city's legislative authority was vested in it, but it was hedged in with many restraints. Important proposals relating to public works required prior approval of a Board of Public Improvements. The most important administrative departments initiated all ordinances governing their work, and the municipal assembly could merely reject their proposals or pass them without amendment. The annual budget originated in the Board of Estimate and Apportionment. Powerless to initiate important measures, the legislators could clog the city government by "hanging up" dubious ordinances or blocking bond issues. The latter was particularly easy, for all financial proposals required the consent of three-fourths of *all* the lawmakers. The "checks and safeguards" placed upon the actions of the Municipal Assembly were so numerous and legislative powers so widely distributed that the charter proved almost unworkable.

The Charter of 1901, which went into effect in 1902, created a unicameral Board of Aldermen. It could pass all the city's ordinances (subject to the Mayor's veto) and eliminate or reduce items in the annual budget. It shared certain administrative powers with the Board of Estimate and Apportionment, such as fixing the salaries of municipal employees and issuing special revenue bonds and corporate stock. It could investigate municipal executive departments and authorize heads of departments to make purchases in excess of $1,000 without public letting. Aldermen served on local improvement boards, which initiated resolutions concerning public works in their respective communities.

The Home Rule Amendment, which became part of the State Constitution in 1923, was an effort to permit cities in New York State to create their own framework of government and to conduct local public affairs with a minimum of interference by State authorities. The Enabling Act of 1924 authorized local legislative bodies to enact laws relating to the "property, affairs or government" of their respective cities. Under this statute the Board of Estimate and Apportionment became the upper house and the Board of Aldermen the lower branch of the Municipal Assembly. The new local legislature was authorized to pass local laws, i.e. laws within this grant of local autonomy, as distinct from ordinances, which the Board of Aldermen alone had been enacting since the Charter of 1901 went into effect.

The Charter of 1936, which went into effect in 1938, divorced administrative and legislative functions. The Board of Estimate became the city's chief administrative body, the City Council the policy-making house. City ordinances were abolished. The Council alone may now pass local laws, subject to the Mayor's veto, but charter amendments require the approval of the Board of Estimate, and, in some cases, the electorate as well. (Certain types of charter amendments may be passed by initiative-petition.) Local laws touching on the administration of municipal affairs or the structure of city departments must also be approved by the Board of Estimate. The Council may reduce or delete items in the expense budget or capital outlay budget. It may investigate any matter relating to the property, affairs or government of the city.

Proportional representation proved the most controversial feature of the charter. In 1936 the electorate was offered two options—majority elections from State Senatorial districts (with three Councilmen at large from each of the boroughs of Brooklyn, Queens, and the Bronx) or the Hare system of P. R., with the borough as the election unit. The latter was adopted at the polls. Each borough would seat one Councilman for every 75,000 valid ballots cast (and an additional representative for a remainder of 50,000 or more). Primaries were eliminated. To be nominated a candidate required a petition of 2,000 voters. The quota for election was 75,000 votes. In the central count losing candidates were eliminated serially, the alternative votes on their ballots being transferred to candidates still in the running. (After a candidate gained the 75,000 quota, the secondary votes on his remaining ballots were similarly distributed.) When the number of candidates was reduced to the borough's share, all continuing candidates were declared elected.

The Constitutional Convention of 1938 offered an amendment to the State Constitution which broadened the powers of cities over their own affairs. After this proposal was ratified at the polls, no special law affecting a particular city could be considered by the State Legislature unless the Mayor and Council of the municipality itself requested it. The Council alone could present the request, if it were approved by a two-thirds vote. Not only did the City Council gain authority to determine the necessity for legislative action on New York City's affairs at Albany, but also it was empowered to enact local laws that would supersede special statutes enacted since 1924.

An Initiative-Referendum to Abolish P. R. was placed on the ballot and adopted by the voters of the city in 1947. Beginning with the campaign of 1949, Councilmen were to be elected by the majority method from the city's 25 Senatorial districts.

Appendix C. MAYORS OF THE CITY OF NEW YORK SINCE CONSOLIDATION

Robert A. Van Wyck	1898–1901	Joseph V. McKee	1932[b]
Seth Low	1902–1903	John P. O'Brien	1933
George B. McClellan	1904–1909	Fiorella H. La Guardia	1934–1945
William J. Gaynor	1910–1913[a]	William O'Dwyer	1946–1950[a]
Ardolph L. Kline	1913[b]	Vincent R. Impellitteri	1950–1953[c]
John Purroy Mitchel	1914–1917	Robert F. Wagner, Jr.	1954–
John F. Hylan	1918–1925		
James J. Walker	1926–1932[a]		

[a] Served until September of last year in office. Mayor Gaynor died; Mayors Walker and O'Dwyer resigned.

[b] Acting Mayor.

[c] Acting Mayor from September to November 1950. Became Mayor after his election, Nov., 1950.

Appendix D. DEMOCRATIC COUNTY LEADERS OF MANHATTAN AND BROOKLYN

1. *Tammany Leaders (New York County)*

William B. Tweed	1867 to 1872
John Kelly and John Morrissey	1872
John Kelly	1872 to 1886
Richard Croker	1886 to 1902
Lewis Nixon (4 months)	1902
Charles F. Murphy, Dan'l F. McMahon, and Louis Haffen (4 months)	1902
Charles F. Murphy	1902 to 1924
George W. Olvany	1924 to 1929
John F. Curry	1929 to 1934
James J. Dooling	1934 to 1937
Christopher D. Sullivan	1937 to 1942
Michael J. Kennedy	1942 to 1944
Edward V. Loughlin	1944 to 1947
Frank J. Sampson	1947 to 1948
Hugo E. Rogers	1948 to 1949
Carmine G. DeSapio	1949 —

2. *Brooklyn Leaders (Kings County)*

Hugh McLaughlin	1861 to 1903
Patrick McCarren	1903 to 1909
John H. McCooey	1909 to 1934
Frank V. Kelly	1934 to 1946
John Cashmore	1946 to 1950
Francis J. Sinnott	1950 to 1952
Kenneth F. Sutherland	1952 to 1954
Joseph T. Sharkey	1954 —

Appendix E. SUMMARY OF P. R. CHARTER USED IN NEW YORK CITY

1. Each of the city's boroughs was entitled to at least one councilman. Without this provision Richmond would not register sufficient votes to elect a single councilman.
2. Each borough was a separate election district.
3. For each 75,000 valid votes cast within the borough it was entitled to one councilman; for a remainder of 50,000 or more it was entitled to an additional councilman.
4. No primaries were held—all nominations were by petition.
5. To be entitled to nomination a prospective candidate had to file a petition containing valid signatures of 2,000 voters who registered in the borough within eighteen months prior to the date of such filing. The signatures had to be obtained within 100 days of the election. Signers did not have to be registered members of the candidate's party nor be authorized to vote in the party's primary. Party emblems were forbidden on the petitions, but party designations could be printed or written on them.
6. The "birdless" ballot was used—party emblems were forbidden, but party designations were printed on the ballots as certified to the Board of Elections by the official county organizations. Candidates who were not officially certified were prohibited from using the party designation.
7. Blank spaces were provided at the bottom of the ballot for writing in names. These spaces were "at least equal in number to the quotient obtained by dividing the number of registered voters in the borough by seventy-five thousand," and each space was preceded by the same voting square which preceded the printed names higher up on the ballot.
8. All candidates who received less than 2,000 votes on the first count were declared defeated. Their votes were transferred to the next choice among candidates who were still in the running.
9. Seventy-five thousand votes elected a councilman. Once he obtained this total, all additional votes cast for him were transferred to the candidates shown as second choice on the ballots.
10. Losing candidates were counted out one at a time, and their votes were distributed to the other candidates still in the running.
11. If two candidates received the same number of votes at the end of a particular count, the tie was broken by continuing in the

running the candidate who was ahead at the end of the preceding count.

12. When all the ballots of already defeated candidates had been transferred, and it was impossible to eliminate another candidate without reducing the total number of candidates still in the running below the number to be elected in the borough, then all of the candidates still in the running were declared elected.
13. Every ballot was supposed to be marked or stamped so that its entire course from candidate to candidate "could be conveniently traced." Whatever errors were corrected or ballots recounted should be "made to take the same course" as in the original count, "unless the correction of an error required (their) taking a different course." See *Prop. Rep.: What It Is and How It Works in N.Y.C.*, pp. 36-37.

PERSONAL INTERVIEWS

THE DEFINITIVE political history of the city in the first half of the twentieth century has not yet been written. An important part of the story may be found in the memories of those who helped make that history. The author gratefully acknowledges the help of the following men and women, who graciously granted him personal interviews:

The Hon. Joseph Clark Baldwin, former Minority Leader of the Board of Aldermen (March 4, 1947); the Hon. Morton Baum, former Republican Alderman (May 28, 1948); Mr. Leo Brasz, of the Board of Elections (June 30, 1947); Professor Joseph P. Chamberlain, Counsel to the Smith Commission and the Thacher Commission (various dates from 1946 to 1950); Mr. Richard S. Childs, Chairman of the Citizens Union (March 9, 1949); Justice Irving Ben Cooper (August 22, 1949); the Hon. Henry H. Curran, former Majority Leader of the Board of Aldermen (January 24, 1947); the Hon. Lambert Fairchild, former Republican Alderman (October 12, 1947); Miss Joan Hamlin, Secretary to the Minority Leader of the City Council (April 17, 1951); Justice Walter R. Hart, former Alderman and Councilman (September 25, 1947); Councilman Stanley M. Isaacs (September 8, 1947); Mr. Gabriel Kaplan, Legal Assistant to Minority Leader Isaacs (May 1, 1951); Mr. Reuben S. Lazarus, Executive Officer of the Board of Statutory Consolidation (March 27, 1947); Mr. William S. Lebwohl, Assistant Corporation Counsel (November 12, 1947); Dr. George H. McCaffrey, Director of Research, Commerce and Industry Association (October 30, 1947); Commissioner Rufus M. McGahen, former Director of the Budget (October 28, 1947); Professor Joseph D. McGoldrick, former Comptroller (March 10, 1947); Mr. James McGowan, campaign manager for the Hon. Francis X McGowan, incumbent and candidate for Assemblyman (October 15, 1950); Professor Arthur W. MacMahon, member of the staff of the Baldwin Commission (February 25, 1949); the Hon. Newbold Morris, former President of the City Council (August 8, 1947); the Hon. James J. Paretti, former Alderman (May 7, 1947); the Hon. William A. Prendergast, former City Comptroller (December 10, 1948); Justice Jacob Gould Schurman (August 1, 1949); the Hon. Murray Stand, former Democratic whip of the Board of Aldermen (June 13, 1947); Mr. Arthur L. Thexton, former campaign manager of the Cincinnati Charter Committee (July 27, 1949); Mr. Leonard M. Wallstein, former Commissioner of Accounts (December 18, 1948).

BIBLIOGRAPHY

BOOKS

Allen, Frederick Lewis. *Since Yesterday: The Nineteen Thirties in America.* New York: Harper, 1940.

Allen, Robert S. (ed.). *Our Fair City.* New York: Vanguard, 1947.

Allen, William H. *Al Smith's Tammany Hall.* New York: Institute for Public Service, 1928.

———. *Why Tammanies Revive: LaGuardia's Mis-Guard.* New York: Institute for Public Service, 1937.

Arndt, Walter Tallmadge. *The Emancipation of the American City.* New York: Duffield, 1917.

Asbury, Herbert. *The Gangs of New York: An Informal History of the Underworld.* New York: Knopf, 1937.

Baker, Abby G., and Ware, Abby Huntington. *Municipal Government in New York City.* New York: Ginn, 1916.

Belous, Charles. *Faith in Fusion.* New York: Vantage, 1951.

Beman, Lamar T. *Proportional Representation.* New York: H. W. Wilson, 1925.

Breen, Matthew P. *Thirty Years of New York Politics.* New York, 1899.

Bryce, James. *The American Commonwealth.* 2 vols. New York: Macmillan, 1941.

Butler, Richard J., and Driscoll, Joseph. *Dock Walloper: The Story of "Big Dick" Butler.* New York: Putnam's, 1933.

Carter, John Franklin. *La Guardia: A Biography.* New York: Modern Age, 1937.

Chambers, Walter. *Samuel Seabury: A Challenge.* New York: Century, 1932.

Childs, Richard S. *Civic Victories.* New York: Harper, 1952.

Cohen, Caryl E., and Alexander, Albert. *New York, Today and Tomorrow.* New York: College Entrance, 1948.

Cohen, Julius Henry. *They Builded Better Than They Knew.* New York: Julian Messner, 1946.

Coler, Bird S. *Municipal Government As Illustrated by the Charter, Finances, and Public Charities of New York.* New York: Appleton, 1900.

Commons, John R. *Proportional Representation.* New York: Thomas Y. Crowell, 1896.

Conkling, Alfred R. *City Government in the United States.* New York: Appleton, 1899.

Curran, Henry H. *John Citizen's Job.* New York: Scribner's, 1924.

———. *Pillar to Post.* New York: Scribner's, 1941.

———. *Van Tassel and Big Bill.* New York: Scribner's, 1923.

Delpech, Henri. *L'Organization Municipale de l'Agglomeration New-Yorkaise.* Paris: Libraire du Recueil Sirey, 1938.

Dillon, John F. *Commentaries on the Law of Municipal Corporations.* Boston: Little, Brown, 1911.

Farley, James A. *Behind the Ballots.* New York: Harcourt Brace, 1938.

Ferber, Nat. *I Found Out: A Confidential Chronicle of the Twenties.* New York: Dial, 1933.

Finegan, James E. *Tammany at Bay* . New York: Dodd, Mead, 1933.

Flynn, Edward J. *You're the Boss.* New York: Viking, 1947.

Foord, John. *The Life and Public Services of Simon Sterne.* New York: Macmillan, 1903.

Forney, Matthias N. *Political Reform by the Representation of Minorities.* New York, 1894.

Fowler, Gene. *Beau James: The Life and Times of Jimmy Walker.* New York: Viking, 1949.

Goodnow, Frank J. *City Government in the United States.* New York: Century, 1910.

Griffith, Ernest S. *Current Municipal Problems.* New York: Houghton Mifflin, 1933.

———. *The Modern Development of City Government in the United Kingdom and the United States.* 2 vols. London: Oxford University Press, 1927.

Gunther, John. *Inside U.S.A.* New York: Harper, 1947.

Hapgood, Norman, and Moscowitz, Henry. *Up from the City Streets.* New York: Harcourt Brace, 1927.

Harlow, Alvin F. *Old Bowery Days: The Chronicle of a Famous Street.* New York: Appleton, 1931.

Herring, Pendleton. *The Politics of Democracy: American Political Parties in Action.* New York: Norton, 1940.

Hirsch, Mark D. *William C. Whitney: Modern Warwick.* New York: Dodd, Mead, 1948.

Hoag, Clarence G., and Hallett, George H. *Proportional Representation.* New York: Macmillan, 1926.

Howe, Wirt. *New York at the Turn of the Century: 1899-1916.* Toronto, 1946.

Isaacs, Julius. *Oath of Devotion.* New York: Dutton, 1949.

Ivins, William M. *Machine Politics and Money in Elections in New York City.* New York: Harpers, 1887.

Kent, Frank R. *The Great Game of Politics.* New York: Doubleday, Doran, 1940.

Key, Vladimer Orlando. *The Techniques of Political Graft in the United States.* Chicago: University of Chicago Libraries, 1936.

Knickerbocker, Jacob. *Then and Now.* Boston: Bruce Humphries, 1939.

La Guardia, Fiorello H. *The Making of an Insurgent: An Autobiography: 1882-1919.* New York: Lippincott, 1948.

Lavine, Emanuel A. *"Gimme": Or How Politicians Grow Rich.* New York: Vanguard, 1931.

Lehman, Herbert H. (Chairman). *The Finances and Financial Administration of New York City.* Recommendations and Report of the Subcommittee on Budget, Finance and Revenue of the City Committee on Plan and Survey. New York: Columbia University Press, 1928.

Lewis, Alfred Henry. *Richard Croker.* New York: Life Publishing Co., 1901.

Limpus, Lowell M. *Honest Cop: Lewis J. Valentine.* New York: Dutton, 1939.

Limpus, Lowell M., and Leyson, Burr W. *This Man La Guardia.* New York: Dutton, 1938.

Lynch, Dennis T. *"Boss" Tweed.* New York: Boni and Liverwright, 1927.

———. *Criminals and Politicians.* New York: Macmillan, 1932.

Macdonald, Austin F. *American City Government and Administration.* New York: Thomas Y. Crowell, 1941.

McGee, Cushman. *The Finances of the City of New York.* New York: Pressprich, 1940.

McGoldrick, Joseph D. *The Law and Practice of Home Rule: 1916-1930.* New York: Columbia University Press, 1933.

Mackaye, Milton. *The Tin Box Parade: A Handbook for Larceny.* New York: McBride, 1934.

MacMahon, Arthur W. *The Statutory Sources of New York City Government.* New York, 1923.

Marx, Fritz M. (ed.). *Elements of Public Administration.* New York: Prentice-Hall, 1947.

Mencken, Henry L. *The American Language.* New York: Knopf, 1931, 1945.

Merriam, C. E., and Gosnell, H. F. *The American Party System.* New York: Macmillan, 1940.

Mill, John Stuart. *On Liberty, Representative Government, the Subjugation of Women.* London: Oxford University Press, 1948.

Millett, John D. *The Works Progress Administration in New York City.* Chicago: Public Administration Service, 1938.

Moley, Raymond. *Our Criminal Courts.* New York: Milton, Balch, 1930.

———. *Tribunes of the People: The Past and Future of the Magistrates' Courts.* New Haven: Yale University Press, 1932.

Moscow, Warren. *Politics in the Empire State.* New York: Knopf, 1948.

Moses, Robert. *Theory and Practice in Politics.* Cambridge: Harvard University Press, 1939.

Municipal Yearbook. Chicago: International City Managers' Association, 1936.

Munro, William B. *The Government of American Cities.* New York: Macmillan, 1920.

———. *Personality in Politics: Reformers, Bosses, and Leaders: What They Do and How They Do It.* New York: Macmillan, 1924.

Myers, Gustavus. *The History of Tammany Hall.* New York: Boni and Liverwright, 1917.

Nevins, Allan. *The Emergence of Modern America: 1865-1878.* (A History of American Life, Vol. VIII.) New York: Macmillan, 1927.

New York Legislative Record and Index. Albany: Legislative Index Co., 1944.

New York State Legislative Annual, 1948. New York: New York Legislative Service, 1948.

Northrop, W. B., and Northrop, John B. *The Insolence of Office: The Story of the Seabury Investigations.* New York: Putnam's, 1932.

Orth, Samuel P. *The Boss and the Machine: A Chronicle of Politicians and Party Organization.* New Haven: Yale University Press, 1919.

Patton, Clifford W. *The Battle for Municipal Reform: Mobilization and Attack, 1875 to 1900.* Washington: American Council on Public Affairs, 1940.

Peel, Roy V. *The Political Clubs of New York City.* New York: Putnam's, 1935.

Penniman, Howard R. *Sait's American Parties and Elections.* New York: Appleton-Century-Crofts, 1948.

Perkins, Frances. *The Roosevelt I Knew.* New York: Viking Press, 1946.

Pink, Louis H. *Gaynor: The Man Who Swallowed the Tiger.* New York: International Press, 1931.

Pleasants, Samuel Augustus. *Fernando Wood of New York.* New York: Columbia University Press, 1948.

Powell, Adam Clayton. *Marching Blacks.* New York: Dial Press, 1945.

———. *Riots and Ruins.* New York: Richard R. Smith, 1945.

Pringle, Henry F. *Alfred E. Smith: A Critical Study.* New York: Macy-Macius, 1927.

Rager, Edward. *The Rat Race.* New York: Vantage, 1952.

Rexford, Frank A. (editor). *Our City—New York: A Book on City Government.* New York: Allyn and Bacon, 1930.

Rhyne, Charles S. (editor). *Municipalities and the Law in Action: 1948.* Washington: National Institute of Municipal Law Officers, 1948.

Riordan, William L. *Plunkitt of Tammany Hall.* New York: Knopf, 1948.

Rodgers, Cleveland, and Rankin, Rebecca B. *New York: The World's Capitol City.* New York: Harper, 1948.

Roosevelt, Theodore. *American Ideals and Other Essays, Social and Political.* New York: Putnam's, 1900.

———. *Autobiography.* New York: Scribner's, 1927.

———. *Essays on Practical Politics.* New York: Putnam's, 1888.

———. *New York.* New York: Longman's Green and Co., 1903.

Salisbury, W. Seward. *New York: The State and Its Government.* New York: Oxford Book Co., 1942.

Salter, J. T. *The American Politician.* Chapel Hill: University of North Carolina Press, 1938.

Seasongood, Murray. *Local Government in the United States: A Challenge and an Opportunity.* Cambridge: Harvard University Press, 1933.

Seidman, Harold. *Investigating Municipal Administration: A Study of the New York City Department of Investigation.* New York: Institute of Public Administration, 1941.

Shaw, Frederick. *The American City.* New York: Oxford Book Co., 1953.

Smith, Alfred E. *The Citizen and His Government.* New York: Harper, 1935.

Steffens, Lincoln. *Autobiography.* New York: Literary Guild, 1931.

Stewart, Frank M. *A Half Century of Municipal Reform: The History of the National Municipal League.* Los Angeles: University of California Press, 1950.

Stoddard, Theodore Lothrop. *Master of Manhattan: The Life of Richard Croker.* New York: Longman's Green, 1931.

Stokes, I. N. Phelps. *The Iconography of Manhattan Island: 1498-1909.* 6 vols. New York, 1915-1928.

Stone, Harold A., Price, Don K., and Stone, Kathryn H. *City Manager Government in the United States: A Review after Twenty-Five Years.* Chicago: Public Administration Service, 1940.

Survey Associates. *Fifteen Outstanding Articles Published by Survey Associates in 1937.* New York, 1937.

Syrett, Harold C. *The City of Brooklyn: 1865-1898.* New York: Columbia University Press, 1944.

Taft, Charles P. *City Management: The Cincinnati Experiment.* New York: Farrar and Rinehart, 1933.

Thomas, Norman, and Blanshard, Paul. *What's the Matter with New York: A National Problem.* New York: Macmillan, 1932.

Train, Arthur. *From the District Attorney's Office.* New York: Scribner's, 1939.

Van Devander, Charles W. *The Big Bosses.* New York: Howell Soskin, 1944.

Walker, Harvey. *The Legislative Process: Lawmaking in the United States.* New York: Ronald Press, 1948.

Walling, George W. *Recollections of a New York Chief of Police.* New York: Caxton Book Co., 1887.

Wallis, J. H. *The Politician: His Habits, Outcries, and Protective Coloring.* New York: Frederick A. Stokes, 1935.

Ware, Caroline F. (ed.). *The Cultural Approach to History.* New York: Columbia University Press, 1940.

Welling, Richard. *As the Twig Is Bent.* New York: Putnam's, 1942.

Werner, M. R. *Tammany Hall.* New York: Doubleday Doran, 1928.

Who's Who in New York, 1938. New York, 1938.

Wilcox, Delos F. *Great Cities in America.* New York: Macmillan, 1910.

Willemse, Cornelius W. *A Cop Remembers.* New York: Dutton, 1933.

Wise, Stephen. *Challenging Years: The Autobiography of Stephen S. Wise.* New York: Putnam's, 1949.

World Almanac and Encyclopedia for 1922. New York: Press Publishing Co., 1921.

Zink, Harold. *City Bosses in the United States: A Study of Twenty Municipal Bosses.* Durham: Duke University Press, 1930.

———. *The Government of Cities in the United States.* New York: Macmillan, 1939.

GOVERNMENT DOCUMENTS AND REPORTS

The Administrative Code of the City of New York. Albany: J. B. Lyon, 1938.

Annual Reports of the Board of Elections in the City of New York for the Years 1917-1949.

Budgets of the City of New York for the Years 1921-1938.

The Charter of the City of New York, with Notes Thereon: Also, A Treatise on the Powers and Duties of the Mayor, Aldermen, and Assistant Aldermen, Prepared at the Request of the City Council by Chancellor Kent, and Published at Their Direction. New York, 1854.

The Constitution of the State of New York to be Submitted to the People at the General Election of 1938. Albany: Constitutional Convention, 1938.

"Fassett Committee Hearings." See *Testimony Taken before the New York Senate Committee on Cities Pursuant to Resolution Adopted January 20, 1890.*

Fifteenth Census of the United States. Washington, D. C., 1931.

Final Report to the Special Committee of the Assembly Appointed to Investigate the Public Offices and Departments of the City of New York and of the Counties Therein Included. 5 vols. Albany: J. B. Lyon, 1900. [The Mazet Committee]

Final Report of Samuel Seabury, Referee in the Matter of the Investigation of the Magistrates' Courts in the First Judicial Department and the Magistrates Thereof, and of the Attorneys-at-Law Practicing in Said Courts. New York: Lawyers Press, 1932.

First Report of the New York State Joint Legislative Committee to Investigate the Affairs of the City of New York. New York: Fremont Payne, December 19, 1921.

General Index and Progressive Register in Detail of All the Proceedings of the Board of Aldermen of the City of New York During the Years 1914 and 1915. New York: Little and Ives, 1916.

The Government of the City of New York. New York: New York State Constitutional Convention Committee, 1915.

The Government of the City of New York. (A Survey of Its Functions Prepared for the Constitutional Convention, 1915, by the Office of the Commissioner of Accounts and the New York Bureau of Municipal Research.) New York: Little and Ives, 1915.

The Greater New York Charter as Enacted in 1897. (Mark Ash, ed.) Albany: Weed-Parsons, 1897.

"Hofstadter Committee Report." See *Report to the Legislature of the Joint Legislative Committee to Investigate the Affairs of the City of New York.*

Investigation of Offices and Departments of the City of New York by a Special Committee of the Assembly: Report of Counsel. December 22, 1899. Albany: J. B. Lyon, 1899.

Joint Legislative Committee to Investigate the Affairs of the City of New York: Transcripts of Hearings, 1931-1932. 71 vols. New York: Marshall and Munson, 1932.

Journal of the Constitutional Convention of the State of New York, 1915. Albany: J. B. Lyon, 1915.

Lee, Henry J. (ed.). *The Charter of the City of New York with Amendments to May 1, 1930; Also the Home Rule Law, Chapter*

363, Laws of 1924, with Amendments to May 1, 1930. Brooklyn: Eagle Library, 1930.

Manuals of the Board of Aldermen, 1918-1936.

"Mazet Investigation." See *Final Report to the Special Committee of the Assembly Appointed to Investigate the Public Offices and Departments of the City of New York and of the Counties Therein Included.*

New York State Constitutional Convention Committee. *Reports.* Vol. V: *New York City Government Functions and Problems.* Vol. VII: *Problems Relating to Legislative Organization and Powers.* Vol. XI: *Problems Relating to Home Rule and Local Government.* Albany: J. B. Lyon, 1938.

Official Directory of the City of New York. New York: Board of City Record, 1937-1953.

Preliminary Report and Draft of the Proposed Charter for the City of New York. New York: New York City Charter Revision Commission, 1936.

Preliminary Report of Charter Revision Commission Appointed by Hon. John P. O'Brien, Mayor. New York, January 2, 1933.

Proceedings of the Board of Aldermen of the City of New York, 1902-1923. New York, 1902-1923.

Proceedings of the Board of Aldermen and Municipal Assembly, Aldermanic Branch, 1924-1937. New York, 1924-1937.

Proceedings of the Council of the City of New York, 1938-1949. New York, 1938-1949.

Proceedings of the Joint Legislative Committee to Investigate the Affairs of the City of New York. 8 vols. [The Meyers Committee]. New York: Marshall and Munson, 1921.

Proposed Charter for the City of New York, Filed with the City Clerk on August 17, 1936, and Report of the New York Charter Revision Commission. New York: New York City Charter Revision Commission, 1936.

Public Papers of Herbert H. Lehman, 1933. Albany: J. B. Lyon, 1934.

Rankin, Rebecca B. (ed.). *New York Advancing: 1934-1935.* New York: Municipal Reference Library, 1936.

———. *New York Advancing: Victory Edition.* New York: Municipal Reference Library, 1945.

———. *New York Advancing: World's Fair Edition.* New York: Municipal Reference Library, 1939.

Record of the Work of the Board of Aldermen, January 1, 1914, to July 6, 1915. New York: M. B. Brown, 1915.

Report and Opinion of Samuel Seabury, Commissioner, in the Matter of the Investigation, under Commission Issued by the Governor of the State of New York, of Charges Made against the Honorable

Thomas C. T. Crain, District Attorney of New York County. New York, August 31, 1931.

Report and Summary of the Evidence of the Joint Legislative Committee to Investigate the Affairs of the City of New York. Albany: J. B. Lyon, 1922.

Report of a Commission to Devise a Plan for the Government of Cities in the State of New York. Assembly Document No. 68. March 6, 1877. New York: Evening Post, 1877.

Report of the Charter Revision Commission of 1907 to the Governor of the State of New York, November 30, 1907. New York: Evening Post, 1907.

Report of the Charter Revision Commission to the Governor of the State of New York with Proposed Amendments to the Greater New York Charter. New York: M. B. Brown, 1900.

Report of the New York Charter Commission with a Draft of a Charter for the City of New York. March 5, 1923. New York: M. B. Brown, 1923.

Report of the New York City Charter Commission to the Legislature. Albany: J. B. Lyon, 1909. [The Ivins Commission]

Report of the Special Committee of the Board of Aldermen of the City of New York Appointed August 5, 1912, to Investigate the Police Department. New York: M. B. Brown, 1913.

Report to the Legislature of the Joint Legislative Committee to Investigate the Affairs of the City of New York. December 28, 1932. [The Hofstadter Committee]

Savona, Francis. *Amendments to the Eagle Library Edition of the Charter of the City of New York from May 1, 1930, to the Close of the Extraordinary Session of the 1934 State Legislature.* Brooklyn: Eagle Library, 1934.

Seabury, Samuel. *In the Matter of the Investigation of the Departments of the Government of the City of New York: Final Report to the Members of the Joint Legislative Committee to Investigate the Administration of the Various Departments of the City of New York.* December 27, 1932.

———. *In the Matter of the Investigation of the Departments of the Government of the City of New York: Intermediate Report.* January 25, 1932.

———. *In the Matter of the Investigation of the Departments of the Government of the City of New York: Second Intermediate Report.* December 19, 1932.

"Seabury Minutes." See *Joint Legislative Committee to Investigate the Affairs of the City of New York: Transcripts of Hearings.*

Special (Senate) Committee to Investigate Organized Crime in Interstate Commerce. *Third Interim Report.* Report No. 307, 82nd Congress, 1st Session, May 1, 1951.

Synopsis of the Greater New York Charter. New York: The Merchants' Association of New York, 1921.

Testimony Taken before the New York Senate Committee on Cities Pursuant to Resolution Adopted January 20, 1890. 5 vols. Albany: J. B. Lyon, 1891. [The Fassett Committee]

To Secure These Rights: The Report of the President's Committee on Civil Rights. Washington: Government Printing Office, 1947.

What "P. R." Is: How It Works. [Prepared for Canvassers in P. R. elections.] New York: Municipal Civil Service Commission, 1937.

PRINTED PAMPHLETS

Annual Reports of the Committee on Legislation of the Citizens Union. New York: Citizens Union, 1930-1934.

An Address to the Members of the Constitutional Convention of the State of New York. New York: Proportional Representation Society of New York, 1894.

Annual Report of the Secretary of the City Club of New York. New York, April 2, 1894.

Arndt, Walter T. *Proportional Representation: "Effective Voting."* 3d ed. New York: Committee of One Thousand, April, 1932.

Caccavajo, Joseph. *Guide to Municipal Government: City of New York.* Brooklyn: Brooklyn Eagle, 1922.

Chadbourne, Ellis. *New York Blazes the Way.* Municipal Affairs Pamphlets, No. 1. New York: Citizens' Movement, 1934.

Charter Revision and Proportional Representation. New York: Women's City Club of New York, 1934.

Charter Revision for the City of New York. (A Plan Prepared by the Division of Research in Public Administration, Department of Government, Washington Square College.) New York: New York University, 1934.

Childs, Richard S. *Best Practices under the Manager Plan.* Rev. ed. New York: National Municipal League, 1939.

———. *The Short Ballot: A Movement to Simplify Politics.* New York: National Municipal League, 1930.

City Affairs Committee Bulletins. 1932-1941.

Civics As It Should Be Taught. New York: National Self Government Committee, November, 1934.

Clark, Evans, and Solomon, Charles. *The Socialists in the New York City Board of Aldermen: A Record of Six Months.* New York: Rand School, 1918.

Cohen, Louis. *P. R. Unmasked.* New York: 1940.

Dewey, John (ed.). *New York and the Seabury Investigations: A Digest and Interpretation.* New York: City Affairs Committee, 1933.

Facts versus Flourishes and Ruffles: What Four Years of Hylan, Hearst and Murphy Have Done to New York. New York: Citizens Union, 1921.

Fiscal Facts Concerning the City of New York: A Twenty Year Statistical Summary of the City's Finances. New York: Citizen's Budget Commission, 1940.

Forney, Matthias. *Proportional Representation.* New York: E. W. Johnson, 1900.

Governmental Organization within Greater New York. New York: Institute of Public Administration, 1931.

Hallett, George. *Proportional Representation—The Key to Democracy.* (1st edition) Washington: National Home Library, 1937. (2d edition) New York: National Municipal League, 1940.

———. *Real Majority Rule.* Brooklyn: Brooklyn Eagle Press, 1935.

Hermens, Ferdinand A. *Democracy and Proportional Representation.* Chicago: University of Chicago Press, 1940. [Public Policy Pamphlet No. 31]

———. *P. R., Democracy and Good Government.* Notre Dame: The Review of Politics, 1943.

Home Rule for Cities. New York: City Club, 1924.

How Our City Laws Are Made. New York: New York City League of Women Voters, 1948.

Keep P. R. Committee. *Danger.* New York, 1947.

Kilroe, Edwin P., Kaplan, Abraham, and Johnson, Joseph. *The Story of Tammany.* New York: Democratic Organization County Committee, 1924.

Lahee, Arnold W. *The New York City Budget.* Pamphlet No. 88. New York: Bureau of Municipal Research, 1917.

Levin, Maurice J. *A Bill Drafting Bureau for the City Council.* New York: City Club, 1938.

Minor, Robert. *Tell the People How Ben Davis Was Elected.* New York: New Century, 1946.

Mitchel, John P. *Address at Annual Dinner of Academy of Political Science, November 19, 1914.* n.p., 1914.

———. *The City and State Constitution.* New York: M. B. Brown, 1914.

The New Tammany. New York Republican State Committee, 1928.

The New York City Charter: Report on Charter Revision. New York: City Club, 1921.

"P. R. Proposal." See *A Proposal to Change the Method of Electing the New York City Board of Aldermen That Every Party May Receive Its Fair Share of Representation.*

Peel, Roy V., and Studenski, Paul. *A New Charter for New York City.* New York: National Municipal League, 1934.

Proportional Representation for New York City. New York: Merchants' Association, 1937.

Proportional Representation ("P. R.")—Effective Voting. Proportional Representation League Leaflet No. 5 (11th edition). New York, 1939.

Proportional Representation: What It Is and How It Works in New York City. (rev. ed.) New York: Chamber of Commerce of the State of New York, 1947.

A Proposal to Change the Method of Electing the New York City Board of Aldermen That Every Party May Receive Its Fair Share of Representation, Submitted to the New York City Charter Commission, October, 1922. New York, 1922.

Reports Adopted by Second Session of Civic Conference on Charter Revision, February 16, 1933. New York: City Party, 1933.

Reports of the Committee on the Board of Aldermen for the Citizens Union for the 1910-1917 Terms. New York: Citizens Union, 1911-1917.

Rowe, L. S. *Reform in Municipal Government.* Boston: George H. Ellis, 1894.

Seabury, Samuel. *Address before the Proportional Representation League, Providence, Rhode Island, November 25, 1935.* n.p., n.d.

———. *The Power of an Ideal.* New York: Committee of One Thousand, 1931.

Selected Bibliography on Revision of the New York City Charter. Princeton: School of Public Affairs, 1933.

Sherman, Philemon T. *Inside the Machine: Two Years in the Board of Aldermen, 1898-1899.* New York: Cooke and Fry, 1901.

Stebbins, Charles M. *Tammany Hall: Its History, Organization and Methods.* Brooklyn: Stebbins and Co., 1921.

Sterne, Simon. *Report to the Constitutional Convention of the State of New York on Personal Representation.* New York: A. Simpson and Co., 1867.

PERIODICAL LITERATURE

Across from City Hall (Citizens Union News), 1946-1953.

Betters, Paul V. "Bolstering Municipal Credit," *National Municipal Review,* XXII, No. 6 (June, 1933), 268-71.

Bird, F. L. "American Cities Face 1933," *National Municipal Review,* XXII, No. 2 (February, 1933), 51-54, 66.

Bone, Hugh A. "Political Parties in New York City," *American Political Science Review*, XL, No. 2 (April, 1946), 272-82.

Boyer, Richard O. "Inquisitor: Profile of Samuel Seabury," *The New Yorker*, VII, No. 19 (June 17, 1931), 20-23.

Childs, Richard S. "The Ballot Is Still Too Long!" *National Municipal Review*, XXXV, No. 2 (February, 1947), 67-70.

———. "The League's Second Stretch," *National Municipal Review*, XXXIII, No. 10 (November, 1944), 514-19, 530.

———. "New York City Elections as a Problem in Political Science," *National Municipal Review*, XXIV, No. 1 (January, 1935), 23-26.

City Council Record, XIV-XXV (1938-1949).

Connery, Robert H. "New York City Cleans House," *National Municipal Review*, XXIII, No. 2 (February, 1934), 100-103.

Cottrell, Edwin. "City Council Organization," *Public Management*, XVII, No. 4 (April, 1935), 95-98.

Creel, George. "The Tammany Take," *Collier's*, CLI, No. 7 (February 8, 1932), 7-8, 30-32.

Curran, Henry H. "Fifty Years of Public Service," *New York Times Magazine*, December 7, 1947.

Davenport, Walter. "Tammany's Own," *Collier's*, No. 9 (March 4, 1933), 16-17, 41-43.

Deutsch, Bernard S. "Charter Revision—The Board of Estimate and the Board of Aldermen," *Real Estate News*, May, 1935, 160-61, 174-77.

Dodds, Harold W. "Model Laws as Aids to Progress," *National Municipal Review*, XXXIII, No. 10 (November, 1944), 531-34, 544.

Douglas, Paul H. "Occupational versus Proportional Representation," *American Journal of Sociology*, XXIX (September, 1923), 129-57.

Eldon, Harry. "The Council—An Estimate," *State of Affairs*, IV, No. 9 (September, 1939), 3-7.

Flynn, Edward J. "Bosses and Machines," *Atlantic Monthly*, CLXXIX, No. 5 (May, 1947), 34-40.

Forbes, Russell. "The Municipal Assembly, New York's Home Rule Legislature," *National Municipal Review*, XVIII, No. 10 (October, 1929), 632-34.

Garrett, Oliver H. P. "One of the Boys: Profile of Ruth Pratt," *The New Yorker*, II, No. 10 (April 24, 1926), 21-22.

Gavit, John P. "La Guardia—Portrait of a Mayor," *Survey Graphic*, XXV, No. 1 (January, 1936), 7-12, 55-58.

———. "New York—The Second Biggest Job," *Survey Graphic*, XXII, No. 3 (March, 1933), 151-55, 192.

Goodnow, Frank J. "The Charter of the City of New York," *Political Science Quarterly*, XVII, No. 1 (March, 1902), 1-23.

Gosnell, Harold F. "The Political Party versus the Political Machine," *Annals of the American Academy of Political Science,* CLXIX (September, 1933), 21-28.

Hallett, George H., Jr. "The Case for P. R." *The American Scholar,* XII, No. 2 (Spring, 1943), 161-73.

Hellman, Geoffrey T. "The Festive Touch: Profile of Joseph Clark Baldwin III," *The New Yorker,* XIX, No. 2 (February 27, 1943), pp. 22-32; XX, No. 3 (March 6, 1933), 26-29.

Hermens, Ferdinand A. "Political Science and Proportional Representation," *Social Science,* XV, No. 1 (January, 1940), 5-19.

———. "Proportional Representation Is a Risk," *Forum,* CVIII, No. 2 (August, 1947), 65-70.

———. "The Trojan Horse of Democracy," *Social Research,* V, No. 4 (November, 1938), 379-423.

Herwitz, Oren C. and Mulligan, William G. "The Legislative Investigating Committee: A Survey and Critique," *Columbia Law Review,* XXXIII, No. 1 (January, 1933), 4-27.

Humphrey, Hubert N. "The Senate on Trial," *American Political Science Review,* XLIX, No. 3 (September, 1950), 650-60.

Johnston, Alva. "Courtroom Warrier: Profile of Emory R. Buckner," *The New Yorker,* VIII, No. 4 (March 12, 1933), 25-28.

———. "The King: Profile of W. Kingsland Macy," *The New Yorker,* VII, No. 30 (September 12, 1931), 25-28.

Jonas, Harold J. "An Alderman in New York City, 1887-8, as Seen in His Journal," *New York History,* XXIX, No. 2 (April, 1948), 187-202.

Jones, Howard P. "The Seabury Revue of 1932," *National Municipal Review,* XXI, No. 3 (March, 1932), 45-47.

Kennedy, Albert J. "The Saloon in Retrospect and Prospect," *Survey Graphic,* XXII, No. 4 (April, 1933), 203-6, 234-40.

Kennedy, John B. "A Tammany Tour," *Collier's,* XCI, No. 6 (February 11, 1933), 10-11, 33-35.

Krock, Arthur. "The Brown Derby and the Bee: Profile of Alfred E. Smith," *The New Yorker,* II, No. 15 (May 29, 1926), 16-18.

La Guardia, Fiorello H. "Bosses Are Bunk: A Reply to Ed Flynn," *Atlantic Monthly,* CLXXX, No. 1 (July, 1947), 21-24.

Lazarus, Reuben A. "The New Administrative Code for New York City," *National Municipal Review,* XXVII, No. 2 (February, 1938), 92-99.

McBain, Howard L. "The New York Proposal for Home Rule," *Political Science Quarterly,* XXXVII, No. 4 (Dec., 1922), 655-80.

———. "Proportional Representation in American Cities," *Political Science Quarterly,* XXXVII, No. 2 (June, 1922), 281-98.

McCaffrey, George H. "New York's 1937 Election and Its Results," *National Municipal Review,* XXVII, No. 1 (January, 1938), 39-45.

MacDonald, Dwight. "Cit: Profile of George Hervey Hallett, Jr.," *The New Yorker,* XXIX, No. 27 (August 22, 1953), 31-49.

McGoldrick, Joseph D. "Again the Tiger Is Challenged," *New York Times Magazine,* June 19, 1932.

———. "The Board of Estimate and Apportionment of New York City," *National Municipal Review,* XVIII, No. 2 (February, 1929), 125-52.

———. "Home Rule in New York State," *American Political Science Review,* XIX, No. 11 (November, 1925), 693-706.

———. "Is the City Manager Plan Suitable for New York?" *National Municipal Review,* XXI, No. 5 (May, 1932), 289-95.

———. "The New Tammany," *The American Mercury,* XV (September, 1928), 1-12.

———. "Our City Councils: New York: The Eclipse of the Aldermen," *National Municipal Review,* XIV, No. 6 (June, 1925), 360-68.

———. "Proposals for the Reorganization of the Government of the City of New York," *American Political Science Review,* XXVII (April, 1933), 336-40.

———. "Storm Warnings in New York City's Finances," *National Municipal Review,* XXI, No. 3 (March, 1932), 168-75.

———. "The Story of New York City in Interest Rates," *National Municipal Review,* XXIII, No. 12 (December, 1934), 672-78.

———. "Tammany Totters But Triumphs," *National Municipal Review,* XXI, No. 11 (November, 1932), 634-36, 640.

———. "What Municipal Home Rule Means Today: New York," *National Municipal Review,* XXI, No. 12 (December, 1932), 671-78.

McInnes, Russell. "New York Legislature Again Impedes a Progressive Governor," *National Municipal Review,* XXIII, No. 7 (July, 1934), 383-88.

Mackaye, Milton. "Out of the Past: Profile of George Brinton McClellan," *The New Yorker,* VII, No. 15 (May 28, 1932), 21-25.

McKenzie, Catherine. "A Portrait of the New York Alderman," *New York Times Magazine,* January 28, 1934.

Maxey, Chester C. "The City Manager Plan and Proportional Representation," *Western Reserve University Bulletin,* XXVII, No. 7 (July, 1924), 5-37.

"Mayor LaGuardia's New York," *Fortune Magazine,* XX, No. 1 (July, 1939), 93-96, 202-208.

Moley, Raymond. "When Politics Seasons Justice," *Yale Review,* XXI (Spring, 1932), 448-65.

Monthly Bulletin of the Chamber of Commerce of the State of New York. XXVIII, No. 1 (May, 1936).

Moore, Barrington. "The Communist Party of the U.S.A., An Analysis of a Social Movement," *American Political Science Review,* XXXIX, No. 1 (February, 1945), 31-41.

Morris, Newbold. "Advantages of the New City Council over the Old Board of Aldermen," *Flatbush Magazine,* XVI, No. 9 (September, 1938), 1, 6.

Moscow, Warren. "Exit the Boss, Enter the Leader," *New York Times Magazine,* June 22, 1947.

Municipal Assembly Record. 1924-1937. (Committee on Legislation, Citizens Union.)

Municipal Reference Library Notes.

Myers, Gustavus. "The New Tammany," *Century Magazine,* CXII, No. 4 (August, 1926), 385-94.

Olmstead, Sophia M. "The Municipal Power of Investigation," *National Municipal Review,* XXV, No. 11 (November, 1936), 649-53.

Owen, Russell. " 'S.R.O.' Sign Out at City Hall," *New York Times Magazine,* Jan. 30, 1938.

Parton, James. "The Government of the City of New York," *North American Review,* CIII, No. 213 (1866), 413-68.

Paterson, Isabel. "Murphy," *American Mercury,* XIV, No. 55 (July, 1928), 347-54.

Peel, Roy V. "The Political Machine of New York City," *American Political Science Review,* XXVII (August, 1933), 611-18.

Philips, Herschell. "Does the Board of Aldermen Earn Its Sizeable Pay Check?" *Real Estate Magazine,* XXI, No. 5 (February, 1933), 19-22, 43.

Pratt, Ruth. "Men Are Bad Housekeepers," *Harpers Magazine,* CLIV, No. 924 (May, 1927), 682-88.

Pringle, Henry F. "Bringing up the City Fathers: Profile of Joseph Vincent McKee," *The New Yorker,* III, No. 30 (September 10, 1927), 19-22.

———. "The Italian Table D'Hôte: Profile of Fiorello H. La Guardia," *The New Yorker,* V, No. 28 (August 31, 1929), 26-29.

———. "Wet Hope: Profile of Henry Hastings Curran," *The New Yorker,* VI, No. 17 (June 14, 1930), 22–25.

Proportional Representation Review.

Haskin, A. H. "Presenting the Phenomenon Called Quill," *New York Times Magazine,* March 5, 1950.

Reichler, Oxie. "The Politician Hates P. R.," *National Municipal Review,* XXXVII, No. 6 (June, 1947), 318-19.

Roher, Miriam. "Mrs. Minority," *National Municipal Review,* XXIX, No. 9 (September, 1940), 585-89, 631.

Ross, Irwin. "Big City Machines and Liberal Voters," *Commentary,* X, No. 4 (October, 1950), 301-8.

Ross, Lillian. "$1,031,961,754.63," *The New Yorker,* XXIII, No. 12, (July 12, 1947), 27-40.

Rovere, Richard H. "The Big Hello: Profile of Peter J. McGuinness," *The New Yorker,* XXII, No. 48 (January 12, 1946), 29-38; XXII, No. 49 (January 19, 1946), 26-38.

———. "Good Citizen: Profile of Newbold Morris," *The New Yorker,* XX, No. 37 (October 28, 1944), 26-36; XX, No. 38 (November 4, 1944), 28-38.

———. "Nothing Much To It: Profile of Edward Joseph Flynn," *The New Yorker,* XXI, No. 30 (September 8, 1945), 28-41.

Schieffelin, William J. "The City Manager Plan Is Suitable for New York," *National Municipal Review,* XXI, No. 5 (May, 1932), 293-95.

———. "P. R. and New Yorkers," *The Survey,* XXVI, No. 7 (July, 1937), 383-86.

———. "P. R. Thwarts Machine Politicians," *Readers Digest,* XXXI, No. 185 (September, 1937), 43-46.

Seabury, Samuel. "Proportional Representation and the Constitutional Convention," *National Municipal Review,* XXVI, No. 12 (December, 1937), 567-71.

Stewart, Frank M. "Milestones of the First Fifty Years," *National Municipal Review,* XXXIII, No. 10 (November, 1944), 520-30.

Tanzer, Eleanor C. "The First P. R. Council: An Experiment in Democracy: 1938-1939," *The Searchlight,* XXIX, No. 1 (October, 1939), 3-15.

Tanzer, Lawrence A. "Municipal Home Rule in New York," *National Municipal Review,* XIV, No. 4 (April, 1925), 246-53.

———. "Political Strategy Nullifies Home Rule in New York," *National Municipal Review,* XXII, No. 1 (January, 1933), 16-18, 23.

Tanzer, Margaret I. "Aldermen Cannot Say 'No'," *The Searchlight,* XXI, No. 1 (September, 1931), 8-10.

Tugwell, Rexford Guy. "Implementing the General Interest," *Public Administration Review,* I, No. 1 (Autumn, 1940), 32-49.

Warner, Richard F. "On the Way Up: Profile of George Upton Harvey," *The New Yorker,* VI, No. 15 (May 31, 1930), 24-27.

Weiner, Joseph L. "Municipal Home Rule in New York," *Columbia Law Review,* XXXVII, No. 4 (April, 1937), 557-81.

White, Andrew D. "The Government of American Cities," *Forum,* X (December, 1890), 357-372.

Woodward, William R., and Hallett, George H., Jr. "Proportional Representation: Objections and Replies," *Forum,* CVII, No. 5 (May, 1947), 392-98.

Woolf, S. J. "Lone Republican Among Our Aldermen," *New York Times Magazine,* June 25, 1933.

Zeller, Belle, and Bone, Hugh A. "The Repeal of P. R. in New York City—Ten Years in Retrospect," *American Political Science Review*, XLII, No. 6 (December, 1948), 1127-1148.

UNPRINTED MATERIALS

Belous, Charles. "A Year Gone By: Being a Report on the Work and Progress of the New York City Council." 1938. (Typewritten manuscript in Municipal Reference Library)

"Board of Estimate of the City of New York." The New York League of Women Voters, 1949. (Mimeographed)

Buchanan, Lucille J. "The New York City Charter Commission of 1934." The New York League of Women Voters, 1934. (Mimeographed)

Childs, Richard S. "Proportional Representation." Radio address over Station WJZ, August 10, 1947. (Typewritten)

———. "Reminiscences." Oral History Project, under the direction of Prof. Allan Nevins, Columbia University, 1950. (Typewritten)

Citizens Union Collection. Nicholas Murray Butler Library, Columbia University.

City Affairs Committee. Press Releases on Matters Related to the Administration and Finances of the City of New York, 1931-1933. Municipal Reference Library. (Mimeographed)

"City Council of the City of New York." The New York League of Women Voters, 1949. (Mimeographed)

Committee of a Thousand. Press Releases and Communications to Members, 1931-1932. Files of National Municipal League. (Mimeographed)

Corporation Counsel of the City of New York. Card index file outlining powers of all governing bodies in the city. Prepared by Board of Statutory Consolidation, 1936-1937.

Custodian of City Hall. "A Thumb Nail Sketch of the City Hall Building." (Mimeographed)

Earle, Genevieve B. Personal Papers. Special Collections, Columbia University, and Municipal Reference Library. (Typewritten and mimeographed)

Fielding, Benjamin. "A Brief Review of the A.L.P. in 1938-1939-1940 at City Hall and the 'Twelve Point' Municipal Program for 1941." Press Release of American Labor Party, January 15, 1941. (Mimeographed)

Greer, Sarah, and Chamberlain, Lawrence. "Outline of Governmental Organization with the Cities of London, Paris, and Berlin with

Explanatory Charts, Prepared for the New York Charter Revision Commission by the Institute of Public Administration." 1935. (Mimeographed)

Gustaferro, Margaret. "The Personnel of the Board of Aldermen of New York: 1918-1928." Master's Thesis, Faculty of Political Science, Columbia University, October 1, 1928. (Typewritten)

Hallett, George H. "Giving the Charter Back to the People." Radio Address over Station WNYC, May 26, 1936. (Typewritten)

———. "The Legislature and Charter Revision." Radio Address over Station WOR, April 28, 1934. (Typewritten)

Isaacs, Stanley M. "Reminiscences." Oral History Project, Columbia University, 1950.

Joint Committee to Investigate the Departments of the City of New York, Minutes of Executive Sessions (April 20, 1931-April 29, 1932). Kent Hall, Columbia University. (Typewritten)

La Guardia, Marie. "Reminiscences." Oral History Project, Columbia University, 1950. (Typewritten)

Lazarus, Reuben A. "The Council: Origin, History, Evolution." Address delivered at College of City of New York, November 18, 1941. (Typewritten manuscript in Municipal Reference Library)

Minutes of the New York City Charter Revision Commission. May-August, 1934. (Mimeographed)

Mitchel, John P. "Speeches: 1914-1916." Municipal Reference Library. (Typewritten)

Morris, Newbold. Correspondence with ex-members of the Board of Aldermen. Office files of Newbold Morris. (Handwritten and typewritten)

———. "Municipal Home Rule under the City Council." Radio Address over Station WHN, January 26, 1938. (Typewritten)

New York City Charter Revision Commission Documents. 10 vols. Kent Hall, Columbia University. The Thacher Commission. (Mimeographed and typewritten)

New York City Charter Commission: Public Hearings, May 7-22, 1936. New York Public Library.

New York City Charter Revision Commission: Records of Public Hearings and Minutes of Executive Meetings: February 18, 1935-August 4, 1936. 4 vols. New York Public Library. (Mimeographed)

Olmstead, Sophia A. "Remarks on the P. R. Election." Radio Address over Station WEVD, December 1, 1937. (Typewritten)

Prince, Helen H. "The New York City Council." Master's Thesis, Faculty of Political Science, Columbia University, May, 1940. (Typewritten)

Pratt, Ruth. "Minority Report on the Budget for 1929." Mimeographed Release in Municipal Reference Library.

Pratt, Ruth. "Speech on the Budget for 1928, Delivered in the Board of Aldermen Meeting of December 5, 1927." Mimeographed Release in Municipal Reference Library.

Rankin, Rebecca B. "New York's Board of Aldermen." Typewritten manuscript at Municipal Reference Library.

"Report Concerning Election of the New York City Council by P. R." New York Commerce and Industry Association, September 24, 1947. (Mimeographed)

"Report of R. Lawrence Siegal, Special Assistant District Attorney General, Relative to the Irregularities Marking the 1937 Election of Councilmen in the Borough of the Bronx to John J. Bennett, Jr., Attorney General of the State of New York." August 30, 1938. (Typewritten)

"Report of Special Committee on Proportional Representation Concerning the Referendum on the Method of Electing the City Council to the Board of Directors, Commerce and Industry Association of New York, Inc." September 17, 1947. (Mimeographed)

"Report of Special Committee on Reorganization of City Government to the Board of Directors, Merchants' Association of New York." February 2, 1933. (Mimeographed)

Schieffelin, William Jay. "Reminiscences." Oral History Project, Columbia University, 1949. (Typewritten)

Schwartz, Asher William. "A Study of the New York City Council." 1940. Typewritten copy in the Municipal Reference Library.

Scrapbooks on the Board of Aldermen, 1922-1935. Citizens Union Scrapbooks, Vols. CXXVII-CXXIX. New York Public Library. (Newspaper clippings)

Stiehl, Laura. "Consideration of the Budget in the New York Board of Aldermen." Master's Thesis, Faculty of Political Science, Columbia University, May, 1927. (Typewritten)

Straus, Dorothy, and Buchanan, Lucille J. "Brief on Charter Revision for the City of New York." League of Women Voters, 1935. (Mimeographed)

Tanzer, Lawrence A. "The Home Rule Situation in New York State." Address before the Women's City Club of New York, 1938. Files of National Municipal League. (Typewritten)

Wallstein, Leonard M. "Reminiscences." Oral History Project, Columbia University, 1949. (Typewritten)

Whitney, Mrs. Harry, and Cunningham, Mrs. John Philip. "Charter Revision." Radio Dialogue over Station WHN, December 28, 1935. (Typewritten)

TABLE OF CASES

INDEX

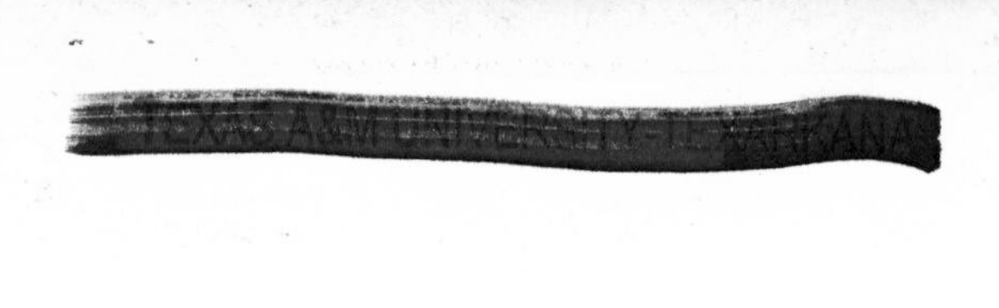